COLLIDE

STYLES, STRUCTURES, AND IDEAS IN DISCIPLINARY WRITING

EDITED BY
BELINDA KREMER
AND RICHARD MCNABB

LONG ISLAND UNIVERSITY,
C.W. POST CAMPUS

PEARSON
Custom
Publishing

Cover Art: Belinda Kremer, "The Gates 1," "The Gates 2," "The Gates 3"

Printed in the United States of America

11 12 13 14 15 16 V0CR 16 15 14 13 12

ISBN 0-536-47326-9

2006240212

KC

Please visit our web site at *www.pearsoncustom.com*

PEARSON CUSTOM PUBLISHING
501 Boylston Street, Suite 900, Boston, MA 02116
A Pearson Education Company

CONTENTS

ACKNOWLEDGMENTS

We would like to thank all of our contributors, each of whom conceived, wrote, revised, and reflected on an original essay specifically for this volume. Their work provides distinctive examples of writing from a range of disciplines, and promotes a rich conversation about, and exploration of, how people form, develop, research, and present ideas in writing. We would also like to thank all of the people at C.W. Post who have used *Collide* in their ENG 2 courses and offered suggestions for revision; they were instrumental in making this 2nd edition a stronger text. We also thank Casmira Boland, Tanya Marin, Edmond Niemczura III, and Mary Pigliacelli for assistance in manuscript preparation. Finally, for substantial revision of the 1st edition's "Rhetorical Considerations" sections, our special thanks to Marie Capasso, Brett Kunsch, and Lauren Weinbrown; many of their revisions appear in the new sections "Think. Write. Ask."

COLLIDE: STYLES, STRUCTURES, AND IDEAS IN DISCIPLINARY WRITING

Richard McNabb and Belinda Kremer

A couple of years ago, a student of ours from a previous semester came to the Writing Center to receive help on a paper he was writing for his anthropology course. The assignment asked students to write up the results of an ethnographic study the class had conducted on language practices of college students. Utilizing the skills learned in freshman composition, the student produced what he believed was a well-organized, well-reasoned, stylistically effective essay. Much to his dismay, he received the essay back with written comments from the instructor asking for extensive revisions. Although the instructor found the essay to be relatively error-free, she objected to the historical narrative he used to begin his essay, to the deductive reasoning that formed the basis of his argument, and to the stylistic features of the essay. Frustrated and confused, he came to the Writing Center to figure out why all the drafting and revision techniques learned in freshman composition failed to help him write a rhetorically effective essay for his anthropology course.

This is not an uncommon experience for students in college. Students are typically faced with a collision of discourses, each with its own set of rules governing analysis, reportage, and argument in a particular discipline. While students are taught how to write in the humanities in freshman composition, they may not be aware that they are writing as "humanists." Though they are not taught the written conventions of disciplines in, say, the social or natural sciences, they may think, simply, that they are learning to write as "college students," and that, having learned this discrete set of skills, they will be prepared for any writing situation. Their composition course—even at an institution with a viable Writing Across the Curriculum program—may be working from the same assumption.

As the instructor's comments in the example above illustrate, a student who produces in an anthropology class an essay appropriate for an English course may fail to communicate effectively—*even if the student understands the material*—because questions, ideas, and forms of presentation work differently in anthropology than in English. In essence, the instructor asked the student to revise the essay using the style and ways of arguing that define her discipline.

In *Genre Knowledge in Disciplinary Communication*, Carol Berkenkotter, Thomas Huckin, and John Ackerman followed a student through his course of study at Carnegie Mellon to track how he learned the discourse conventions of a field. As in the situation with our student, they determined that to write successful papers, students must understand the conventions of the genre in which they are writing—whether an ethnographic study in an anthropology course, a narrative essay in a literature course, or a lab report in a chemistry class. Whatever the genre, Berkenkotter et al. found that students must use the appropriate written conventions to communicate effectively in a particular discipline.

A first-year composition course cannot begin to teach students to think and write as accomplished historians, geologists, or nurses. But it can teach students to begin to read for similarity and difference within and between disciplinary scholarship, a kind of reading necessary for their intellectual advancement and a kind of reading whose stakes will get higher as students advance, in academe or in professional endeavors. As Edward Said aptly puts it, "You have to pass through certain rules of accreditation, you must learn the rules, you must speak the language, you must master the idioms . . . of the field . . . to which you want to contribute" (7–8).

The purpose of *Collide* is to introduce students to some of the different written conventions and rhetorical approaches they will encounter throughout a college curriculum. The text teaches by showcasing seventeen original, research-type, discipline-specific responses generated by our contributors on the theme *collide*. Each essay is followed by a reflective piece that discusses the process of the author's thinking and writing and relates this process to disciplinary styles and structures. Representing disciplines from the Humanities, Education, Natural Sciences, Social Sciences, and Visual and Performing Arts, the contributors explore how ideas collide in their fields.

By natural extension, the responses are reflective of the collision of discourses students encounter in their college courses. Students will be exposed to different disciplinary writing styles, for the kind of question that interests the biologist and the psychologist, for instance, will differ, the content of their texts will differ, and the rhetorical conventions that guide their writing will differ. Students will learn how an author's perspective, organizational patterns, and rhetorical choices are representative of larger disciplinary expectations. As well, students will learn, particularly through the reflective pieces, that contributors identify themselves as individuals, as thinkers and writers in relationship with conventions—not merely as adherents to them.

Resistance, individual choice, and writers' effect on disciplinary rules are part of the formation and evolution of conventions in any field. The case can be made that resistance to conventions and the competing values of various discourse vocabularies and communities mean that students need not learn how to read what is "expected" or "conventional" at all. *Collide* works on the assumption that students can make informed scholarly and structural choices—including resisting or abandoning conventions—only when they can first truly read the field.

The book is organized around three acts of colliding: collision of bodies, collision of motives, and collision of languages. Each section contains an introductory discussion contextualizing the contributors' essays within the concept of collision. The contributors follow their essays with a short reflective piece on the writing process. In these pieces, they identify the purpose of their essays and explain how and why they wrote the essays as they did. In addition, the contributors discuss the effect of such strategies on a typical audience in their field. The goal of these reflective pieces is to give students a glimpse into how scholars and professionals construct discipline-specific essays as well as to provide a framework for identifying and understanding "moves" within the content and structure of essays.

To help stimulate discussion and writing, questions on rhetorical considerations and on connections to other essays accompany each contributor's piece. The first kind of question is designed to help students think more critically about how a writer's stylistic and rhetorical choices affect the reading of an essay. These questions ask students to consider the essay as a unique text. The other kind of question makes connections to other essays in the volume, asking students to look for relationships among writings in various disciplines. The two kinds of questions, therefore, prompt students to think about the ways in which an author's writing process is shaped by disciplinary convention and the ways in which it overlaps with other disciplines across the curriculum. Put differently, these questions ask students both to analyze and to synthesize textual and rhetorical elements of essays.

In addition to discussion questions, the volume contains ideas for writing assignments. At the conclusion of each section, a series of writing projects gives students models of how they might explore further the types of collision raised in the essays. The goal is to have students apply what they have learned about textual and rhetorical elements of essays to their own writing.

Collide is intended to help students grasp the rhetorical conventions used by writers and also to recognize subject matter and methodologies of varied disciplines. We want to caution readers, however, that one needs to know more than the formal conventions of a field. As Charles Bazerman comments in his study of genres in scientific discourse, by teaching students the "formal trappings of the genres they need to work in, we offer them nothing more than unreflecting slavery to current practices and no means to ride the change that will inevitably come" in a discipline (320). That is to say, teaching the conventions of a field cannot mean teaching a set of rigid, prescribed procedures. The goal is to teach students to identify *and* locate a field's conventions within the range and meaning of current disciplinary practices. Students should understand how the acquisition of this advanced literacy is the result of both cognitive processes and sociocultural ones. Having helped students to understand how these conventions are embodied in certain practices, we can then suggest ways of using them appropriately and thus persuasively within specific contexts.

Works Cited

Bazerman, Charles, and James Paradis, eds. *Textual Dynamics of the Professions: Historical and Contemporary Studies of Writing in Professional Communities*. Madison: U of Wisconsin P, 1991.

Berkenkotter, Carol, and Thomas Huckin. *Genre Knowledge in Disciplinary Communication*. New Jersey: Erlbaum, 1995.

Said, Edward W. "Opponents, Audiences, Constituencies, and Community." *Critical Inquiry* 9 (1978): 1–26.

WHEN BODIES COLLIDE

What happens when bodies—physical beings or conceptual objects—collide with one another? The essays in this section explore such collisions: what drives them and what the resulting impacts suggest about our culture.

In "So Close Yet So Far: Time-Space Convergence and the Prospect of a Global Village," Mark Pires uses collisions of time and space to discuss the notion of an emerging global village. Pires questions "convergence" and "connection" and "global" and "village"; he then runs these ideas, and others, into each other. The result is a thoughtful consideration of planetary bodies—literal and metaphorical, individual and collective, and human and technological—as well as a critique of our received notions of progress.

In "Colliding Upward: Approaching Equity in the Superintendency," Estelle Kamler focuses on individual, boundaried bodies in the workplace. Using data from the field of educational administration, Kamler argues that our bodies' markers—particularly markers of gender and "race," or ethnicity—have, historically, correlated strongly with career paths and outcomes. Kamler establishes that career paths and outcomes for aspiring superintendents continue to track differently along lines of gender and ethnicity. She then presents data supporting a proactive approach to mentorship networks structured to produce equitable outcomes in educational administration. Thoughtful collision, Kamler shows, can change mentorship outcomes, replacing selective promotion and advantage with equal access for all bodies entering the field.

When what one wants (desire) and what one gets (result) diverge, how does one determine what's gone wrong? Simone Weil Davis proposes that the desire for contact often results instead in collision; she asks that we consider collisions of various kinds as life-affirming impulses gone off course or crashed. The first scene in "Crush: Collision and Contact" is an actual car wreck; Davis then drives us through, among other things, boxing, 70s TV, NASCAR racing, Princess Di's

1

limo, and the work of artist Carlos Almaraz. Along the way, Davis builds a case—a wish, she calls it—that we might less often collide with, and more often contact, who and what we are trying to touch.

Nicholas Ramer, on the other hand, seeks exactly the collision of bodies in "Simulating the Collision of β-Poly(vinylidene fluoride) with Infrared Light." Discussing this carefully simulated collision, which runs on software, Ramer writes: "Our vibrational frequencies are in very good agreement with both the experimental and semi-empirical values," and elsewhere notes for us the value of the information to be gained from such simulations, and the real-world applications of such information in improving and developing devices like SONAR. In Ramer's case, collision is not only not to be avoided; it is to be created where it does not "really" exist, for our benefit.

Finally, Barbara Shorter's article, "Patients Hoping to Alleviate Pain Collide with the Unknown Forces of a Disease," written for this anthology and differently presented to the Journal of Urology *and appearing in its July 2007 issue, presents us with a distinct but related idea of benefit, one tied closely to the human body. In her reflective piece, Shorter tells the story of hundreds of thousands of women suffering from a specific syndrome, in pain, with shared symptoms and shared diagnosis, colliding with a lack of medical knowledge regarding their affliction, and all coming up empty-handed in terms of treatment. Read on to learn what happened to Shorter and these patients, and to see how she shapes the story of their collision with the unknown.*

SO CLOSE YET SO FAR: TIME-SPACE CONVERGENCE
AND THE PROSPECT OF A GLOBAL VILLAGE

Mark Pires, Earth and Environmental Science

"Time" has ceased, "space" has vanished. We now live in a global village.

Marshall McLuhan (1964)

INTRODUCTION

In the fall of 1620, William Bradford and his fellow Pilgrims set sail aboard the Mayflower from Plymouth, England, on a voyage that eventually made landfall at Plymouth Harbor on Cape Cod Bay. The approximately 2,750-mile journey took sixty-six days. Three centuries later, during another momentous era of migration to the New World, waves of European immigrants made trips of similar distance by steamship in about two weeks. In the late twentieth century, a different class of transatlantic voyager, one with deep pockets, could make the crossing in less than three and a half hours traveling at twice the speed of sound aboard the Concorde; others, whose pockets were not so deep, would arrive about five hours later by subsonic aircraft. Overland travel has also seen similar change. For example, journeys between New York and Boston that required three or four days to complete by stagecoach in the early nineteenth century now take as little as three and a half hours by rail aboard Amtrak's Acela Express service. In a manner of speaking, Europe and North America, as well as New York and Boston, are "closer" to each other today than they have been at any time in history.

The circumstances described above reflect what geographers call "time-space convergence," a concept that helps to explain how "the deterrent or inhibiting effect of distance on human activity" has been reduced over time (Knox and Marston 2003, 39). Throughout history, innovations in transportation and communication technology have steadily eroded the so-called "tyranny of distance" that impeded interaction between people and places located, variously, at opposite ends of town, country, continent, and planet. With the rate of change in such innovations having accelerated in recent decades, separation, via time and distance, of different cultures and societies around the world has seemingly collapsed, resulting in greater global interaction accompanied by both positive and negative consequences.

This chapter explores the concept of time-space convergence (TSC), its place in the discipline of geography, and its influence in shaping the contours of an emerging global village. We begin with a definition of TSC and examine its application in contemporary human geography. We will then go on to consider the relevance of TSC for the future of an increasingly interdependent world in the twenty-first century. Here the discussion shall focus on questions of whether we can expect the changing nature of time-space relationships to contribute to more widespread, mutually beneficial human interaction, or whether we instead might find ourselves on a collision course with our own destiny whereby we suffer the consequences of a failure to harness technological gain for the greatest possible good. In other words, are we, the inhabitants of the global village, bound to live together in a single, more equitable world, or in worlds apart segregated by the dangerously divisive forces of socioeconomic injustice and inequity?

THE PLACE OF TIME-SPACE CONVERGENCE IN GEOGRAPHY

A discussion of the concept of time-space convergence is commonly found in most introductory texts in human or cultural geography.[1] A standard definition reads as follows: "The reduction in the travel time between places and the decline in the importance of distance brought about by improvements in transport and communication. It is an important concept in understanding changing spatial distributions, interactions, and relationships" (Small and Witherick 1989, 227). Innovations in transportation and communications typically play the pivotal role in reshaping patterns of spatial interaction between places by virtue of their impact on altering the geography of transportation costs. As Knox and Marston (2003, 43) point out, cost reduction and infrastructure improvement in air travel, satellite communications, electronic-mail software, and other technologies give rise to a shrinking world in which places are brought "closer" together.

Among the five organizing themes in geography—place, location, movement, human-environment interaction, and regions—TSC is most closely associated with the location and movement themes (Geography Education Standards Project 1994). With respect to location, TSC helps to illustrate the idea that while places remain equidistant from each other in absolute terms, their relative locations vis-à-vis one another are subject to change with changing economic and technolog-

---

1. On occasion, one may come across various synonyms for time-space convergence, including "T-S compression," "T-S collision," and "T-S implosion."

ical circumstances. For example, although New York City has been and always will be physically closer to Bismarck, North Dakota, than it is to San Francisco, it can be considered closer to San Francisco than to Bismarck if measured by criteria such as travel time via scheduled airline service. Similarly, the movement theme is concerned with spatial interaction among places and regions and considers diverse flows of people, goods, capital, and ideas within and between different locations at various scales from the local to the global. The volume, frequency, and direction of these flows are subject to change and reflect the dynamic nature of transportation and communication technology, political economy, and cultural influences as these evolve over time.

Examples of how geographers apply the TSC concept range over a broad spectrum of topics. Situated in the domains of location, movement, and spatial interaction, TSC is perhaps most often employed by specialists in the subfield of economic geography. It is also popular among social theorists as a conceptual framework to explore the changing world of social relations now emerging in the postmodern era of rapid globalization (Harvey 1989, 1990), a topic addressed later in this essay. In an historical context, Stein (1996) illustrates the utility of TSC to examine changes in the response time of urban service provision associated with the modernization of fire fighting in late nineteenth-century Canada. Innovations in modes of transportation and the expansion of transportation networks that facilitate the movement of goods and people have traditionally garnered the attention of economic geographers interested in the dynamic relationships between cities and regions (Pawson 1992, Carstensen 1981, Dovey 1998, Wood and Lee 1980). The TSC concept has also been incorporated into the work of geographers who focus on issues of global governance and political economy in a world of constantly shifting international capital flows, territorial configurations, and strategic alliances (Corbridge 1993, Agnew 2000, Jessop 2000, Brunn and Jones 1994). As noted below, questions related to the impact of global capitalism and Westernization on issues of ethnicity, identity, and culture change are also examined through the lens of TSC (Ormrod 1990, Goehring and Stager 1991, King 1997).

Although primarily from the realm of economic geography, the literature cited above illustrates the variety of situations in which TSC is used to interpret the dynamic relationship between time and space. In the next section of the chapter, we turn our attention to the TSC concept as it relates to the notion of the global village.

TSC IN THE CONTEMPORARY GLOBAL CONTEXT

In a book with the intriguing title *The Death of Distance*, a senior editor with *The Economist* of London suggests that the unfolding communications revolution is poised to shepherd in a world where, among other things, "most people on earth will eventually have access to networks that are all switched, interactive, and broadband; inexpensive communications may reduce some of the pressure to emigrate from poor countries; and, [one effect of economic globalization] will be to increase understanding, foster tolerance, and ultimately promote worldwide peace" (Cairncross 1997, xi–xvi). Despite these appealing propositions, one might well ask whether the author isn't being somewhat overly optimistic. As Janelle (1991, 69) cautions, "time-space convergence is not universally applicable to everyone," and one need look no further than the volume of passengers ever transported by the Concorde to find evidence to support this claim.

For some in the global community, we are entering an era of more convenient, less expensive, and seemingly limitless opportunity for the exchange of goods and services and the movement of people across space. In a time-space-compressed global economy, borders no longer present barriers to exchange thanks to "free trade" agreements; capital flows between hemispheres in "dizzying constellations of buying and selling" (Gregory 1994, 98), and the remote wildernesses of the North Pole and Amazon rainforest are transformed into popular tourist destinations. For many others, however, the promise of a hyperlinked world remains, for all intents and purposes, confined to their geographical imaginations. Despite technological innovations in transportation and communication, the majority of people today live in a Janus-faced world where societies are both much closer to and much farther apart from one another than ever before. In considering these circumstances and the question of whether the benefits of TSC can be extended as widely as possible, de Blij and Murphy (2003, 450) suggest, insightfully, that "the scale of our political institutions has not caught up with the scale of our interactions, making it difficult to harness interdependence for the good of the greatest number of people." In other words, our ability to use technological innovations in transportation and communications intelligently and purposefully for the greatest good has not caught up with their ability to bring us so much closer together.

To consider some of the implications of TSC for a global village quickly becoming saturated with too much technology too fast, let us examine some of the ways in which rapid globalization manifests itself in the different economic, political, environmental, and cultural spheres of international affairs. As will be illustrated in the discussion, the costs and benefits of TSC are rarely distributed equally among inhabitants of the village.

Economic Sphere

Perhaps the most important issue of all is the gaping and growing economic divide that separates the people of the world into the "haves" and the "have-nots." While one might suggest that such disparity is simply the manifestation of an inescapable Darwinian reality, I argue that in a modern world shaped by time-space convergence it possesses more serious threat than it ever did in earlier periods of history. Data from the United Nations Development Program (cited in Knox and Marston 2003, 94) on the disparity in wealth among the world's people show that over the last forty years the "gap between the poorest fifth of the world's population and the wealthiest fifth increased more than three-fold." Several associated statistics are clearly alarming. In 1999, for example, the fifth of the world's population living in the highest-income countries had 74 percent of world income while the bottom fifth had just 1 percent; the top fifth controlled 82 percent of world export markets while the bottom fifth had just 1 percent; and the top fifth had 74 percent of world telephone lines, one component of the information superhighway, while the bottom fifth had just 1.5 percent. Clearly, such polarization cannot be a good thing, and it is unwise—not to mention unethical—to ignore how such disparity can contribute to civil unrest, terrorism, and flows of illegal migration, despite Cairncross's contrary optimism, that spill across borders more easily in a time-space-compressed world. Consequently, rich countries would do well to realize that the more their economic well-being is based on exploiting lower labor costs and unsustainably extracting natural resources from poor countries, the more they render themselves vulnerable to the social dislocation and potentially violent political disruption that often ensue when the gap between rich and poor widens.

Political Sphere

As noted above, the world's political institutions have had difficulty keeping up with ever more intense global interactions. We now live in an exceedingly complex and complicated world, one that is far more intricate than the over-simplified binary configuration that prevailed during the Cold War era. Politically speaking, the world's nations are struggling to come to terms with the rapidly evolving geopolitical chessboard of the early twenty-first century, and

despite the optimism for a more secure future that emerged after the fall of the
Berlin Wall, uncertainty, apprehension, and fear have quickly reassumed prominent positions in world affairs.

In commenting on the devastating attacks on the United States in September 2001, Conley (2001) evokes the language of TSC to illustrate its effect in the
geopolitical arena. He said, "Distance has totally collapsed, and the twin towers
are the ultimate metaphor for that collapse. Afghanistan is New York. Palestine
is New York." The metaphor echoes Gregory's discussion of TSC as it relates to
the interaction between places. Quoting Giddens (1990), Gregory (1994, 99)
observes how TSC "connotes a chronic and deeply unsettling change in our
everyday experience of time and space, in the course of which, so Giddens claims,
place becomes 'phantasmagoric': places are 'thoroughly penetrated by and shaped
in terms of influences quite distant from them.'" Indeed, on 11 September 2001,
lower Manhattan was thoroughly penetrated by a most distant influence, one that
effectively collapsed not only the twin towers, but also the distance between
Kabul and Canal Street. Later, in March 2003, the wonders of TSC technology
once again shrank the distance between two places: Iraq and any place in America with a television set. Although these events certainly mark watersheds in
international relations, one cannot say with any certainty what the outcome of
the newly emerging geopolitical alignments will be five, ten, or twenty years
from now. Instead, one might only concede a certain degree of trepidation given
that our political institutions seem to be somewhat poorly prepared to cope with
such brutal change.

Environmental Sphere

Great strides have been made over the last generation to help people reach a
deeper understanding of the inextricable linkages and dynamic interconnections
that exist between human and natural systems on planet Earth. Interestingly,
these efforts, represented by ideas such as the Gaia hypothesis (Lovelock 2000)
and the notion of "Spaceship Earth" (Ward 1966), result in part from the technologies associated with our exploration of the moon and beyond. Early 1970s
photographs taken by NASA's Apollo missions of Earth from the perspective of
outer space provide a powerful symbol of how small the world really is and how
all of humanity is ineluctably "in this together" (Cosgrove 1994).

Insofar as the global village is concerned, signs are both reassuring and trou-
bling about whether we are moving in the right direction with respect to environmental issues. For example, concrete progress has been made in arresting the

depletion of the atmosphere's protective ozone layer through the establishment of the 1987 Montreal Protocol to phase out the use of ozone-depleting chlorofluorocarbons, and it is encouraging to note that considerable international attention is now focused on issues such as global climate change, biodiversity protection, and the promotion of environmentally sustainable economic development.

However, efforts to meet the challenges of the global environment are often stymied by political and economic factors. Examples here include the reluctance of some countries to engage in the Kyoto Protocol on limiting greenhouse gas emissions that contribute to global warming and the introduction of new threats stemming from the recent explosion of wealth in certain countries that affect how people interact with the natural environment. One such threat is associated with the potentially destructive impacts of the ecotourism phenomenon (Vaughan 2000, O'Neill 2002). The challenge of ecotourism, or sustainable tourism as it is sometimes called, is "to [protect] resources of international importance while at the same time facilitating economic growth in both the developed and developing worlds" (O'Neill 2002, 501). Ironically, with forecasts for exceptionally strong growth in ecotourism well into the future, concerns are being raised about whether we risk loving nature to death through the new paradigm that brings larger numbers of people ever closer to some of the most sensitive regions of the natural world. Here again TSC forces are at work, subjecting "remote" places worthy of vigilant protection to more frequent visitation and potentially degrading human activity. As de Blij and Murphy (2003, 421) point out, "as more and more people travel, tourism's social and environmental implications will have to be viewed alongside its economic potential."

Cultural Sphere

One of the great challenges that will confront any movement toward a global village is reconciling the world's enormous cultural diversity with the ostensibly desirable goal of global unity. The global village comprises many different neighborhoods, each with its own set of values, customs, traditions, and aspirations. Although it is often said that good fences make good neighbors, the current trend associated with the globalization process is to dismantle rather than reinforce such fences. How will global villagers respond to living in an increasingly fenceless cultural landscape?

As if this challenge were not difficult enough to begin with, it is further complicated by the existence of certain dominant cultures that are able to project their value and belief systems farther and wider than others by virtue of their access to and control over communication technology (Brunn and Jones 1994). For example, as a satellite dish feeds its signal to a battery-powered television in the middle of the Sahara bringing the world into the Bedouin's tent, the distance that once separated Hollywood or Paris from Timbuktu is obliterated. But what is gained, and by whom, in this transaction? In this example, the collapse of distance is essentially unidirectional: Western culture makes its way into the psyche of the viewers, usually projecting images of the unattainable or undesirable, while those who sent the message are no wiser about the lives and cultures of their global audience. Such exchanges, while not always unhelpful, do underscore the point that some benefit more than others under the current structure of global interdependence facilitated by space-adjusting technology.

The rapid pace of change in communication technology, its usually unidirectional trajectory, the sender's power to filter messages and determine the nature of what is and isn't transmitted (and sometimes the recipient's ability to do the same), and the often limited capacity of recipients to digest, interpret, and respond to the content of the messages received is part of the problem of trying to reconcile cultural differences in the global village. Another part of the problem is the gap in access to technology, the so-called "digital divide," which, for now, strongly determines who does and who doesn't get the message (U.S. Department of Commerce 1999). The prospect that "most people on earth will eventually have access to networks that are all switched, interactive, and broadband" (Cairncross 1997) belies the uphill struggle that will first have to be waged to bring "most people" on Earth on-line. Landing thousands of computers on the tarmac in Tanzania is not the problem. The problem is getting them out of the box and switched on in front of people who are both trained in their use and, preferably, free from the preoccupation of worrying about where their next meal is coming from. Unlike McLuhan's vision of a global village in which its inhabitants are linked to one another via an extended central nervous system of advanced telecommunications, at the present time it appears that most villagers, depending on which side of the gap they currently reside, are either suffering a Toffleresque nervous breakdown due to information overload or starving from information deprivation of Dickensian proportions.

Conclusion

Is humanity on a collision course with its own future? The shape of the world to come and the prospect of a global village will be determined in part by how different societies manage the circumstances of living on a shrinking planet. The effects of time-space convergence on the interactions between various places and the people who live in them have the potential to be rather positive. We have before us an opportunity to do the right thing in the mutual best interests of the global community by bringing more people together, more often, and more conveniently than ever before through the prudent and purposeful application of space-adjusting technology. As Janelle (1991, 79) suggests, such technology "could help to free the innovative potentials of peoples in all parts of the world to solve their basic problems and to share more fully in the benefits of life." However, managing a time-space-compressed world for the greater good is a tall order. Today's world is a risky place, and there is ample evidence of our increasing vulnerability to the multiple threats of political instability, terrorism, global climate change, cultural imperialism, and the possibility of a cascading collapse in the global economy. To avoid such collisions with our own destiny, it is incumbent upon the nations of the world to summon the courage to act with greater determination to effect positive change. Achieving social and economic justice, political stability, environmental sustainability, and tolerance and respect for a multicultural global community will demand that we focus much greater attention on controlling the negative consequences of the widening gap between haves and have-nots, environmental degradation, and political conflict that have so far marked the present era of globalization. To ignore such consequences only increases the risk that humanity will fail to harness the potential of space-adjusting technology, and in the process contribute to the demise rather than the development of the global village.

References

Agnew, J. 2000. Understanding of the changing nature of space and the future of global governance. *Geography Research Forum* 20: 1–13.

Brunn, S., and J. Jones. 1994. Geopolitical information and communication in shrinking and expanding worlds: 1900–2100. In *Reordering the world: Geopolitical perspectives on the twenty-first century*, ed. G. Demko and W. Wood, 301–322. Boulder, CO: Westview Press.

Cairncross, F. 1997. *The death of distance: How the communications revolution will change our lives.* Boston: Harvard Business School Press.

Carstensen Jr., L. 1981. Time-distance mapping and time-space convergence: The southern United States, 1950–1975. *Southeastern Geographer* 21. 67–83.

Conley, D. 2001. Distance has totally collapsed. *The New York Times*, September 16, sec. 14.

Corbridge, S. 1993. Marxisms, modernities, and moralities: Development praxis and the claims of distant strangers. *Environment & Planning D* 11: 449–472.

Cosgrove, D. 1994. Contested global visions: *One-World, Whole-Earth*, and the Apollo space photographs. *Annals of the Association of American Geographers* 84: 270–294.

de Blij, H., and A. Murphy. 2003. *Human geography: Culture, society, and space*. New York: John Wiley & Sons.

Dovey, K. 1998. Multiplicities and complicities: Signifying the future at Euralille. *Urban Design International* 3: 89–99.

Geography Education Standards Project. 1994. *Geography for life: National geography standards 1994*. Washington, DC: National Geographic Research & Exploration.

Giddens, A. 1990. *The consequences of modernity*. Stanford, CA: Stanford University Press.

Goehring, B., and J. Stager. 1991. The intrusion of industrial time and space into the Inuit life-world: Changing perceptions and behavior. *Environment & Behavior* 23: 666–679.

Gregory, D. 1994. Social theory and human geography. In *Human geography: Society, space, and social science*, ed. D. Gregory, R. Martin, and G. Smith, 78–109. Minneapolis: University of Minnesota Press.

Harvey, D. 1989. *The condition of postmodernity*. New York: Basil Blackwell.

Harvey, D. 1990. Between space and time: Reflections on the geographical imagination. *Annals of the Association of American Geographers* 80: 418–434.

Janelle, D. 1991. Global interdependence and its consequences. In *Collapsing space and time: Geographic aspects of communication and information*, ed. S. Brunn and T. Leinbach, 49–81. London: HarperCollins Academic.

Jessop, B. 2000. The crisis of the national spatio-temporal fix and the tendential ecological dominance of globalizing capitalism. *International Journal of Urban and Regional Research* 24: 323–360.

King, A. 1997. *Culture, globalization, and the world-system: Contemporary conditions for the representation of identity*. Minneapolis: University of Minnesota Press.

Knox, P., and S. Marston. 2003. *Places and regions in global context: Human geography*. Upper Saddle River, NJ: Pearson Education.

Lovelock, J. 2000. *GAIA: A new look at life on Earth*. London: Oxford University Press.

McLuhan, M. 1964. *Understanding media*. New York: McGraw-Hill.

O'Neill, A. 2002. What globalization means for ecotourism: Managing globalization's impacts on ecotourism in developing countries. *Indiana Journal of Global Legal Studies* 9: 501–527.

Ormrod, R. 1990. Local context and innovation diffusion in a well-connected world. *Economic Geography* 66: 109–122.

Pawson, E. 1992. Time-space convergence in New Zealand: 1850s to 1990s. *New Zealand Journal of Geography* 94: 14–19.

Small, J., and M. Witherick. 1989. *A modern dictionary of geography*. London & New York: Edward Arnold.

Stein, J. 1996. Annihilating space and time: The modernization of fire-fighting in late nineteenth-century Cornwall, Ontario. *Urban History Review/Revue d'Histoire Urbain* 24: 3–11.

U.S. Department of Commerce. 1999. *Falling through the Net: Defining the digital divide*. http://www.ntia.doc.gov/ntiahome/fttn99/contents.html (accessed July 7, 2003).

Vaughan, D. 2000. Tourism and biodiversity: A convergence of interests? *International Affairs* 76: 283–297.

Ward, B. 1966. *Spaceship Earth*. New York: Columbia University Press.

Wood, L., and T. Lee. 1980. Time-space convergence: Reappraisal for an oil short future. *Area* 12: 217–222.

MARK PIRES, REFLECTIVE PIECE

Take a geography professor committed to enhancing students' communications skills, team him up with a number of colleagues from other disciplines who share that commitment, and ask them to determine a common theme upon which they can frame essays to represent the discursive conventions of their respective fields. Having agreed upon the idea of "collision" as the thread that will bind their collective efforts, each individual is left to decide how to interpret this theme in writing. The geographer at first finds himself a little perplexed, having preferred a competing trope that better matched his specific area of interest. After some reflection, however, he recalls a geographic concept that, with some poetic license, could be used to conform with the common theme and that could also address a topic of broader significance.

This is how I arrived at my decision to write about Time-Space Convergence (TSC) and to use it as a context to discuss the notion of an emerging global village. Geography is concerned primarily with understanding, from an interdisciplinary perspective, the relationships between planet Earth and its inhabitants. Although Earth remains constant in size over time, recent centuries have witnessed a dramatic increase in its human population and phenomenal growth in technological innovations that bring people, goods, capital, and ideas together more easily, quickly, and efficiently than ever before. Consequently, more frequent collisions (i.e., interactions) now take place among members of the human race with important implications for the quality of life that each of us enjoys. The technological changes responsible for our increasing interaction have the potential either to facilitate improvement in the human condition or to exacerbate the predicament in which a majority of humanity already finds itself. To be prepared to take on the challenges of living peacefully in a global village, we need to become better acquainted with the nature of the collisions now taking place and to understand their consequences for our collective future. TSC helps us to see how the world gets smaller with time, the consequences of this process, and why it might behoove us to take notice of what is happening in our village.

I envisioned this essay to represent an exploratory rather than an analytical piece of work, raising questions and evoking themes that I currently engage in some of my teaching. Although time-space convergence and the global village are not new concepts in geography, I considered it worthwhile and timely to combine these ideas in the context of the currently fashionable theme of globalization. Introduction of the topic was accomplished in part by using at the head of the paper the felicitous quotation from McLuhan that speaks succinctly to the overall theme of the essay. The main introductory section begins with an historical vignette that offers an easily understood illustration of TSC. This is followed by paragraphs that explain briefly the TSC concept and how I attempt to use it to explore the idea of the global village. The section also indicates where I intend to take the reader and the specific questions that will be discussed throughout the chapter.

After defining time-space convergence, situating it within the overall themes of geography and providing a very brief literature review, I then move on to present the substance of my argument in the section headlined "TSC in the Contemporary Global Context." In presenting my case I use a variety of sources and styles to introduce and reinforce the points I wish to make. For example, I open this section with reference to a piece from the popular literature (Cairncross 1997) that provides fodder for critical review later on as suggested by the quote that immediately follows from Janelle (1991), a recognized authority on TSC. The section continues with a narrative discussion based primarily upon informal observations bolstered at regular intervals by direct quotations from and citations of scholarly work. I use a multidimensional framework based on economic, political, environmental, and cultural "spheres" of international affairs to examine TSC in the context of the contemporary globalization process. This framework recognizes the interdisciplinary approach that is one of the hallmarks of geographic inquiry. Although somewhat unusual for articles published in scholarly journals, I draw upon information from two textbooks (de Blij and Murphy 2003, Knox and Marston 2003) both to bolster the exploratory questions and to provide some statistical data that support one of my substantive arguments. I am confident in my decision to refer to these sources, given the succinct encapsulation of my position in the first sentence quoted from de Blij and Murphy and the provocative and convincing statistical data cited in Knox and Marston. Metaphor, as related in an article published in *The New York Times* (Conley 2001) and discussed in a more scholarly work (Gregory 1994), is also employed at one point in the text to emphasize an important idea.

In summarizing the discussion, I reconsider the main exploratory question that frames the essay. The tenor of my concluding remarks is equivocal: space-adjusting technologies have both potential and pitfalls insofar as the future of the global community is concerned. I close with an exhortation to be mindful of the consequences of maintaining the status quo, a warning of sorts that speaks to our relatively unquestioning confidence in technological fixes to resolve problems that I would argue require more attention to political and social root causes. Again, the statements made here together with others throughout the essay provide food for thought to fuel debate on the merits of my interpretation of time-space convergence and the prospect for a global village.

While writing the essay I tried very carefully to keep in mind the general tone and structure of what I have come to associate with published work in the mainstream scholarly outlets in my field. Since my contribution is exploratory rather than analytical, the essay does not demonstrate many of the typical conventions used to report the findings of original research such as hypothesis statements, data presentation, statistical analysis, graphs, charts, tables, etc. It does, however, follow a general pattern or sequence of introductory illustration and statement of purpose, a review of relevant literature, a main discussion, and concluding remarks. In one sense, the essay is an example of what might be included under a "commentary" rubric sometimes found in the relevant journals where authors either posit original ideas for consideration by the general readership or respond critically to work published previously.

Insofar as stylistic and mechanical aspects of the essay are concerned, I sought guidance from the "Information for Authors" section of a recent edition of the *Annals of the Association of American Geographers*, one of two flagship journals of the Association published in the United States. Citations in the main body of the text and entries in the reference list conform to the standard author-date parenthetical style used in the journal. Finally, since no piece of writing is perfect upon the first draft, I circulated my work among both the editors of this volume and several colleagues who were willing to review it. The comments and suggestions I received as feedback were very useful in helping me to improve the final draft.

"THINK. WRITE. ASK."

1. Mark Pires tells us that his essay is meant to "represent an exploratory rather than an analytical piece of work." In the text, what suggests that this work is an exploratory one?
2. Although Pires uses statistical data from two textbooks to support his argument, he mentions that this is unusual for academic articles in geography. How do textbooks differ from other types of support, such as journals, articles, or books? Why might textbooks be an unusual choice of information in a research article in Pires's discipline?

3. The paragraph "Although primarily from the realm of economic geography . . ." and the paragraph "To consider some of the implications . . ." are constructed similarly and have a similar purpose. What do these two paragraphs accomplish? Do you find them useful in understanding the text, and if so, why?

4. Pires, Estelle Kamler, and Simone Davis all state that they use narration as a mode of discourse in their essays, whether it is by making informal observations, by embracing the narrative "I," or by sharing relevant personal stories. Try to identify the passages from these essays that represent a *narrative* organizational pattern. How do the narrative techniques used by a geographer, an educational administrator, and a cultural studies critic differ from one another?

5. Pires, Erica Frouman-Smith, Jerome Tognoli, and Barbara Fowles use various approaches in writing their conclusions. What are some of the similarities and differences between them? Which of the four conclusions feels most like your natural style? Why do you think you tend to write that way?

COLLIDING UPWARD: APPROACHING EQUITY
IN THE SUPERINTENDENCY

Estelle Kamler, Educational Leadership and Administration

"Woman will learn the power of association and she will learn the value of herself."

New York Working Women's Protective Union 1863 (Cited in Berg, 1978, p. 143)

INTRODUCTION—THE HUMAN IMPACT

Individuals who become school superintendents enter a world where their values and actions can leave an indelible imprint on the entire school community. These chief executive officers are responsible for shaping the goals of the school system and providing professional leadership and direction for all educational programs and extra-curricular activities. In speaking of the superintendency, Bullard and Taylor (1993) said, "America's children have entrusted us [superintendents] with their dreams. . . . We are the stewards of their future . . ." (p. 410).

Given the power and influence inherent in the superintendency, it would appear that gifted educators of both genders and all ethnic backgrounds who have vision for and deep commitment to the profession would vie for this role. The percentage of males and females as well as the racial composition in the superintendency would therefore reflect the gender and race distributions in other teaching and administrative positions. However, this is far from reality.

The drastic decline of women in the superintendency from approximately 11% nearly a century ago to a low of three percent in the 1970s and the limited rise in the number of women superintendents to today's national percentage levels of 12 to 15 percent (Archer, 2003) can be analyzed through a spectrum of social, political, and economic lenses with multiple and complex factors converging as determinants. There is, however, one consistent thread in career advancement throughout the decades, and that is the clout of influential people— the network of support and linkage to those who are prominent in the hiring process.

The web of connections—the "old boys" network—that has traditionally propelled white men up the career ladder has long been recognized (Moody, 1983). The advantages of being included in this exclusive "club" are access to role models, one-on-one or multiple mentors who provide psychosocial nurturing as well as career development counseling—not to mention the initial self-esteem benefit of being invited into a privileged enclave. Being tapped on the shoulder, supported, coached, and sponsored are dynamic forces that can be equated to a human collision affecting not only the destiny of the individual but also the future of education.

Blount (1998) views the current status of women and confirms the role of advocates and networks in women's reemergence into the superintendency. She states:

> Slowly, they [women] are also assuming more school superintendencies. This gradual change is not an accident, but rather is the result of persistent, courageous, collective efforts by activists determined to see equitable distribution of power in school employment. It is also a tribute to the women and men who have mentored and encouraged women onward. (pp. 147–148)

The role of the mentor and the proactive functions of both informal and formal networks have been acknowledged as key components in preparing and promoting individuals for advancing their careers. The political activism of the suffragettes and the rebirth of the women's movement which led to the 1972 passage of Title IX resulted in more women assuming the superintendency.

The educational literature is replete with references to the significance of networking—the impact of one person or a group of people on an aspirant in attainment of a superintendency. In an effort to clarify this human domino effect as it relates to the past and present state of the superintendency, I will discuss in this essay what is known about mentors and networks and review current research about networking models as well as specific strategies that have been cited as being important for women and people of color to secure the superintendent's position. In addition, a new kind of network, one that is inclusive and designed to encourage and support talented leaders regardless of gender and race to seek the superintendency, will be presented to illustrate an innovative solution implemented by one collaborative group of educators to elevate equity in the superintendency.

Although the superintendency is fraught with a myriad of challenges such as the implementation of federal and state mandates for higher standards and the accompanying rigorous assessments, this top administrative post, even with extensive internal and external political pressures from unions, parents, and the community, still provides the foremost pathway to advance an educational system. This prominent and visible position also affords individuals the opportunity to become role models for children as well as adults and to promote beliefs and leadership approaches that underscore democracy. With America's ever-growing multicultural population, as well as a reported dearth of applicants for the superintendency, it appears to be more important than ever to ensure access to this position by equal representatives of our society, including women and people of color.

STATISTICS—INEQUITY EXISTS

In a recent study of American school superintendents, Glass, Bjork, and Brunner (2000) found that 86.6 percent of American school superintendents are males and 13.2 are females, with 91.6 percent of the women being white. These numbers represent national averages; however, the percentages of women superintendents have in recent years increased beyond the national average in some states. Wolverton (1999) noted that the Association of California School Administrators in 1997 identified the state of Delaware as having the highest percentage of women superintendents with 26 percent. In 2000, The New York State Council of School Superintendents published the results of a study of New York State superintendents. The report found that gender diversity in New York had increased, with the percentage of female superintendents rising from 12.1% to 18.4% in three years. In addition, the study noted that nearly 30% of new superintendents were women; however, also referenced was the fact that ethnic diversity was less than 1.5 percent.

Based on the latest findings, there appears to be a steady increase in at least the percentage of women who have been appointed to the superintendency. However, these statistics do not uncover the full story and should not comfort us with the notion that we have turned the corner with equal access to the super-intendency. To fully understand gender equity in the superintendency, it is help-ful to know that presently 65 percent of the teachers and 43 percent of the principals are female. Also of note, 10.9 percent of the public school teachers and 12.3 percent of the principals are people of color (Shakeshaft, 2000, pp. x-xi). Clearly in the superintendency, women are underrepresented. Bjork (2000) pro-vides a perspective regarding the percentage increases of women in the superin-tendency in recent years. He tells us that women have increased in all administrative positions; however, at the senior levels such as the superinten-dency there has been "little significant progress." The U. S. Census Bureau char-acterized the superintendency as being the "most male-dominated executive position of any profession" (p. 8).

HISTORY—HOW FAR HAVE WE COME?

In 1909 when Ella Flagg Young was appointed as the first woman superintendent of Chicago schools, she proudly stated:

> Women are destined to rule the schools of every city. I look for a large majority of the big cities to follow the lead of Chicago in choosing a woman for superintendent. In the near future we will have more women than men in executive charge of the vast educational system. It is woman's natural field, and she is no longer satisfied to do the greatest part of the work and yet be denied leadership. (p. 515)

Blount notes that in the earlier decades of the twentieth century, thousands of women succeeded in attaining school leadership positions. She refers to Hansot and Tyack's label of the "golden age" for women administrators when "hundreds of women waged successful campaigns for superintendencies. By 1930 women accounted for 28 percent of county superintendencies and 11 percent of all superintendents nationwide" (p. 61). The growth in the number of women in the superintendency coincided with women's visibility on the political scene, winning them greater economic, social, and political power. Blount credits the strength of the women's movement and the web of connections among women superintendents, teachers, women's association members, and suffrage activists as "providing the essential network for women's rise to school leadership positions" (p. 81). However, this initial period of promise did not persist with women's representation in most school administrative positions—"quietly, but rapidly declining" from the end of World War II to the 1970s where the percentages "plummeted from 9 to 3 percent . . ." (p. 2).

Evidently, the gains achieved in the early twentieth century did not foreshadow equal access for women in this position. With the G. I. Bill's support for teaching and for administrative certification for veterans, the demise of the women's movement, American's urbanization and the resulting consolidation of school districts, and an increased sex stereotyping of "management" as a male domain, women administrators were a vanishing breed (Schmuck, 1995).

MENTORS AND NETWORKS—PATHWAY TO ACCESS

Through the centuries, mentoring has been recognized for ensuring that selected novices would have an easier road to career fulfillment. We are first introduced to the term mentor in Homer's epic *The Odyssey*. Odysseus, leaving for the Trojan War, gave the responsibility of nurturing his son Telemachus to Athena, goddess of wisdom, who took Mentor's form. Mentor educated and guided Telemachus, providing for his physical, intellectual, spiritual, social, and administrative development (Crow & Matthews, 1998; Schwiebert, Deck, Bradshaw, Scott, & Harper, 1999).

Educational as well as business literature indicates that effective mentors provide valuable career and psychosocial assistance for aspirants as they progress in the profession from initiation to mastery (Hall & Klotz, 2001; see also Kram, 1983; Shakeshaft, 1989). Career functions advance the mentee's career through "sponsorship, exposure, and visibility, coaching and protection, and challenging assignments." The psychosocial aspect is affective in nature where the mentee is supported to meet both psychological and emotional challenges. This aspect of mentoring includes "role modeling, acceptance and confirmation, counseling and friendship" (Kram, 1983, pp. 613–614).

From my personal experiences as a woman who served in the superintendency for nine years, I can attest to the importance of a mentor. As I moved from one administrative post to the next in my "climb up the ladder" to the superintendency, there were both prejudicial roadblocks and ongoing mentoring and sponsorship by men in positions of power. I can remember my first interview for a fledgling administrative position where the superintendent told me that he would only hire me as a kindergarten teacher. By contrast, the superintendent who supervised me during my administrative internship continued his guidance, encouragement, and active sponsorship, and assisted me through the labyrinths of my career. It is very clear to me that one does not advance by just ability and skill (Kamler, 1995). A mentor who buoys the aspirant's self-esteem and forwards the individual through connections to a wider group of sponsors (networks) may very well make the difference between that individual always being the aspirant or becoming the superintendent.

In actuality, a mentor's sponsorship of a mentee into a network of other potential sponsors may be the key for the aspirant in securing a superintendency. Shakeshaft (1989) further clarifies:

> Related to sponsorship is the need to have access to a network that provides one with information on job openings and administrative strategies as well as visibility and a support group. Women have traditionally been excluded from these networks and thus have not heard about administrative positions, have not been known by others, and have had few people to approach for counsel. (p. 176)

Sharp, Malone, Walter, and Suppley (2000) confirm this belief in their three-state study of female superintendents in which several barriers including a lack of professional networks, membership in the "old boys" network, and influential sponsors were identified as preventing women from accessing the superintendency. Moody (1983) and Alston (1999) also cite these obstacles as problematic for both Afro-American male and female aspirants.

Certainly, the "old boys" network has been viewed as advantageous to those who have been taken into its fold. However, to increase access for women and people of color into the superintendency, the "old boys" network needs to be transformed into a more inclusive environment (Blount, 1998; Gardiner, Enomoto, & Grogan, 2000; Grogan, 1996; Tallerico, 2000). Studies have been conducted to determine the specific needs of women and people of color to assist their entrance into the superintendency. In addition, individuals and organizations have taken a lead by implementing different strategies and creating new structures that change historical networking patterns to promote greater access for women and people of color. It may serve to advance the network transformation process by identifying those elements in these newly established practices as well as further considering the role that women in leadership are playing in support of other women for the superintendency.

FORCES FOR CHANGE—INDIVIDUAL
AND ORGANIZATIONAL INTERVENTIONS

Keller (1999, para. 1) states that "if women are to increase their representation at the top levels of their profession they must have help from those who have gone before." She reports that 17 percent of Washington State's 296 districts were headed by women. Credit for the state of Washington becoming so "open to women superintendents" was given to three women superintendents who bring "national reputation to their districts and have helped clear the way by working with groups such as the Women's Caucus of the American Association of School Administrators (AASA) for other women leaders" (para. 8). Blount also refers to the AASA's related research publications, annual meeting, and Women's Administrators' Conference, which "enjoy a growing social and political presence within the larger association and offer support for women serving as administrators or seeking such positions" (p. 148). In addition, Schmuck (1995) highlights the importance of a significant number of regional and state organizations of women administrators which advocate for women in educational administration.

Research has supported the need for white women and those of color to mentor other women, to provide role models for a leadership approach that focuses on relationship and team building—the style of leadership most identified with successful women superintendents (Brunner, 2000; Enomoto, Gardiner, & Grogan, 2000; Grogan, 1996). In addition, according to the Association of American Medical Colleges Project Committee (1996):

> Increasing the number of prominent women as role models would add diversity and balance to leadership, benefiting both sexes. . . . The presence of women seeking to combine family and professional responsibilities is making it easier for men to play a greater role in their children's lives as well. . . . (p. 802)

Although there is merit in promoting women through women's organizations in educational literature, some concerns regarding these organizations have been examined. Mainly these issues focus on: (a) the level of participation of women leaders; (b) whether the web of connections within these women's organizations extends to those who have the "power" to sponsor and support women aspirants for the superintendency effectively; and (c) whether these organizations serve as exemplary models of leadership to advance democratic educational systems.

Sobehart and Giron (2002) note that "research indicates current women administrators are not carrying their weight as mentors to other women" (p. 44). In recent conversations with the organizer of the Women's Conference for AASA as well as with a prominent member of the New York State Association of Women Administrators, I was told that in actuality only a limited number of women superintendents are present and/or speak at the major networking events sponsored by these organizations. Bell and Chase (1996) explored women superintendents' professional relationships, including colleagues, mentors, informal networks, and professional organizations. They found that women's connections to other women in which they not only gave but also received nurturing were deemed positive. However, women-to-women connections could be considered precarious since women who associate with women's groups may be criticized, unlike men who affiliate with all male associations. Bell (1995) noted that, in male-dominated professions, "pressure to disaffiliate from other women arises from women's need to prove themselves different from the negative stereotypes of others like them" (p. 308). It therefore appears that although women leaders are an important cog in the mentoring and networking process to promote other women into the superintendency, based on women's concerns about further discrimination, an all-female network may not attract those who are essential to changing the current status.

In comparing the "old boys" network to women organizations, there is also the concern of exclusivity and whether in actuality one structure better serves not only those who are trying to gain access to the superintendency, but also the educational community as a whole. Gardiner, Enomoto, and Grogan (2000) speak to the conflict that women and minorities experience with mentoring and networking:

> Traditional mentoring may have been their [women's and minorities'] only means to enter the ranks of administration, but once they are within the network, how do they keep themselves from succumbing to the attitudes and beliefs that discriminate against so many others like them? . . . The power to include or exclude potential administrators, to reward or punish them, lies not at the hands of individuals . . . but in the effects of participating in the network and in the outcome of activities that sustain it. (p. 189)

In contrast to a network based on exclusion, Gardiner et al. (2000) encourage a "new discourse on leadership" which includes "openness and outreach" (p. 194) and is founded on "an ethic of caring to mentor others actively" in a "collaborative structure" (p. 199).

Bell and Chase (1996) found that women superintendents' professional connections to white men were positive in their being included in the "power structures" and "support networks of educational administration" (p. 129). As noted in a study by Enomoto, Gardiner, and Grogan (2000), which focused on issues of race and gender as 18 women respondents described their mentoring relationship, "women of color need to (a) gain political savvy; (b) access networks; (c) find mentors who are similar to their protégés; (d) seek mentors who are different from their protégés, and (e) secure alternative support systems" (p. 577) to address the challenges of being minority.

It is apparent that although the "old boys" network in its exclusive form has not well served women and people of color, an exclusive female network may not be the answer to achieving greater access for females and aspirants of color. Emerging from the research, there appears to be a need for men to work in partnership with women leaders to provide career counseling and emotional support to females and aspirants of color. The female and male leaders' perspectives of political "know how," their collective connections to both men and women in power, and their modeling of different leadership styles and problem-solving methods may prove to increase both the interest of potential superintendent aspirants and the access to the position. An example of this type of network has recently been established in New York State.

NETWORK TRANSFORMATION—ALTERING THE BLUEPRINT OF OPERATION

In 2001, the Nassau County School Superintendents Council in partnership with the Long Island School Leadership Center designed and implemented an Aspiring Superintendents' Study Group—a unique group that uses mentoring and networking to tap promising administrators and promote their interest in the superintendency. The Aspiring Superintendents' Study Group combines an intimate setting for personal dialogue with a larger forum for capturing multiple perspectives on a variety of issues to enhance learning, forge connections, and provide a safe and secure place to nurture leadership. Aspirants are treated to a closer look at how leaders in the field differ in style while discussing philosophical and practical aspects of the superintendency. Here both male and female superintendents work collaboratively to inspire and prepare future superintendents. It may also be interesting to note that the majority of aspirants who have been tapped for participation are women, although there are some male aspirants and people of color.

As the coordinator of this formalized structure, I have been in the process of gathering data regarding the effectiveness of this group. The enthusiastic responses from those in attendance and their continued and active participation indicate that these sessions have proven to be worthwhile. It will be important, however, to examine the long-term effects of this initiative to determine if the efforts of this group increase the field of potential candidates and provide them with the knowledge and skills to be impressive competitors for the superintendency. If so, this model may prove to be one that other groups can replicate to transform the culture of current networks into an all-encompassing and equitable structure for access.

Conclusion—Influencing the Future

The transfer of energy from one person to another is a potent charge that has life-altering results. Women and men alike who have achieved influential positions have the responsibility to collaborate with each other to ensure that *all* people of talent and potential will have access to the superintendency. A network comprised of prominent female and male educators from all racial backgrounds who embrace the principles of democracy by joining forces to create broad and caring connections respectful and appreciative of diversity can only result in greater equity for all, lighting the way for a stronger, inclusive nation. To quote Blount (1998):

> If we continue to support schools that systematically distribute power unequally by sex and gender, we send a forceful message to students about women's worth, their potential, and their place in society. Gross inequities in one part of the educational system will inevitably be perpetuated in others. A truly fair system for female and male students will not exist until we question the deeply rooted tradition of denying women power in public schooling. (p. 169)

References

Alston, J. A. (1999). Climbing hills and mountains: Black females making it to the superintendency. In C. C. Brunner (Ed.), *Sacred Dreams: Women and the superintendency* (pp. 79–90). Albany, NY: State University of New York Press.

American Association of University Women Educational Foundation. (1996). *Girls in the middle: Working to succeed in school.* Washington, DC: Author.

Archer, J. (2003). Survey studies barriers to women leaders. *Education Week on the Web.* Retrieved April 25, 2000, from http://www.edweek.org/ew/newstory.cfm?slug=25AASA.h22

Bell, C., & Chase, S. (1996). The gendered character of women superintendents' professional relationships. In K. Arnold, K. Noble, & R. Subotnick (Eds.), *Remarkable women: Perspectives on female talent development* (pp. 117–131). Cresskill, NJ: Hampton.

Bell, C. R. (1996). *Managers as mentors.* San Francisco, CA: Berrett-Koehler Publishers.

Bell, C. S. (1995). "If I weren't involved with schools, I might be radical:" Gender consciousness in context. In D. M. Dunlap & P. A. Schmuck (Eds.), *Women leading in education* (pp. 288–312). Albany, NY: State University of New York Press.

Berg, B. (1978). *The remembered gate: Origins of American feminism.* New York: Oxford University Press.

Blount, J. M. (1998). *Destined to rule the schools: Women and the superintendency 1873–1995.* Albany, NY: State University of New York Press.

Bjork, L. G. (2000). Introduction: women in the superintendency—advances in research and theory. *Educational Administration Quarterly, 36*(1), 5–17.

Brunner, C. C. (1997). Working through the "riddle of the heart": Perspectives of women superintendents. *Journal of School Leadership, 7*, 139–164.

Brunner, C. C. (2000). *Principles of power: Women superintendents and the riddle of the heart.* Albany, NY: State University of New York Press.

Bullard, P., & Taylor, B. O. (1993). *Making school reform happen.* Boston: Allyn & Bacon.

Crow, G. M., & Matthews, L. J. (1998). *Finding one's way: How mentoring can lead to dynamic leadership.* Thousand Oaks, CA: Corwin Press.

Enomoto, E., Gardiner, M., & Grogan, M. (2000). Notes to Athene: Mentoring Relationships for Women of Color. *Urban Education, 35*(5), 567–583.

Gardiner, M., Enomoto E., & Grogan, M. (2000). *Coloring outside the lines.* Albany, NY: State University of New York Press.

Glass, T., Bjork, L., & Brunner, C. (2000). *The study of the American school superintendency.* Arlington, VA: American Association of School Administrators.

Grogan, M. (1996). *Voices of women aspiring to the superintendency.* Albany, NY: State University of New York Press.

Hall, L., & Klotz, J. (2001, November). *A regional study of gender differential perceptions of mentoring functions in accessing the superintendency.* Paper presented at the annual meeting of the Mid-South Educational Research Association, Little Rock, Arkansas.

Kamler, E. (1995). *Gatekeeping: The relationship between the search consultant, women and the superintendency.* Unpublished doctoral dissertation, Hofstra University.

Keller, B. (1999, November 10). Women superintendent credit support from colleagues. *Education Week on the Web.* Retrieved November 14, 2002, from http://www.edweek.org/ew/ewstory.cfm?slug=11seattle.h19

Keller, B. (1999, November 10). In Washington state. A welcoming hand for women chiefs. *Education Week on the Web.* Retrieved May 28, 2002, from http://www.edweek.org/ew/ewstory.cfm?slug=11wash.h19

Kram, K. E. (1983). Phases of the mentor relationship. *Academy of Management Journal, 26*(4), 608–625.

Moody, Sr., C. D. (1983). On becoming a superintendent: contest or sponsored mobility? *Journal of Negro Education, 52*(4), 385–389.

New York State Council of School Superintendents (NYSCOSS). (2000). *Snapshot 2000: A study of school superintendents in New York State.* Albany, NY: Volp.

Schmuck, P. A. (1995). Advocacy organizations for women school administrators, 1977–1933. In D. M. Dunlap & P. A. Schmuck (Eds.), *Women leading in education* (pp. 199–224). Albany, NY: State University of New York Press.

Schwiebert, V. L., Deck, M. D., Bradshaw, M. L., Scott, P., & Harper, M. (1999). Women as mentors. *Journal of Humanistic Counseling, Education and Development, 37,* 241–253.

Shakeshaft, C. (1989). *Women in educational administration.* Newbury Park, CA: Sage.

Shakeshaft, C. (2000). Foreword. In C. C. Brunner, *Principles of power: Women superintendents and the riddle of the heart* (pp. ix–xvi). Albany, NY: State University of New York Press.

Sharp, W. L., Malone, B. G., Walter, J. K., & Suppley, M. L. (2000). A three-state study of female superintendents. Paper presented at the annual meeting of the Mid-Western Educational Research Association, Chicago, IL.

Sobehart, H. C., & Giron, K. L. (2002, November). Athena as mentor. *Women Administrators Conference 2002 Monograph, 43–48*. School of Education Leadership Institute and American Association of School Administrators.

Tallerico, M. (2000). *Accessing the superintendency.* Thousand Oaks, CA: Corwin Press.

Wolverton, M. (1999, Spring). The school superintendency: Male bastion on equal opportunity? *Advancing Women in Leadership Journal, 1.* Retrieved July 3, 2002, from http://www.advancingwomen.com/awl/ spring99/Wolverton/wolver.html.

ESTELLE KAMLER, REFLECTIVE PIECE

For me the word *collide* corresponded to my research regarding women's entrée into the superintendency and the potent relationship between a network of sponsors and aspirants. That is, having such a network results in upward career mobility. Initially, the essay began with a short personal story, followed by research-based remarks to provide authority for my viewpoint. However, I changed the organization of the piece after I delved further into the educational research. By reviewing conference papers and recently published journal articles and books in educational administration, I became more informed about the topic and decided that it was important to frame the discussion for the reader with references from the professional literature. It seemed to me that the description of my personal experiences would better punctuate my point of view and clarify the link between theory and practice if embedded in a theoretical context. In addition, I began to reflect on the informal and formal conversations I was having with aspirants and superintendents in my role as Coordinator of the Nassau County Aspiring Superintendents' Study Group and on the significance of this networking environment on both the aspirants and the participating superintendents. With the encouragement of several peer reviewers, I added this information to provide another authentic connection to the field of educational leadership and administration.

To set the stage for my argument, I used both statistical information and educational literature to provide a retrospective about women in the superintendency. I also used multiple sources to underscore the value of mentors and networks for securing the superintendency. In addition, I included some personal reflections from both my experiences as an aspirant to the superintendency and my experiences as a superintendent.

To strengthen my argument, I described the Aspiring Superintendents' Study Group, which provides for the reader a working model of an inclusive network. However, I acknowledged that the data collection for this venture was in its infancy and that, to state definitively the merit of this model, it would be necessary to analyze further the data that has been collected to date as well as to gather additional information and examine the longitudinal effects of this configuration.

In the final section of the essay, I revisited the metaphor of collision and stated its connection to the powerful forces of the human dynamics of a network and aspirants. Rather than ending with my own words, I decided to use a quotation from a respected researcher whom I believed captured the full picture of unequal access to the superintendency and succinctly as well as artfully related this concern to the broader issue of education.

Throughout the essay my voice was integrated with the voices of researchers from the field of educational administration. In the process of revision, I paraphrased more readily, rather than using lengthy quotations that I believed interfered with the point I was trying to clarify. In my first draft I used questions to launch each section of the essay; however, in the revision, I eliminated this stylistic approach and substituted direct statements grounded in research to strengthen the lead as well as to continue to provide the reader with reputable data to support my stance. I did notice that I like to group ideas and that my sentences are complex, highlighting vocabulary enriched by my readings.

"THINK. WRITE. ASK."

1. Estelle Kamler uses a quotation prior to her introduction that is implicitly related to the purpose of her essay. In what way does this quotation comment on the entire essay? As a reader, how did you respond to the quotation?

2. What is the purpose of Kamler's essay? How can you tell? Does Kamler explain her purpose explicitly, or must you observe the essay as a whole and use context to determine the purpose?

3. Kamler tells us that in an earlier draft she began the essay with a personal story about her mentoring experiences, but ultimately revised the essay to the structure in which you see it now. How would a return to the original drafting, that is, starting with a personal story, affect the tone and organization of the article?

4. Kamler uses a variety of evidence (statistical data, case-studies, personal experiences) to support her argument. Identify these types of evidence in her essay. What type of evidence do you find most convincing in argumentative writing? In what situation would this type of evidence not be as successful or appropriate?

5. Compare Kamler's sentence structure patterns (sentence length and variation) with Barbara Fowles's and Cara Gargano's. What similarities and differences can you find in the sentence patterns of these three writers? Does this help you draw any conclusions about disciplinary writing? Which choices do you tend towards in your own writing?

CRASH: COLLISION AND CONTACT

Simone Weil Davis, English

"Damn," I think. No, I say it out loud. In eight minutes my class starts, I'm still 20 miles from campus, and this jam is going nowhere. It's not like I can afford another absence: I'm the teacher. The traffic starts up and immediately stops, over and over, trying and failing, an irregular heartbeat. In the last hour and a half, I've traversed maybe three miles. I strike the steering wheel with the side of my hand, as if that did any good. "Damn!" My feet play at the clutch, the brake, and the gas pedals like some impotent church organ.

A curve rounded, I finally see what's caused the horrendous snarl. Of course: a smash-up. A black Nissan Sentra is tilted at a nauseating diagonal across the far-left lane, its front end crumpled and the windshield shattered. Eerily, the other car in the crash is exactly the make and model I'm driving: a blue, late 80s Honda Civic is off to the side of the road, with its right rear bumper and passenger door just annihilated, caved in. The police and ambulances are firmly on the scene, the flares have been set, the proper authorities are at work. The traffic permits me to move up a few feet and I am able to see a stretcher being lifted into the back of one of the ambulances. Sitting on the guardrail, a woman in shorts and a "Twin Towers" T-shirt is hunched up, curled in on herself. A cop squats in front of her, talking her up earnestly. I wonder if she was the Honda's driver. Yes, I am staring. As the minutes careen forward and I jerk only inches, I reflect on the class full of students waiting for me and entirely beyond my reach, and I continue to stare. In fact, when I finally catch up to the scene unfolding in the collision's aftermath, I risk generating a fender-bender of my own, as I crane my neck to look sideways. Everyone does just the same thing, slowing down a hair more than is technically required, in order to see. That, above all, is what has caused this remarkable fifteen-mile back-up that began in Brooklyn and now has us well into Nassau County: multiplied by a thousand drivers, an unseemly but uncontrollable impulse to rubberneck supersedes all else, to peek, to take in whatever rich detail one's moment of passing will offer up. It's our due, after having waited so long in a crawling line of cars. It's our due, having taken the same risk the Nissan's and Honda's drivers took, but having gotten away with it today. It's our due, to slide past the crash and stare. Having gawked, gratefully, we accelerate and the jam disperses. The accident victims stay where they are, and we speed off.

**

We are a people accustomed to the spectacle of collisions. From the action TV of the 70s and 80s (*Streets of San Francisco, The Mod Squad, Miami Vice*), past any video game or digitally enhanced blockbuster of today, straight through to *Jackass* and *World's Wildest Police Videos*, we take our entertainment with as much explosive impact as the stunt drivers, pyro-technicians, and special effects department can provide us. NASCAR has pulled out way in front (if you'll pardon the automotive imagery) as the most popular spectator sport in America, and at its heart lies not just speed, but the very real possibility of collision. The Daytona 500 has taken many drivers' lives, perhaps most famously that of NASCAR champ Dale Earnhardt in February 2001. *USA Today* allows interested web readers to use its graphic feature to "follow the path of Earnhardt's fatal crash" for themselves.[1] From James Dean in his tortured Porsche to Princess Di's limo, there is nothing more glamorous to us than a beautiful celebrity mangled and made myth by a terrible car crash. Andy Warhol's paintings weren't all of soup cans, Elvis, and Marilyn Monroe: in 1963 and 1964 he created his influential print series *Death and Disaster*, which turns graphic crash scenes into "celebritized" pop art. Run through the blockbusters you saw this summer, or even the ads for upcoming Hollywood action movies you saw on TV this month. How many images of collision did you see? Too many to count? In this essay, I'd like to ask what marriage of yearning and terror this is that lurks behind our culture's horrified fascination with collision. What makes us crave and compulsively revisit what we most fear? Perhaps, too, we fear that which we most crave. But I am getting ahead of myself.

One visual artist who turned to the car crash in a number of his paintings was Carlos Almaraz (1941–1987). Almaraz was one member of a Chicano art collective known as Los Four that, between 1973 and 1983, had an enormous impact on the Latino art world and the urban landscape of Los Angeles with their many large murals and public art installations. In the early eighties, Almaraz put up a show entitled *L. A. Parks and Wrecks*; as the name suggests, many of the canvases depicted car crashes. In one segment of a 1986 interview with the Smithsonian's Margarita Nieto, Almaraz talked about the show and what inspired it. "In Echo Park [by which he lived] you have this very serene lake facing you, a sense of something totally fictional. And then to the left of you, you've got the Hollywood freeway, which literally has crashes going on every few hours. . . . I

---

1. http://www.usatoday.com/sports/motor/earnhardt/2001-02-19-ccover.htm

used to wake up to the sound of metal crunching . . . and the contrast between the two had a lot to do with my own life" (Almaraz). The wrecks depicted in Almaraz's paintings were often multiethnic, and often involved a police car and a low-rider (the latter associated, of course, with Chicano culture). The smash-ups in his work often crossed the line between accidental collisions and the wreckage caused by very intentional shoot-outs: in each case, "metal crunched" and smoke billowed.

> People say, "Well, why do you paint such terrible things?" I said, ". . . I've been given this power to make images and . . . I can't just paint pretty pictures, because I have fears [like] everyone else does, and sometimes I have to make a picture of these fears." I know that children understand that very well. If they show cars crashing or airplanes crashing, it's because they're frightened. They have to get into a plane with mommy and daddy and they don't under-stand. . . . They do understand that this thing could fall! They've seen it on television. So in school they sit down and they draw that anxiety and make a rendering out of it, and somehow it's less frightening when you see it there in front of you, than it is inside your heart and inside your head. (Almaraz)[2]

Almaraz felt that the crashes he saw and heard from his Echo Park apartment were an integral part of Los Angeles life, more than they were its accidental byproducts. Along related lines, in 1970, Mexican poet Octavio Paz wrote that "the Accident is not an exception or a sickness . . . nor is it a correctable defect of our civilization: it is the natural consequence of our science, our politics, and our morality" (112). He called the nuclear bomb "the universal Accident," an apocalypse that always threatened but that, like a car crash, couldn't be sched-uled into anyone's calendar (111). And by that token, it is no accident, then, that we are what Mikita Brottman calls a "car crash culture."

As if in direct contrast to Almaraz's notion that "somehow it's less frighten-ing when you see it right in front of you," images of this country's *military* col-lisions are typically strangely buffered, supplanted not by "pretty pictures," but by palatable ones. The American mass media often bolster the government's public image by keeping the bloody consequences of our military actions out of sight and providing us with other, more soothing images to put in their place. During the first Gulf War, Desert Storm, we watched "smart bombs" penetrat-

---

2. Interview with Carlos Almaraz conducted by Margarita Nieto of the Smithsonian Institute at the Archives of American Art Southern California Research Center in Los Angeles, CA. 6, 13, & 20 February and 31 July 1986, and 29 January 1987.

ing air-shafts again and again, marveling over the precision of these surgical strikes; the destruction that left more than 100,000 Iraqis dead, many of them women and children, meanwhile went unseen.[3] In March 2003, we watched and heard the "shock and awe" fireworks that kicked off the second Gulf War and then several weeks later were invited to feel our bosoms swell with patriotic pride as George W. Bush announced the war's successful "conclusion" from the aircraft carrier upon which he'd just landed. Again, images and reportage of dead and injured civilians were declared vulgar and were barely disseminated, although somewhere between 6,000 and 7,700 civilian deaths have been reported so far, as I write this.[4]

This antiseptic packaging of the actual collisions of war runs concurrent with pop culture's nonstop crashes and "kaBOOMs," ever-theatricalized, ever-present, that keep us always face to face with the spectacular force of colliding bodies. Perhaps Almaraz was right. Perhaps, like the children in his quotation, we are frightened and in our movies, rock concerts, TV shows, and bestsellers are "rendering our anxiety" with a crash. Is this what drives us to stage wrecks and explosions, to pay to see cars and planes tumble and burn (hopefully with an attractive cast along for the ride), even while shirking the carnage and consequences of actual collision?

Poet and essayist Anne Carson says: "As members of human society, perhaps the most difficult task we face daily is that of touching one another—whether the touch is physical, moral, emotional or imaginary. Contact is crisis" (130). In her article on ideas about female pollution and marriage practices in antiquity, Carson reflects upon the rituals developed by the ancient Greeks in order to make contact seem safer somehow, to hem in its danger, and to deal with their fears about it. Maybe our own culture's continuous gawking at collisions, whether real or staged, could itself be seen in part as a ritualized obsession with the scariness and inherent risk of contact. I remember that in college we used the word "collision" to refer to particularly unfortunate one-night stands suffered by friends: contact had been sought and achieved, but it had turned out messy, regrettable.

We have all heard that (horribly unfair) saying: "There's no such thing as an accident." Sigmund Freud argued that it was the death drive that "drove" us not

---

3. Accounts of the Iraqi death toll from the first Gulf War vary wildly, but most of the reliable estimates chime in at over 100,000. Beth Osborne Daponte, a demographer at the US Census Bureau, estimated that 158,000 Iraqis, half of them women and children, were killed in the war and its aftermath. See the *Iraq Resource Information Site* at <http://www.geocities.com/iraqinfo/index.html?page=/iraqinfo/home.html>.

4. See *The Iraq Body Count Project* at <http://www.iraqbodycount.net/background.htm>.

only to theatricalize violence in our cultural expressions but even to career right into literal collisions that were not at heart accidental. For Freud, even though we ostensibly fear death and do everything in our power to keep it at bay, on some deep level, our subconscious yearns for it—for its unknowability and its resolutions.

But is it only our own deaths that we run to greet, thus? Perhaps our culture's constant staging of collisions reflects not only Freud's death drive, but also a drive toward contact with the "Other," with those people we are conditioned to fear or distrust, but about whom we are curious unto death, those "other" people for whom we are, on some level, starving. For a collision is by definition a coming into contact.

"What?," you may be asking. "Aren't we too close already?" And indeed, the proximities of the twenty-first century can seem dramatic: technology and new migrations are leading to a shrinking globe, the false intimacy of Reality TV turns private lives into public spectacle, and an ever more diverse American population is changing our demographics forever. Nonetheless, we can live whole lives without any intimate exchange with those we have branded as different.

The anonymity of urban life is oft-lamented. We hurtle past one another, alone in the faux privacy offered by our glassed-in sedans or SUVs. (Would I ever have apprehended the human-ness of that woman on the guardrail, if an accident hadn't stopped her cold, mid-commute?) Further, pop culture is at least as rife with stereotypes about ethnic and class groups as it is with "things that go boom." (Gangstas in cop shows; evil, devouring mothers in Disney cartoons; "funny" bad-guy Arabs in Hollywood comedies . . . and the list goes on.) These stereotypes blind us: we can look at each other and see only cartoon projections, ridiculous, sinister, or both. Wanting contact with those beyond our work world, our neighborhood, and our market niche but also deeply fearing or misunderstanding it, we grow addicted to the spectacle of collision—the impact of a forceful coming-together.

This essay is a wish more than a declaration. Maybe I am just desperate to believe that something big within us counters or mitigates our xenophobia.[5] I make my claims hesitantly, rushing with a broad stroke, hoping that at heart they are valid. But look, if you will, at how sexy collision is made to be in J.G. Ballard's 1973 novel *Crash* and David Cronenberg's movie of the same name. The plot line of *Crash* centers around a cluster of people, a loose, self-forming underground of people, who actively seek out car crashes and the strange intimacies between

---

5. Xenophobia: The fear or hatred of strangers, foreigners, or anything that is foreign.

strangers (and between human and car bodies) that they bring about. The pain endured is an acceptable price for these starkly real, extraordinary experiences; quickly, the pain itself becomes an integral part of the erotic pleasure. While I myself, as a reader/viewer, find both Ballard's novel and Cronenberg's movie almost unbearably morbid and self-important, I present them as evidence here that the lust for collision in our culture supersedes class lines. Each of these "arty" works has drawn a great deal of highbrow attention, both hip and scholarly. Clearly, a compulsive fascination with crashes cannot be pigeonholed as a lowbrow phenomenon and is not at all limited to blue-collar NASCAR devotees. Ballard's novel and Cronenberg's movie are often discussed in terms of Freud's death drive, social malaise, and the merging between man and machine that we are exploring in these days of "late capitalism" and high technology. I want to augment these readings with the simple notion that part of what a collision represents is the bringing together of people. Emphatically, a collision is not a *successful* kind of contact, as it results in some destruction and possibly even death, but it is an *impulse* toward contact, rendered violent by its entanglement with deep-seated fear of the "other." As we saw, Octavio Paz believes that the accident is in fact a logical consequence of our society's mode of functioning. Deep-seated prejudices and the social forces that encourage them habitually preclude *constructive* contact between people, but the impulse toward contact remains. This leaves us trapped in a systemic, suicidal aggression, making do, dangerously preoccupied with the brutal contact that is collision.

One of the most startling openings to a novel in all of American literature is the outset of Ralph Ellison's 1950 masterpiece *Invisible Man*. Within a page (the third paragraph, to be exact), the unnamed narrator, who has only just become our "host," is beating the crap out of a surly, abusive stranger in the night. It's not the fact of a violent scene that so surprises the reader, not even a violent narrator, but *our* violent insertion into a moment of aggression so soon after having picked up a book and embarked upon a read. It's like pulling out of the driveway—and immediately getting blindsided. I quote at length:

> One night I accidentally bumped into a man, and perhaps because of the near darkness he saw me and called me an insulting name. I sprang at him, seized his coat lapels and demanded that he apologize. He was a tall blond man, and as my face came close to his he looked at me insolently out of his blue eyes and cursed me, his breath hot in my face as he struggled. I pulled his chin down sharp upon the crown of my head, butting him as I had seen the West Indians do, and I felt his flesh tear and the blood gush out, and I

yelled, "Apologize! Apologize!" But he continued to curse and struggle, and I butted him again and again until he went down heavily, on his knees, profusely bleeding. I kicked him repeatedly, in a frenzy because he still uttered insults though his lips were frothy with blood. Oh yes, I kicked him! And in my outrage I got out my knife and prepared to slit his throat, right there beneath the lamplight in the deserted street, holding him in the collar with one hand, and opening the knife with my teeth—when it occurred to me that the man had not *seen* me actually; that he, as far as he knew, was in the midst of a walking nightmare! And I stopped the blade, slicing the air as I pushed him away, letting him fall back to the street. I stared at him hard as the lights of a car stabbed through the darkness. He lay there, moaning on the asphalt; a man almost killed by a phantom. It unnerved me. I was both disgusted and ashamed. I was like a drunken man myself, wavering about on weakened legs. Then I was amused. Something in this man's thick head had sprung out and beaten him within an inch of his life. I began to laugh at this crazy discovery. . . . (4–5)

Invisible Man is about a black man in mid-twentieth-century America who must negotiate the "peculiar disposition of the eyes" of those around him, all those who cannot see him because they're blinded by their ideas about race (3). When the narrator collides with the blue-eyed man on a darkened street, he knows from the man's reaction that, due to racism more than to the shadows of the night, he cannot really see the narrator for who he is. The tense drama unfolds, and the narrator finds himself kneejerkingly enacting the white man's nightmare of getting "mugged" by a wild black "hoodlum." The narrator explains to his new readers that

it is sometimes advantageous to be unseen, although it is most often rather wearing on the nerves. . . . Or again, you often doubt if you really exist. You wonder whether you aren't simply a phantom in other people's minds. Say, a figure in a nightmare which the sleeper tries with all his strength to destroy. It's when you feel like this that, out of resentment, you begin to bump people back. . . . You ache with the need to convince yourself that you do exist. (3–4)

Dreads, dramas, and drives that lurked in each man's breast as they moved through the night unimpeded burst into violent play the second that they collide. And we are off on the breakneck chase of Ellison's novel.

** **

Okay. We must interrupt the discussion underway. If this is an essay about catastrophic crashes, we cannot proceed indefinitely without mentioning the towers, can we? Weren't the collisions of 9/11/2001 among the most cataclysmic and raw in history? *(The sickening, silky, unimpeded, wrong, wrong glide of each plane as it cut through each tower.)* Only some of us saw it live that day, in the perfectly clear, Indian summer, Tuesday morning air, but even so we *all* saw it again and again, inside our heads and out, on the TV and behind our eyes. In the days and weeks after 9/11, CNN and all the networks tape-looped those sickening clips of the moment of collision with a hypnotic, compulsive, grim frequency. For a time, we thought we would never stop seeing these flights, these slippery, gliding, unendingly wrong encounters between planes and towers. Even more than the Pentagon with its gaping hole, far more than the plane in Pennsylvania, with its onboard heroes who prevented the further tragedy of collision by taking the plane down, the World Trade Center being hit was *the* visual fed us by the media in the wake of that morning's tragedies. There is an enormous amount to say about 9/11, of course, in terms of historical and political analysis, in terms of lament, of individual life stories changed forever, in terms of economic impact, global change—I could go on, but I won't, as I have only a small hope of a contribution to make here to that mountain of talk.

Alas, some elements of the post-9/11 conversation have already become cliché, one prime example being the following plaint: "Why do they all hate us so much?" Let's look at this query, uttered so often in the aftermath. What stands out for me is the question's confidence that there is a definable "they," a definable "us." "Us": our beleaguered nation-state, beleaguered despite being the most powerful country in the world, unified against attack despite our population's astonishing diversity? "They": everybody else, painted as indeterminate Muslim zealots for the sake of a formulation we can hang on to? Students posed this question in one class I held, and other students answered it readily. "They all hate us so much, because they are jealous of our freedom." I would answer the question very differently, and my answer would involve terms like corporate greed, Third World rage, domination, religious conviction, economic oppression. What I'd like to do here, though, is just to ask whether Ralph Ellison's words can bring anything to our understanding of those planes and of the "shock and awe" that we inflicted upon Iraq a year and a half later, and of the culture we have all been inhabiting ever since. Here I speak to the motivations not of the White House and Pentagon, but of American citizens living in history, washed through with it, participants, not puppet-masters.

Remembering Ellison: if "we" and "they" each carry "nightmare" projections of the other, if we are each cast as phantoms in the other's nightmare, then have we "begun to bump people back" in part because we "ache with the need to convince [ourselves] that [we] do exist"? No one can bear being cast as the devil in someone else's dramatic rendering of a black-and-white moral universe. Both Americans and Arabs have experienced that slight. And beyond and beneath the desire to prove that we exist and our perspectives matter, isn't there *somewhere* in the mix a yearning for contact, alas, warped into the most fatal sort of hate? Think how much we haltingly learned about Islam after 9/11, how many images of "embedded" reporters wearing kuffiyeh[6] and standing in sandstorms, or studio experts marching over three-dimensional floor maps of Afghanistan or Iraq we saw, since September 11. In the last couple of years, perhaps as many young Americans and Britons have been dancing to club DJs spinning grooves with Arabic vocals and a Middle Eastern riff as have been volunteering for military service. In the wake of our incursion into Afghanistan, Arab-American restaurants were deluged with interested new customers. Though badly distorted by enmity, superficiality and self-righteousness, this fascination with people with whom we share the planet, whom we had tried to forget but whom we were forced now to consider, seems to me to bespeak in part a genuine, salvageable, even salvational curiosity.

My argument here is counterintuitive. As colliders and stagers of collision, we are driven by so very much besides the wish to get close to one another. We are compelled toward collision by vengeance, by greed, by ideas about justice and martyrdom, by the drive to conquer, and probably even by the death drive. Hatred, fear, and blindness combine, combust, and mutate into the desire to destroy, even at our own peril, and in addition to the aggressive violence that we watch or support, *accidents* happen. Accidents happen that no one has intended, and they draw our attention because we are helpless before bloodshed, can think of nothing to do but watch. These factors all play a role in the culture's fascination with the smash-up, the crash, and the explosion.

In the essay mentioned earlier, Anne Carson quotes anthropologist Ernest Crawley, who believed that people were invariably rather threatened by one another, that we all feel a need to guard against the "invasions" of contact. He wrote in 1902: "Every touch is a modified blow" (130). I am asking, is the reverse also true? Is every blow a modified touch? I do not think we can look at the deeply entrenched reasons for conflict and the deep-seated hatreds in our world and concur.

---

6. Traditional black and white head scarves worn by Muslim men. Women's veils are called hijab.

Perhaps, though, *some* of the blows, *some* of the collisions we watch again and again in all our entertainment, indicate a curious desire for touch, for contact, with those individuals or groups from whom we are separated by terror, hostility, and blindness, by what Ellison would call "a peculiar disposition of the eyes." The hope extended by this essay is that somehow this curiosity about each other might be disentangled from the kamikaze drive toward collision. Carson's essay ends with Dorothy Parker's whimsical idea for her gravestone epitaph: "If you can read this, you've come too close" (152). We have all seen that sticker on the bumper of a car we're following. Somewhat aggressively, its message wards off collision. While I like to keep the right number of car-lengths between my own jalopy and the cars around me, I hope that in other realms we can all learn to come close enough to "read" each other, bypassing collision in favor of contact.

Works Cited

Almaraz, Carlos. Interview with Margarita Nieto. *Smithsonian Archives of American Art*. 11 July 2002. 17 July 2003 <http://artarchives.si.edu/oralhist/almara86.htm>.

"Autopsy of a Disaster: The U.S. Sanctions Policy on Iraq." *Iraq Resource Information Site*. 13 Nov. 1998. 12 July 2003 <http://www.geocities.com/iraqinfo/index.html?page=/iraqinfo/home.html>.

Ballard, J. G. *Crash*. NY: Farrar, Starus, and Giroux, 1996.

Brottman, Mikita, ed. *Car Crash Culture*. New York: Palgrave, 2001.

Carson, Anne. "Dirt and Desire: Essay on the Phenomenology of Female Pollution in Antiquity." *Men in the Off Hours*. New York: Vintage, 2001. 130–57.

Crash. Dir. David Cronenberg. Perf. James Spader and Holly Hunter. Columbia Tri-Star, 1996.

Crawley, Ernest. *Mystic Rose: A Study of Primitive Marriage and of Primitive Thought in Its Bearing on Marriage, 1902*. New York: Kessinger, 2003.

Ellison, Ralph. *Invisible Man*. New York: Vintage, 1989.

Paz, Octavio. *Conjunctions and Disjunctions*. Trans. Helen Lane. New York: Arcade, 1991.

SIMONE WEIL DAVIS, REFLECTIVE PIECE

This essay is more an example of the conventions and writing style of a "cultural studies" project than of an English essay, per se. Cultural Studies is an interdisciplinary field aligned most closely with English and History departments, but enjoying practitioners from other areas of the humanities and social sciences, as well. Cultural Studies allows us and encourages us to make leaps between genres and media, between "high" and "low" culture. (So, in my piece, I am free to look to literature, TV, movies, tabloid journalism and visual art for my "evidence.") Cultural Studies invites us to think about world events in terms of their representations and interpretations in the media. A cultural studies approach asks: What is our cultural landscape? What human-made signs surround us? What are the sources of the messages we can read there? What do these messages bespeak? What do they only hint at? What do they suppress or distort?

My essay also exemplifies some conventions of form that are common in cultural studies projects. I begin with an anecdote: this has the merit of drawing in the reader, one hopes. It also establishes a respect for the "story-weaving" element in all scholarship. Rather than claiming a scientific objectivity, I try to assert what authority I can *via* the capacity for storytelling and the open acknowledgment of the narratorial "I." There is room for an "I" in some academic writing, in other words. One can even structure one's essay around that "I"'s thought process. Ask a big question and attempt to answer it, being careful to make one's motivations and strategies apparent as one goes. Seems awfully personal for an academic paper? Well, if approached with care, the posing and answering of a question that matters, even with the retreats, the contradictions, the doubts, and the wishes apparent, can shape a very coherent, rationally structured argumentative essay.

When I teach Reading and Composition, I often urge students to imagine a smart but rather contentious reader remarking upon their paper and to incorporate that reader's hypothetical objections directly into the paper. If you imagine what a reasonable person might raise as objections to your argument and incorporate those right into your discussion, you essentially beat the critical reader to the punch, and thereby you strengthen your argument. In this paper, the "hypothetical objector" takes the form of a rather self-doubting narrator who is very ready to hem in her argument and circumscribe her claims. Remember: the caveat is one option available to the writer of the argumentative essay. As a writer, you can describe and defend *partial* claims, if that's what makes sense, rather than feeling compelled to make a case for something so full-blown it strikes you as preposterous even as you write it.

One other quality makes this piece typical of a cultural studies project: at heart, the essay identifies a social hope. While cultural studies projects are exercises, above all, in critical thinking, they very often revalue and celebrate elements in our culture and lives that go overlooked or undervalued. In my essay, I am reflecting upon and analyzing a cultural phenomenon—our obsession with the crash—and seeking within this phenomenon a glimmer of hope—the hope that this obsession is fueled in part by a more life-affirming impulse, the impulse toward contact.

"THINK. WRITE. ASK."

1. Simone Weil Davis begins her essay with an anecdote, or a brief story from her own experience. How does this anecdote help frame her essay? What benefits and risks potentially come with beginning an argumentative piece of writing this way?

2. Davis tells us that it is necessary to consider hypothetical objections when constructing an argument. She thinks of these hypothetical objections as coming from a "self-doubting narrator" who may point out weaknesses, contradictions, or inconsistencies in order to deflate the validity of her argument. What are some instances where she takes on the role of the self-doubting narrator? What objections does she identify? By pointing out these objections, does she strengthen or weaken her own argument?

3. Davis's voice is present throughout the essay. What specific instances can be identified as a glimpse into Davis's personality? Does the presence of her personality in a piece of argumentative writing help or hurt the validity of her argument?

4. Davis uses star-like symbols (* *) called asterisks to break apart the text of her essay. When she uses these symbols, what is happening within the text? In what ways do the symbols affect the flow of the essay?

5. Lori McNeil's, Barbara Fowles's, and Davis's essays draw upon media images and texts as sources of evidence for collisions. How does Davis' "cultural studies" approach to these sources differ from the sociologist's (McNeil) or the media arts scholar's (Fowles)? What are some examples of these differing approaches?

6. Think about Davis's tone, and make a list of adjectives that describe it; then narrow your list to the few most accurate adjectives for her tone. Consider Susan Dinan's tone in the same way, and then compare the two. How does the tone of each author relate to the presentation of her argument?

WHEN BODIES COLLIDE

SIMULATING THE COLLISION OF β-POLY(VINYLIDENE FLUORIDE) WITH INFRARED LIGHT

Nicholas J. Ramer, Chemistry

ABSTRACT

The collision of the ferroelectric polymer β-poly(vinylidene fluoride) with infrared radiation is simulated using density-functional theory. We have determined the resulting vibrational frequencies from the collision. With the use of the generalized gradient approximation and periodic boundary conditions, we find excellent agreement between our theoretical results and experimental values. We contrast our methods with those of a previous Hartree-Fock density-functional determination. The form of this work can be used as a template for the study of other ferroelectric polymers or their co-polymers.

INTRODUCTION

Some crystalline materials possess the property of *ferroelectricity*: a spontaneous polarization whose magnitude is variable and whose direction is "switchable" based upon an applied electric field. This spontaneous polarization is caused by the differences in electronegativity (or the ability to attract an electron) of the atoms that comprise the material. Ferroelectricity was first found in Rochelle salt (potassium sodium tartrate tetrahydrate) in 1920 [i]. Barium titanate, $BaTiO_3$, was subsequently found to be ferroelectric in 1952 [ii]. The discovery of ferroelectricity in this material ushered in the use of similar perovskite materials and their solid solutions in device applications like actuators and transducers. There is a constant effort to create new ferroelectric materials that are cheaper and easier to produce. Along those lines, the ferroelectric behavior of the polymer poly(vinylidene fluoride) or PVDF was first reported by Furukawa *et al.* [iii]. PVDF and its co-polymers are ideal materials for applications in which soft transducers (or electromechanical converters like those used in SONAR devices) are needed, due to their good acoustic impedance.

PVDF or $(-CH_2-CF_2-)_n$ exists in different forms with only the β and δ phases exhibiting ferroelectricity. It is the presence of the highly electronegative fluorine atoms and their corresponding electron attraction away from the carbons they are attached to that largely provide this material with its ferroelectric behavior. The spontaneous polarization in β-PVDF material lies perpendicular to the polymer chain (see Figure 1).

Several researchers have studied the crystal structure of β-PVDF. Lando *et al.* determined a structure containing a planar-zigzag chain (all hydrogens and fluorines are pointed 180° with respect to the carbon chain) [iv]. They confirmed their structure by nuclear magnetic resonance.

Atomic motions accompany the polarization switch and indicate its magnitude and direction. Understanding and modeling this underlying atomic origin for the ferroelectricity in β-PVDF has centered on the determination of its vibrational spectrum. A vibrational spectrum originates from the collision of particular frequencies of light, typically in the infrared region of light (400 to 4000 cm^{-1}), with a sample of a material. The corresponding atomic motions or vibrations give rise to the absorbencies in the spectrum. One of the first vibrational studies focused on the confirmation of the planar-zigzag structure for β-PVDF [v]. Enomoto *et al.* completed a vibrational mode analysis for β-PVDF using

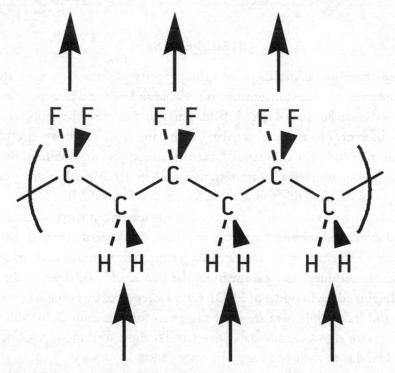

Figure 1   Planar-zigzag structure for β-poly(vinylidene fluoride). Arrows indicate direction of spontaneous polarization within the molecule.

modified force constants transferred from polyethylene and tetrafluoroethylene [vi]. They were able to assign peaks within their infrared spectrum based upon this analysis. Beorio and Koenig also utilized force constants from polyethylene and tetrafluoroethylene to assign the peaks in their Raman spectrum to specific vibrational motions [vii].

A subsequent determination by Tadokoro *et al.* [viii] used modified valence force field intramolecular force constants from Boerio and Koenig [vii,ix] (see below). Intermolecular force constants were also determined and included in the computations. The calculated vibrational frequencies were compared to experiment and found to have excellent agreement.

These previous studies utilized experimental results in order to determine force constants from which vibrational frequencies were calculated. Recently, a first-principles determination of the vibrational spectrum of β-PVDF has been completed. Using a restricted Hartree-Fock self-consistent field method, a structurally optimized 11 monomer β-PVDF chain was studied and its vibrational spectrum reported (see below) [x].

Since previous vibrational frequency determinations for β-PVDF have utilized either semi-empirical methods based on experimental results or density-functional methods that do not consider several important characteristics of the system, a more thorough and complete first-principles treatment is warranted. We have previously determined the structure of the planar-zigzag structure using the experimental lattice constants and have found excellent agreement with experiment for its bond lengths and angles [xi]. Building on that study, a fully relaxed structure (both in atomic coordinates and lattice constants) can be determined and from this structure, the vibrational frequencies for β-PVDF can be found.

METHODOLOGY

Using the ABINIT software package [xii,xiii], we have applied density-functional theory (DFT) within the generalized-gradient approximation (GGA) [xiv] to determine the exchange-correlation energy and periodic boundary conditions. Optimized atomic pseudopotentials [xv] were generated using the OPIUM code [xvi] for use with a plane-wave basis set cut-off energy of 50 Ry [xvii]. We have previously used these same pseudopotentials to study planar-zigzag β-PVDF at the experimentally determined lattice constants [xi].

In order to determine the vibrational frequencies for β-PVDF, it is important to allow relaxation of all internal atomic coordinates along with the structural parameters. It has been previously shown that a structure found by constrained relaxation (i.e., atomic relaxation at fixed or experimental lattice constants) yields slightly different vibrational frequencies than a structure found by free relaxation (i.e., atomic and structural relaxation) for $PbTiO_3$, a perovskite ferroelectric material [xviii]. The freely relaxed structure, however, gives a theoretical energy minimum with respect to strain and is more appropriate for the computation of elastic properties and strain-phonon couplings. Initially, we chose the experimentally determined lattice constants according to Hasegawa *et al.* [xix] along with the atomic positions found in our previous work [xi]. By computing the stresses for different unit cell dimensions, it is possible to relax the lattice constants to achieve a fully relaxed crystal structure. The full relaxation was terminated when the total stress on the unit cell was less than 1 MPa.

Density-functional perturbation theory has been applied for the determination of the vibrational frequencies [xx, xxi, xxii, xxiii, xxiv]. First, a dynamical matrix is determined from systematic atomic displacements. This dynamical matrix contains the force constants that result from a fitting of the forces due to displacement versus the magnitude of the displacement for each atom in the unit cell. Diagonalization of this dynamical matrix will yield eigenvalues (vibrational frequencies) and eigenvectors (vibrational modes). These vibrational modes will be some linear combination of the normal modes of the system.

RESULTS AND DISCUSSION

Fully relaxed structure for planar-zigzag β-PVDF

As stated above, in order to determine accurate vibrational frequencies, a fully relaxed structure, both in atomic positions and lattice parameters, must be found. Table 1 summarizes the bond lengths and angles in our fully relaxed structure along with its lattice constants. We have also included the bond lengths and bond angles for our previously determined theoretical structure with experimentally determined lattice constants [xi] and the experimental results according to Hasegawa *et al* [xix]. In our fully relaxed structure, we find lattice constants a few percent larger than the experimentally determined values. This amount of overestimation is common with DFT-GGA calculations [xxv]. However, the bond lengths and angles are almost identical to those of our previous theoretical results, which were in excellent agreement with the experimental results. It is interesting to note that in our present study the C-C-C bond angle is closer to the experimental value. This results from the slight increase of the c lattice constant from 2.56 Å to 2.60 Å.

Table 1   Theoretical and experimental lattice constants, bond lengths and bond angles for planar-zigzag β-poly(vinylidene fluoride)

	Present Theory	Previous	
		Theory[a]	Experiment[b]
Lattice constants			
a	8.88	8.58	8.58
b	5.09	4.91	4.91
c	2.60	2.56	2.56
Bond lengths			
C–H	1.10	1.10	1.09
C–F	1.39	1.39	1.40
C–C	1.54	1.53	1.54
Bond angles			
H–C–H	107.6	107.5	111.9
F–C–F	105.2	105.3	101.2
C–C–C	112.3	113.6	112.6

Lattice constants and bond lengths are given in Angstroms and bond angles in degrees.

[a] From Ref. [xi.].

[b] From Ref. [xix].

Vibrational frequencies for planar-zigzag β-PVDF

Based upon the crystal symmetry, there should be fourteen normal modes plus three translational modes and one lattice librational mode around the chain axis [v, viii, xxvi]. Those fourteen normal modes can be divided into five modes with A_1 symmetry [$v_s(CH_2)$, $v_s(CF_2)$, $v_s(CC)$, $\delta(CH_2)$, $\delta(CF_2)$], two modes with A_2 symmetry [$t(CH_2)$, $t(CF_2)$], three modes with B_1 symmetry [$v_a(CC)$, $w(CH_2)$, $w(CF_2)$], and four modes with B_2 symmetry [$v_a(CH_2)$, $v_a(CF_2)$, $r(CH_2)$, $r(CF_2)$] [xxvii]. The librational mode will have B_2 symmetry.

Table 2 contains the infrared vibrational frequencies for β-PVDF from the present study. We have grouped the frequencies according to their symmetry. These values were determined from the diagonalization of the dynamical matrix and therefore should be equal to the infrared experimental values. In addition, we have included the infrared experimental values and those from semi-empirical force constant analysis [xxvi]. For the librational lattice mode, we have used the frequency reported in Ref. viii. For completeness, we have included the Raman vibrational frequencies for the infrared silent modes (A_2) also from Ref. viii. The semi-empirical values were found from solving the dynamical secular equations described in terms of the mass-adjusted Cartesian displacement coordinates. Thirty experimentally determined intramolecular force constants of valence force field type were used from previous studies [vii,ix]. In addition, four intermolecular force constants were determined from the addition of second derivative of the potential energy given by a Lennard-Jones potential (to model the van der Waals interaction) and a Coulombic force constant (to model the electrostatic interaction between chains). For the former term, only the H···F atomic pairings were included since their interatomic distances were less than 3 Å. For the latter term, partial charges for the C and F atoms were deduced from the C-F bond length and dipole moment. An assumed dielectric constant was also needed. Table 2 also includes the potential energy distribution analysis for each vibrational frequency in order to identify the combination of specific normal modes that gives rise to the absorbance at a given frequency.

Table 2 Theoretical and experimental vibrational frequencies for planar-zigzag β-poly(vinylidene fluoride)

| Species | Present | Previous[a] | | PED (%)[b] |
		Observed	Calculated	
A_1	3015	2980	2975	$\nu_s(CH_2)$ (99)
	1424	1428	1434	$\delta(CH_2)$ (81)
	1213	1273	1283	$\nu_s(CF_2)$ (40) $-\nu_s(CC)$ (22) $+\delta(CCC)$ (26)
	810	840	844	$\nu_s(CF_2)$ (59) $+\nu_s(CC)$ (17)
	482	508	508	$\delta(CF_2)$ (98)
A_2	1022	980[c]	980	$t(CH_2)$ (100)
	258	260[c]	265	$t(CF_2)$ (100)
B_1	1325	1398	1408	$w(CH_2)$ (58) $-\nu_a(CC)$ (34)
	1139	1071	1074	$\nu_a(CC)$ (53) $+w(CH_2)$ (25) $-w(CF_2)$ (22)
	430	468	471	$w(CF_2)$ (90)
B_2	3069	3022	3024	$\nu_a(CH_2)$ (99)
	1159	1177	1177	$\nu_a(CF_2)$ (71) $-r(CF_2)$ (18)
	856	880	883	$r(CH_2)$ (62) $-\nu_a(CF_2)$ (18) $-r(CF_2)$ (19)
	419	442	444	$r(CF_2)$ (70) $+r(CH_2)$ (24)
	81	70[d]	72[c]	Librational lattice mode

Frequencies are given in cm^{-1}.

[a] From Ref. [xxvi]. Observed values are infrared spectral data unless noted.

[b] Potential energy distribution from Ref. [xxvi]. See Ref. [xxvii] for notation. The sign (+/-) indicates the phase relation among the symmetry coordinates.

[c] Raman spectra data from Ref. [viii]. These modes are not infrared active.

[d] Infrared spectra data from Ref. [viii].

Our vibrational frequencies are in very good agreement with both the experimental and semi-empirical values. The errors in the vibrational frequencies are expected for DFT-GGA calculations for non-metallic insulating systems. More specifically, we find generally lower frequencies than experiment and the semi-empirical values. This underestimation of the vibrational frequencies originates from the increased unit cell volume. An exception to the underestimation occurs in the highest frequency modes, specifically $v_s(CH_2)$ and $v_a(CH_2)$. The origin of this overestimation may lie in the smaller bond angle within the $-CH_2-$. The largest amount of error occurs in the librational mode (~16%). It is important to note that our determination did not use any empirical parameters of any kind (other than atomic numbers and masses of the atoms).

As previously stated, a Hartree-Fock DFT determination has been completed for the vibrational frequencies for β-PVDF [x]. No tabulated results were reported for the Hartree-Fock study. Since their study was based upon an 11-monomer chain, bands of frequencies were found. Although numerical comparison is not possible, several comments can be made between our results and theirs based upon the location of these bands. First, the locations of the narrow bands assigned to the anti-symmetric and symmetric CH_2 stretches (respectively, bands I and II, using notation from Ref. [x]) are approximately 300 cm^{-1} higher than our values. Band III, which corresponds to CH_2 bending and wagging predominantly, lies 200 cm^{-1} higher than our reported values for these modes. These differences underscore the inherent concerns with Hartree-Fock calculations of converged monomers. Our calculations incorporate not only the correlation energy of the system but employ periodic boundary conditions. These conditions permit the inclusion of intermolecular effects, which will not be present in a converged monomer study. Lastly, it is important to consider the chain-terminating groups that are present in the chain. Although their identity is not reported in the Hartree-Fock study, these groups will have an effect on a finite chain's dipole moment and may contribute to some of the difference between the theoretical and experimental results [xxviii]. This is avoided in the present study due to periodic boundary conditions.

In a recent vibrational study of PVDF thin films with high β-phase content, an absorption peak at 600 cm^{-1} has been found [xxix]. This peak was assigned to belong to β-PVDF as compared to the other phases present in the films. This peak was not found in our present study of β-PVDF. Furthermore, this peak has been found in previous vibrational studies of β-PVDF samples; 599 cm^{-1} [v], 598 cm^{-1} [vi], 600 cm^{-1} [viii]. In the latter study, the absorption is assigned to noncrystalline portions of the sample due to its appearance in the infrared spectra of the α, β and γ forms as well as in molten samples. Based upon our findings, this explanation seems reasonable.

Conclusions

The vibrational frequencies for planar-zigzag β-poly(vinylidene fluoride) have been determined from first principles using density-functional theory and periodic boundary conditions. This determination has included electron correlation effects by employing the generalized gradient approximation. Our vibrational frequencies are in very good agreement with the experimental and semi-empirical theoretical results. In addition, our results are in better agreement with experiment than those of a previous Hartree-Fock density-functional study. Using these methods, it will be possible to predict more accurately the vibrational properties for other ferroelectric co-polymers, when experimentally-determined intramolecular and intermolecular force constants are not available.

References

[i]   Valasek J. Phys Rev 1921;17:475.

[ii]   Megaw HD. Acta Cryst 1952;5:739.

[iii] Furukawa T, Date M, Fukada E, Tajitsu Y, Chiba A. Jpn J Appl Phys 1980;19:L109.

[iv]   Lando JB, Olf HG, Peterlin A. J Polym Sci Part A-1 1966;4:941.

[v]   Cortili G, Zerbi G. Spectrochim Acta 1967;23A:285.

[vi]   Enomoto S, Kawai Y, Sugita M. J Polym Sci A-2 1968;6:861.

[vii] Boerio FJ, Koenig JL. J Polym Sci A-2 1971;9:1517.

[viii] Kobayashi M, Tashiro K, Tadokoro H. Macromolecules 1975;8:158.

[ix]   Boerio FJ, Koenig JL. J Polym Sci A-2 1969;7:1489.

[x]   (a) Li JC, Wang CL, Zhong WL, Zhang PL, Wang QH, Webb JF. Appl Phys Lett 2002;81:2223. (b) Wang CL, Li JC, Zhong WL, Zhang PL, Wang QH. Synth Met 2003;135–136;469.

[xi]   Ramer NJ, Stiso KA. Polymer 2005;46:10431–6.

[xii] The ABINIT programs is a common project of the Université Catholique de Louvain, Corning Incorporated and other contributors (see http://www.abinit.org).

[xiii] For a description of the ABINIT project, Gonze X, Beuken JM, Caracas R, Detraux F, Fuchs M, Rignanese GM, Sindic L, Verstraete M, Zerah G, Jollet F, Torrent M, Roy A, Mikami M, Ghosez P, Raty JY, Allan DC. Comp Mat Sci 2002;25:478; Gonze X, Rignanese GM, Verstraete M, Beuken JM, Pouillon Y, Caracas R, Jollet F, Torrent M, Zerah G, Mikami M, Ghosez P, Veithen M, Raty JY, Olevano V, Bruneval F, Reining L, Godby R, Onida G, Hamman DR, Allan DC. Zeit Kristallogr 2005;220:558.

[xiv] Perdew JP, Burke K, Ernzerhof M. Phys Rev Lett 1996;77:3865.

[xv]   Rappe AM, Rabe KM, Kaxiras E, Joannopoulos JD. Phys Rev B 1990;41:R1227.

[xvi]   For OPIUM pseudopotential generation programs, see http://opium.sourceforge.net.

[xvii]   At 50 Ry plane-wave energy cut-off, there exists some core overlap between the C and F atoms. A set of 60 Ry pseudopotentials was constructed and atomic relaxations for the planar-zigzag structure were repeated. The relaxed 60 Ry structure was identical to the 50 Ry structure.

[xviii] García A, Vanderbilt D. Phys Rev B 1996;54:3817.

[xix]   Hasegawa R, Takahashi Y, Chatani Y, Tadokoro H. Polym J 1972;3:600–610.

[xx]   Baroni S, Giannozzi P, Testa A. Phys Rev Lett 1987;58:1861.

[xxi]   Gonze X, Allan DC, Teter MP. Phys Rev Lett 1992;68:3603.

[xxii]   Gonze X. Phys Rev B 1997;55:10337.

[xxiii] Gonze X, Lee C. Phys Rev B 1997;55:10355.

[xxiv]   Baroni S, de Gironcoli S, Dal Corso A, Giannozzi P. Rev Mod Phys 2001;73:515.

[xxv]   Grinberg I, Ramer NJ, Rappe A. Phys Rev B 2001;63:R201102.

[xxvi]   Tashiro K, Itoh Y, Kobayashi M, Tadokoro H. Macromolecules 1985;18:2600.

[xxvii] Normal mode notation: v_a (antisymmetric stretching); v_s (symmetric stretching); δ (bending); w (wagging); t (twisting); r (rocking).

[xxviii] Springborg M, Kirtman B, Dong Y. Chem Phys Lett 2004;396:404.

[xxix]   Bormashenko Y, Pogreb R, Stanevsky O, Bormashenko E. Polym Test 2004;23:791.

WHEN BODIES COLLIDE

A scientific research article is nothing more than a report of results from either a series of experiments or from a theoretical simulation of a physical phenomenon. In a very basic sense, the author is telling a story. To construct the most compelling (and interesting) story about the results, the article must be the blueprint for the entire research process, from conception of the project and choice of methods to ideas for future work. This transparency and completeness are paramount to all scientific writing because others who read the article will not only want to understand your results and the implications for their own research but may also want to repeat your work.

CHOOSING TOPICS AND ORGANIZATION

The most important decision that I make as a scientist is the choice of my research topic. Some research topics originate as part of discussions with peers in my field and also from reading articles written by other researchers. My interest in the subject of ferroelectric polymers originated almost ten years ago while attending a conference. I have spent a considerable amount of time researching whether someone had already done similar work to what I was proposing, and if so, how they did it. I also read as much as possible on the subject so that I could gradually become an expert and be able to write effectively. When I execute a research project, I am very mindful of the fact that eventually I will need to communicate what I find in an article. This means making notes during the research process and organizing those notes according to the article sections. In addition, I like to categorize relevant articles that will be cited in my article. This makes the writing process easier since I can access those articles as needed.

KNOWING YOUR AUDIENCE

Prior to starting to write a scientific research article, it is very important to know the target audience. Some questions I keep in mind are:

- Will most of the audience have a fundamental understanding of the underlying physical phenomenon on which my research is based?
- What kind of motivation will I need to provide to compel my audience to view my results as important to their own research goals?
- Will most of the audience know my methods?

- Which result(s) will be the most important to my audience? How best can the important result(s) be framed in terms of answering my research questions?

The answers to these questions will guide choices about content, level of detail and, in some cases, the exact language (diction) used in the article. An article written for a technical journal with an audience that does research similar to the research being written about will not contain extended background information; instead, it will describe the methods and results more fully. An article written for a general scientific audience will contain very little technical information; instead, it will offer a broader presentation of the results and how those results relate to larger issues or research problems in the field. The original article upon which the *Collide* article was based was very technical and relied on the audience having a firm understanding of prevailing theoretical methods in materials science. For *Collide*, the audience is quite different and the introduction was rewritten to remove some technical language and to define or explain some other terms.

As with anything else, experience ultimately becomes the best guide in constructing an article for a particular audience. In the absence of experience, or when writing a first article in a new research area, I review articles that have previously been written on the subject. Ideally I read these articles from the same journal in which I want my article will eventually appear. This simple step can help answer many questions about audience, and also helps with technical issues of sectioning, formatting, length and reference style.

CONSTRUCTING THE ARTICLE

Before beginning to write, I like to outline the article so that I will achieve a clear and concise presentation of the research results. This means laying out which references (to either my previous work or to the work of others) I will use as background for my results. I read those references to get a clear idea of how their work supports my results or how my results will further or refute their research. In addition, I create any figures, tables or graphs that will be used to illustrate my results. These are, in a sense, major landmarks that I will need to describe, and then use to demonstrate, my results; I write the captions or descriptions that accompany them outside of the main text of the article.

The article is topped by a *title* and a summary, or *abstract*. The body of the article contains an *introduction* to the research, a description of the *methodology* or *procedures* employed, a reporting of the *results* from using those methods, an interpretation or *discussion* of the results, and finally a *conclusion* that summarizes the findings and reinforces their importance in answering the research questions.

The Title and Abstract

The most important parts of any scientific research article are the *title* and the *abstract*. This is mostly because scientific articles (like articles in other disciplines) are cataloged in databases, and an article's title and abstract are searched by keyword by most database search engines. I typically leave writing these parts of the article to the end. This is because over the course of writing the article, the interpretation of the results becomes clearer and in some cases, the argument for the importance of my results strengthens. I attempt to make the titles of my articles as short as possible. This is sometimes easier said than done. It should state the specific subject of the research and give the methods used if they are novel when compared to previous research. The abstract should concisely summarize the article; typically there is a word or line limit imposed. It is a personal style choice whether to write the opening in the first person. I like to end my abstracts with a statement that appeals to the largest audience. I always keep in mind that the abstract could be the only part of the article that a researcher will see. It should have as great an impact as reading the entire article.

The Introduction

The *introduction* is a summary of previous work that relates to the article's research. The opening sentences or paragraph describe why the study was important to undertake. These opening sentences are typically general, broad statements about the main subject of the research (later statements will have to be much more specific). The information in the introduction's opening will be widely accepted as valid by the audience. This portion of the introduction "sells" why it was important to study a particular subject. I like to revise an introduction several times throughout the writing process, or write it last. Sometimes as I revise I add citations to previous work that better support my interpretations of my own results.

The remainder of the introduction is devoted to discussing in a very compact way all the previous work that has been done relating to the main research of the article. I like to organize the introduction historically, starting with the earliest research and working forward in time. It is all right for these paragraphs to seem disjointed, without anything clearly relating one paragraph to the next. I am setting the stage for what I will discuss in the latter parts of the article. These paragraphs all point to why my work was necessary, and how it differed from previous work. If there are seminal articles that I will discuss in greater detail in the "Discussion" section, I will only refer to them in the introduction, since I do not want to repeat information.

The last paragraph of the introduction serves as a transition, and is one of the most important paragraphs of the entire article. It can be written in the first person. Here I state exactly what I did in my research, i.e., the research objectives. I do not mention any interpretation or conclusions that I have drawn from the research. Instead, I generalize the results and leave the details for "Results" and "Discussion." The order of these sentences mirrors the order of the latter sections of the article. Depending on your personal style, the future or past tense may be used.

The Methodology or Procedure

The *methodology* or *procedure* is by far the most technical writing. I prefer to write this section first. For others who want to repeat my research or use the same methods for their own work, the details of this section are the most important. Since my research is theoretical, details of the software I use and its settings need to be given. In addition, given the way the software functions, I need to give the criteria I used to assess my results, such as tolerances and errors. I also need to address any assumptions or approximations I make to do my research and justify their use by providing examples of previous research.

For research that employs laboratory experiments, I would need to write a detailed description of the entire research method or protocol. Typically this protocol has been used throughout the project so it is simply a matter of writing it in a paragraph form. I need to justify the choice of methods providing any relevant citations to others that have used similar or different methods. I would provide names and models of equipment used along with the quality or grade of chemicals used. I would also need to include information on any statistical analysis and how I insured the quality of the data I obtained.

The Results and Discussion

The *results* and *discussion* are the core of the article. After setting the stage and describing my methods, I finally divulge the results and what those results mean. In some articles, the results and the discussion appear separately. I prefer to combine them, since understanding the discussion of some results helps the presentation of further results.

I begin this section by describing my results via tables and graphs. Even though a caption accompanies each table and graph, I repeat which data each contains. If previous studies have determined these same results in a different way, I include those results in the table or graph. I also must include a more detailed description of these previous studies even if they were mentioned in the Introduction. I compare my results via percent error and describe why my results differ from previous results by others. I may need to justify why my results are more accurate or more rigorous as compared to the earlier work. Again, this is the motivation as to why I undertook this project and why the reader should take notice of my work.

Once the results have been presented and compared, it is important to include how these results can be viewed in terms of answering other research questions. This is how science is furthered in the writing. Simply presenting results without any discussion leaves the reader wondering what to do with the results and how to place them into the larger context of the subject. There may also be a need to address errors that exist in the data, and the possible sources of error; here *methodology* issues relating to approximations and accuracy may be revisited. I am very careful not to "shoot myself in the foot." In any scientific research there are errors—they are an accepted part of data collection and interpretation. In my discussions, I must be aware of the errors, identify their sources, quantify them when possible, and provide ways to minimize them in the future.

Prior to concluding the article, I like to include a paragraph on ways in which these results can be built upon in future work. This is somewhat speculative but allows the reader to envision how my results are valuable to furthering the field as a whole. I am not reinventing the wheel—I am merely looking ahead to the next logical step in the research process and hopefully whetting the appetite of the reader to look for my next article.

The Conclusions

The *conclusions* summarize the main findings of the article. I like to write my conclusions section by rewording the last paragraph of the introduction and including the actual results in some detail. I keep in mind that I want to show how my research objectives have been met with my results. The last sentences of the conclusions should connect the ideas expressed in the Introduction with my overall research goal. This section is typically written in the first person.

CLOSING THOUGHTS

Scientific writing is unlike writing in humanities or social science disciplines. Scientific articles are highly technical and logically structured. Every statement made in the article must be substantiated either in previously published work or by a reasonable and well-educated interpretation of your results. In addition, the language used in scientific articles is very specific to the particular field. These same considerations can guide writers of other types of scientific writing such as laboratory reports and library research papers on scientific topics.

"THINK. WRITE. ASK."

1. Nicholas Ramer tells us that he addresses both a primary and secondary audience. Who do you think is the primary audience?—the secondary? Once you've decided on the primary audience, locate a passage that addresses this audience specifically. Do the same for the secondary audience, and then describe exactly how these passages differ.

2. As he writes, Ramer keeps in mind the need to make his audience receptive to his research. How does Ramer create such receptivity? What passages in his article indicate his attempts to captivate his two audiences?

3. Ramer tells us that his use of first-person plural ("we") in the abstract and introduction is a matter of personal style. In what "person" does he speak in "Methodology"?—in "Results"? How does the point of view affect the reading of each section for you?

4. Compare Ramer's style and formatting in "Simulating the Collision . . ." with Todd Zimmerman's in "Natural history, food preference, and competitive interactions . . ."; what sorts of landmarks or structures does each offer to readers unfamiliar with, on the one hand, chemistry, and on the other, biology? Similarly, look at Belinda Kremer & Angela Pisano's *All Begin Guy Walks into a Bar*; what sorts of landmarks or structures help readers through this "graphic poem"?

5. Ramer states that the title is one of the more crucial elements of a chemistry article. What is his reasoning? Ramer's use of "collide" in his title clearly refers to the theme of this anthology. If he was going to publish this piece in, say, the *Journal of Chemical Theory and Computation*, do you think he would need to change his title? If so, propose a title you think he could use.

PATIENTS HOPING TO ALLEVIATE PAIN COLLIDE WITH THE UNKNOWN FORCES OF A DISEASE

Barbara Shorter, Nutrition

ABSTRACT

TITLE: THE EFFECTS OF FOODS, BEVERAGES AND SUPPLEMENTS ON THE SYMPTOMS OF INTERSTITIAL CYSTITIS

AUTHORS: Barbara Shorter,* Leslie Kushner, Robert M. Moldwin

*CW Post Campus, Long Island University, Brookville, NY, Long Island Jewish Medical Center, New Hyde Park, NY

LEARNING OUTCOME: To determine if certain foods, beverages and dietary supplements are perceived as increasing or decreasing the symptoms of Interstitial Cystitis.

TEXT: The etiology of Interstitial Cystitis (IC), a debilitating, multifactorial syndrome of the bladder, eludes doctors. Various causes have been speculated. Consequently, IC is a complex condition to treat. Among the non-traditional approaches, dietary changes seem to improve symptoms in some individuals. Most of the data gathered on diet as it affects IC symptoms is anecdotal. A questionnaire designed to detect whether foods, beverages or dietary supplements have an effect on bladder symptoms was developed and administered to patients meeting NIDDK criteria for IC (n=37). In addition to answering general questions about the effect of comestibles on IC symptoms, subjects were asked to indicate whether each of over 150 individual items worsened symptoms, slightly worsened symptoms, had no effect, slightly improved symptoms, improved symptoms, or was not eaten by the subject; responses were recorded as −2, −1, 0, +1, +2, respectively, and a mean value for each item was generated. Nearly three quarters (73%) of the IC patients surveyed indicated that consumption of certain foods or beverages exacerbated symptoms. The rank order of specific comestibles that worsened symptoms was coffee, grapefruit, cola, vinegar, alcoholic beverages, tomatoes, tomato products, lemons, orange juice, chili, strawberries, pineapple, oranges, onions, pizza, chocolate, decaffeinated coffee; coffee ranked as most bothersome with a mean value of −1.85. Results of this study indicated that there is a large cohort of IC patients whose symptoms are exacerbated by ingestion of specific comestibles. Diets designed to avoid certain comestibles would be beneficial for IC patients.

INTRODUCTION

Interstitial Cystitis (IC) is a debilitating, multifactorial syndrome of the bladder that affects over 700,000 Americans, predominantly women[3,4]. The etiology of IC is still unknown, as is the cure. This disease that has baffled physicians for years is a syndrome characterized by pain of the bladder and the surrounding pelvic region, urinary urgency, frequency and nocturia. Its symptoms and severity vary from person to person. Although it often mimics a bacterial infection, there are no bacteria present in the urine. There is no blood or urine test to diagnose IC, and IC has symptoms similar to bacterial cystitis, bladder cancer, sexually transmitted diseases, and vaginitis. Thus, these other illnesses must be ruled out as part of the diagnostic workup; in other words, IC is diagnosed more through exclusion than identification. IC often vacillates between flare-ups and remission. It has been speculated that causes of IC include abnormalities of the bladder surface, abnormalities of the bladder's blood supply, undiagnosed microorganisms, autoimmunity, and an increased activation of mast cells.[5–9]

Because the etiology of IC eludes doctors, it is a complex condition to treat. Numerous therapies have been tested; however, no single modality has been successful for all patients. Medications and treatment algorithms must be individualized. Mitigation of pain has been successful at various levels when using antidepressants, antihistamines, immunosuppressives, GAG layer substitutes, transcutaneous electrical nerve stimulation, bladder instillation, and bladder distention.[5–7, 10–11].

Among the non-traditional approaches used for IC, dietary changes seem to improve symptoms in some people, although not all foods and beverages have the same effect on patients. Most of the data gathered on diet as it affects IC pain is anecdotal. Only a few studies are cited in the literature. One of the first publications suggesting dietary restrictions was based on statements made by patients attending the Women's Clinic for IC between 1984 and 1985. Gillespie[12] noted that alcohol and foods high in acid and arylalkylamines increased discomfort in some people. Following this, in 1992, after asking 240 IC patients to ingest as many of the offending foods as they could, Gillespie studied the metabolites in their urine. Most of the patients (83%) reported increased pain and frequency during the study. When compared to the control subjects, their urinary metabolites differed. The controls noticed significant reduction in their pain and frequency, and when re-challenged could identify the onset of their symptoms, in some instances as soon as 30 minutes after ingestion[12]. However, the effect of individual foods was not addressed.

Additionally, Koziol[13] surveyed 374 patients and determined that more than half of them were affected by acidic and spicy foods, alcoholic or carbonated beverages, coffee and tea. Again, individual foods were not specified. Studies on the constituents of foods that precipitate bladder pain are scant, and many publications describing dietary implications for IC patients refer to the aforementioned findings[5, 9-11, 14, 15]. Generalizations regarding the effects of consuming different types of foods have been made. Therefore, patients may try to eliminate more foods than necessary to avoid increasing painful symptoms; however, this could result in degrees of malnutrition. A well-balanced diet is essential for the optimal functioning of the human body. Nutrients serve to enhance immune response, nerve transmission, the healing of wounds, and blood flow. These processes are particularly important to the IC patient[6].

There is no substantial scientific evidence indicating that acidic foods exacerbate bladder pain, but some patients report relief when ingesting alkalizing agents such as calcium glycerophosphate[16] and sodium bicarbonate. In contrast, Nguan et al.[17] found insignificant changes in the intensity of pain following intravesical pH acidification in IC patients.

The purpose of this study is to determine the prevalence of IC patients whose symptoms are exacerbated by the consumption of certain foods and/or beverages, to develop a list of specific foods and food categories that intensify or ameliorate symptoms, and to indicate which foods are most problematic for these subjects.

METHODS

A questionnaire (see Appendix I for sample pages) was designed to detect whether foods, beverages and supplements have an effect on bladder symptoms. In order to address this question, patients were asked if they felt that comestibles caused an increase in urinary symptoms. Then, in order to determine which foods might exacerbate bladder symptoms, lists of typical foods were generated. Subjects answered general questions about the effects of comestibles on IC symptoms. For each of over 150 individual items, subjects chose a category: worsened symptoms, slightly worsened symptoms, had no effect, slightly improved symptoms, improved symptoms, not eaten. Responses were recorded as −2, −1, 0, +1, +2, DE, respectively, and a mean value for each item was generated. Added to the questionnaire were two pain indices questionnaires: The O'Leary-Sant Interstitial Cystitis Symptom Index and Problem Index (OSPI) and the Pelvic Pain and Urgency/Frequency Patient (PUF) Symptom Scale. The OSPI asks questions about severity of frequency, urgency, nocturia and bladder pain. The PUF addresses severity of frequency, nocturia, dyspareunia, and pelvic pain. The questionnaire was reviewed by a panel of experts for content validity, and then given to patients on two separate dates, one week apart, and tested for test-retest reliability. In total the questionnaire was administered to thirty-seven patients meeting NIDDK criteria for IC. Data was analyzed using frequencies and Chi-square. Correlations were made between foods and OSPI and PUF scales. Additional correlations were made with bothersome comestibles and allergies and medications.

RESULTS

Nearly three quarters (73%) of the IC patients surveyed indicated that the consumption of certain foods or beverages caused an exacerbation of symptoms: 5% indicated that foods or beverages did not exacerbate symptoms and 22% did not know. Eighteen percent of the subjects indicated that the consumption of certain foods or beverages reduced symptoms of IC. More than 75% of subjects reported exacerbation of IC symptoms after ingestion of coffee, cola, grapefruit and vinegar; 50–75% reported exacerbation of IC symptoms after ingestion of spicy foods, pizza, alcoholic beverages, strawberries, and tomatoes. Subjects tended to avoid the most bothersome foods, indicating that they did not eat chili (50%), orange juice (41%) lemons (41%), spicy foods (41%), pineapple (36%), decaffeinated coffee (36%), grapefruit (32%), alcoholic beverages (32%), coffee (27%), oranges (27%), cola (27%), or vinegar (27%). The rank order of specific comestibles that exacerbated symptoms is coffee, grapefruit, cola, vinegar, alcoholic beverages, tomatoes, tomato products, lemons, orange juice, chili, strawberries, pineapple, oranges, onions, pizza, chocolate, and decaffeinated coffee; coffee ranked most bothersome with a mean value of −1.85.

CONCLUSIONS

There is a large cohort of IC patients whose symptoms are exacerbated by the ingestion of specific comestibles. Although this data is preliminary, it is consistent with the anecdotal reports previously noted by urologists. The most frequently reported, and the most bothersome, comestibles include items containing caffeine, citrus fruits and juices, tomato and tomato products, items containing vinegar, and alcoholic beverages. Further research is needed to evaluate which specific components of foods are the offenders. However, until more information is available, nutritionists can develop diets for patients excluding the aforementioned foods and beverages. This will enable nutritionists to develop varied and healthy diets for IC patients, excluding the bothersome foods.

References

1. The Interstitial Cystitis Association. Poised for a breakthrough: researchers are now pursuing dozens of potential IC treatments. *ICA Update*. 2004;Jan: 4.

2. Leedy P, Ormrod J. *Practical Research Planning and Design*. Upper Saddle River, NJ: Merrill Prentice Hall; 2001.

3. Rosenberg M, Hazzard M. Prevalence of interstitial cystitis symptoms in women: a population in the primary care office. *J Urol*. 2005;174(6):2231–2234.

4. Clemens J, et al. Prevalence and incidence of interstitial cystitis in a managed care population. *J Urol*. 2005;173(1):98–102.

5. Erickson DR. Interstitial cystitis: update on the etiologies and therapeutic options. *J Womens Health Gender-Based Med*. 1999;8,(6):745–755.

6. Moldwin R. *The Interstitial Cystitis Survival Guide*. California: New Harbinger Publications; 2000.

7. Interstitial Cystitis, NIH Publication No. 02-3220. National Institute of Diabetes and Digestive and Kidney Diseases. Available at: http://www.niddk.nih.gov/health/urolog/pubs/cystitis/cystitis.htm. Accessed April 10, 2003.

8. Nickel JC. Interstitial cystitis: etiology, diagnosis and treatment. *Can Fam Physician*. 2000;46(12):2430–2434,2437–40.

9. Whitmore K. Self-care regimens for patients with interstitial cystitis. *Urol Clin of North Am*. 1994;21:1,121–130.

10. Metts JF. Interstitial cystitis: urgency and frequency syndrome. *Am Fam Physician*. 2001;64:1199–1206,1212–1214.

11. Peters KM. The diagnosis and treatment of interstitial cystitis and clinical conversations: nurses who work with patients with interstitial cystitis. *Urol Nurs*. 2000;20:2,101.

12. Gillespie L. *You Don't Have to Live With Cystitis!* New York: Rawson Associates; 1986.

13. Koziol JA, Clark DC, Gittes RF, Tan EM. The natural history of interstitial cystitis: a survey of 374 patients. *J Urol*. 1993;149:465–469.

14. Cunningham E. Are there special dietary guidelines for interstitial cystitis? *J Am Diet Assoc*. 2002;102:3,379.

15. Misunderstood bladder disease symptoms may be linked to diet. *Environmental Nutrition*. 2002;25:7.

16. Bologna RA, Gomelsky A, Lukban JC, Tu LM, Holzberg AS, Whitmore KE. The efficacy of calcium glycerophosphate in the prevention of food-related flares in interstitial cystitis. *Urology* 2001;57:119.

17. Nguan C, Franciosi LG, Butterfield N, et al. A prospective, double-blind, randomized crossover study evaluating changes in urinary pH for relieving the symptoms of interstitial cystitis. *Br J of Urol Int.* 2005;95(1):86–90.

APPENDIX I

CODE #: _____

The Effects of Foods, Beverages and
Supplements on the Symptoms of Interstitial Cystitis

Please return this questionnaire within one week of receipt

Sex: Male/Female_____   Age_____

(Please circle answer)

1. Do you feel that consumption of certain foods and/or beverages has ever caused you to have increased urinary urgency and/or frequency and/or pain or worsening of bladder symptoms? *

    Yes   No   Don't Know

*When we refer to bladder symptoms we are referring to pain, frequency and urgency.

2. Do you feel that consumption of certain foods and/or beverages has ever caused you to have a reduction in urinary urgency and/or frequency and/or pain or lessening of bladder symptoms?

    Yes   No   Don't Know

3. If you feel that certain foods and/or beverages and/or supplements trigger bladder symptoms, list the five foods and/or beverages that have ever caused you the worst bladder symptoms.

    List five foods and/or beverages and/or supplements that have ever caused a decrease in bladder symptoms.

    _____   _____

    _____   _____

    _____   _____

    _____   _____

    _____   _____

4. Read through the following lists of foods on the next few pages. **Circle** the number that relates to the effect the food or beverage has ever had on urinary urgency, frequency and/or bladder pain.

Skip this question if you feel foods never cause urinary urgency, frequency and/or bladder pain.

Food	I Have Never Eaten This	Effect on Symptoms				
		worsens symptoms	*slightly worsens symptoms*	*no effect*	*slightly improves symptoms*	*improves symptoms*
Fruits						
apples		−2	−1	0	+1	+2
apricots		−2	−1	0	+1	+2
bananas		−2	−1	0	+1	+2
blackberries		−2	−1	0	+1	+2
blueberries		−2	−1	0	+1	+2
cantaloupe		−2	−1	0	+1	+2
cherries		−2	−1	0	+1	+2
dates		−2	−1	0	+1	+2
figs		−2	−1	0	+1	+2
grapefruit		−2	−1	0	+1	+2
grapes		−2	−1	0	+1	+2
guava		−2	−1	0	+1	+2
honeydew melon		−2	−1	0	+1	+2
kiwi		−2	−1	0	+1	+2
lemons		−2	−1	0	+1	+2
nectarines		−2	−1	0	+1	+2
oranges		−2	−1	0	+1	+2

Circle Answer

5. Have you ever eaten any foods, beverages or supplements that you knew would increase your symptoms?

Yes   No   Don't Know

6. Have large meals ever caused more bladder symptoms than small meals?

Yes   No   Don't Know

7. Do you purchase any reduced acid foods such as reduced acid orange juice or reduced acid tomatoes?

Yes   No   Don't Know

What do you purchase?_____

8. If you do consume some reduced acid foods do you feel that they cause you less symptoms than the same foods that are not acid reduced?

Yes   No   Don't Know

9. Do you have any allergies such as seasonal (hay fever, ragweed, etc.) or allergies to medications, animals or foods?

Yes   No

If yes, What allergy medications do you take?

_____

How many times a day do you take the allergy meds?

_____

10. Do you feel that certain medications cause a change in your symptoms?

Yes   No   Don't Know

List all meds that increase symptoms:	List all meds that decrease symptoms:	List any other medications that you take:
_____	_____	_____
_____	_____	_____
_____	_____	_____
_____	_____	_____
_____	_____	_____
_____	_____	_____

BARBARA SHORTER, REFLECTIVE PIECE

How many times have you heard of someone becoming a health professional because that person or a loved one has developed a chronic disease? The all-consuming ramifications of the illness change the life of the afflicted as well as many significant others. Those involved inevitably become experts in the etiology and treatment of the disease. Oftentimes the pathology is well known, the diagnosis simple and direct. A test is taken, and the results give definitive answers. However, sometimes patients are not as fortunate; there are symptoms but no rationale for them. The frustration and anxiety the patient and loved ones experience can become overwhelming. The desire to find answers becomes a quest. This may lead individuals to do whatever they can to become involved in research. The following story relates to a disease called Interstitial Cystitis/Painful Bladder Syndrome, and how one woman's persistence continues to spur research.

For many years, female patients suffering excruciating pain in the perineal area, accompanied by the strong urge to urinate often, traveled from internist to gynecologist to urologist. These women commonly said they had to urinate every half hour, although only a small amount of urine was produced. The likely explanation was bacterial infection in the urinary system, but bacteria were never found in urine tests. Physical exams and laboratory results were inconclusive. Doctors were baffled. No reasons for the symptoms could be identified. A woman coming for medical help would often be told that the problem was in her head; she must be "stressed." Some doctors tried what they could: they prescribed antibiotics, stretched the urethral opening, suggested meditation, all in the hopes of offering some relief, but to no avail.

Some women went to five, six, eight, ten doctors over the course of years, then decades, always looking for an answer. Some women were unable to maintain employment because of the pain, or because of their repeated trips to the bathroom. Some women could not stand the pain, and contemplated suicide.

Why didn't anyone figure out what was wrong? We live in the twenty-first century; doctors are supposed to determine the cause of a problem, offer a treatment, and give advice. However, patients hoping to alleviate this particular pain collided with the unknown forces of a disease called Interstitial Cystitis/Painful Bladder Syndrome (IC/PBC). Although "interstitial cystitis" received its name in 1887 from Dr. A. Skene, who described a disease manifested by bladder inflammation and ulceration, for almost a hundred years little study of it was undertaken.

Every once in a while in our health world, an issue erupts that makes scientists realize there is another mystery that needs to be solved, another pain-causing disease for which hundreds of thousands of people seek answers but end up colliding with an illness whose etiology and subsequent treatment have not been discovered. In the sciences, this is something we have to expect: new, curious illnesses. What to do? First, we have to determine if there is, in fact, a problem, based partly on the magnitude of the illness. The discovery of the magnitude of IC is an interesting story.

Over twenty years ago a female orthopedic surgeon, Dr. Vicki Ratner, suffered severely with the symptoms of IC, and she realized that other women did too. After years of seeking treatment and numerous doctor's visits without any determination of her illness, she was invited to speak on a TV show where she discussed the symptoms. The network received over 10,000 letters in response to her appearance. Thus, acknowledgement of an unknown health concern was evident. After much devotion to this issue, Dr. Ratner organized the Interstitial Cystitis Association in 1984. Today, this organization is flourishing. It is responsible for federal funding for IC research. Another fact of interest is that in the 1970s a mere 54 publications appeared in the medical journals; in the 1980s, 111 articles, in the 1990s, 452 articles, December 2003, 1,136 articles[1], and in 2006, a search of the National Library of Medicine's PubMed indicated 1,382 published articles on IC. Clearly, there is the realization of a problem without a solution. Furthermore, estimates of the number of women experiencing IC are over one million, and this is considered a low estimate. There is no doubt that IC is real and affects a segment of our population.

Now, how do we handle the collision with the unknown? How does a scientist alter that event? This feat is attained through research. A scientist must seek out possible answers through a methodical process. Studies must be undertaken so as to clinically determine a cause and effect relationship between an action and a reaction. Initially, a researcher must survey peer reviewed literature so as to determine what is already known about the condition. This gives one insight into our current depth of knowledge. A hypothesis must be decided upon. Then, a research report is planned.

In the case of IC, despite the fact that the etiology of the disease is still unknown, there is anecdotal information about factors related to comestibles that affect the symptoms. Patients have often mentioned to their doctors that certain foods, beverages and supplements exacerbate their symptoms. To those with expertise in nutrition, this information is particularly noteworthy. It would be valuable to develop a testing instrument to be used in a clinical trial that would provide valid and reliable information regarding comestibles and their effects on IC symptoms. Determining the effects of comestibles on the symptoms of IC is the purpose of the study. Considering the debilitating pain that patients often suffer, any mitigation of symptoms would be welcomed. Furthermore, once a list of offensive comestibles is determined then further research into why these foods and beverages act as they do can be researched.

A questionnaire must evolve into a useful instrument through a process. First, it must be evaluated by a panel of experts who can determine if it will in fact measure what the researcher intends it to measure. Then, it must be completed by patients who will ascertain clarity and readability. Finally, it must be given to patients on two separate occasions to measure test-retest reliability. At this point the questionnaire is considered to be a worthwhile tool to help researchers seek answers to the unknown. (See Appendix I Abbreviated Sample Questionnaire.)

The population receiving the survey must be those who have been diagnosed with IC. This population consists of patients attending the Interstitial Cystitis Center at The North Shore-Long Island Jewish Health System. Patients who meet the diagnostic criteria for IC as set by the National Institute of Diabetes, Digestive and Kidney Diseases (NIDDK) are asked to complete the questionnaire. Upon completion of the surveys, data must be entered and statistical analysis must be undertaken. Now, the results can be evaluated and conclusions drawn.

When writing research a particular format is followed. According to Leedy and Ormrod[2] a research report should achieve four objectives:

1. It should give the readers a clear understanding of the research problem and why it merited an in-depth investigation.
2. It should describe exactly how data were collected in an attempt to resolve the problem.
3. It should present the data completely and precisely. The data presented in the report should substantiate all the interpretations and conclusions that the report contains.
4. It should interpret the data for the reader and demonstrate exactly how the data resolve each research problem.

The scientific writing process begins with an Abstract. This is an abbreviation of the paper. There are various abstract styles that can be used. The research article begins with an Introduction. Following this, the body of the paper includes Methods, Statistical Analysis, Results and Discussion. Finally, it is completed with a Summary and Conclusion. American Medical Association (AMA) style is used for some scientific manuscripts.

The data used for this paper is preliminary data obtained from the test questionnaires. It is not that which will be obtained from the 200 participants completing the final revised surveys. This data is available in the *Journal of Urology* July 2007 article entitled "Effect of Comestibles on Symptoms of Interstitial Cystitis."

Thus, we have seen how a scientist would proceed in order to be able to answer questions. That is, how a scientist would develop a research study, and how it would be presented. In the case of a patient who is in need of treatment to mitigate pain for a disease with unknown etiology, this is a step a researcher can take so as to prevent future collisions with the unknown forces of a disease.

"THINK. WRITE. ASK."

1. Barbara Shorter tells us that the data collected in her article is preliminary, and that when the study is complete, the full data set will be published in a peer-reviewed journal. What's a peer-reviewed journal?

2. Why would Shorter want to publish her full data in a peer-reviewed journal, but not in a composition anthology like *Collide*? How does publication in peer-reviewed journals affect the significance of people's research and writing?

3. Will Shorter have to make any changes in formatting or style to submit her article to a peer-reviewed journal in nutrition? If you're thinking, "I have no idea," and you didn't have Shorter's reflective piece to guide you, where could you look for information that would help you build an answer?

4. In her reflective piece, Shorter outlines for us the features of writing a research paper in nutrition. What are some of the features she identifies?

5. Find, and take a close look at, Shorter's presentation of her research problem. Do the same for Nick Ramer's presentation in his chemistry article, Anke Grosskopf's in her political science essay, and Susan Dinan's in "Restriction, Circumvention . . .," which is a chapter from a history text. Do you prefer any one disciplinary style over the others? Why?

6. Shorter uses the American Medical Association citation style in her article. How does this citation style differ from MLA and APA? Why do you think citation styles differ from one another?

A. Each of the authors in this section writes about collisions between bodies. After considering how "bodies" is used both literally and metaphorically in the preceding sentence, look for an incident on campus that includes a collision of "bodies."

 Write an editorial for your school newspaper expressing your opinion on the subject (suggested length: 300 words). When you've finished writing your editorial, write a short essay reflecting on the rhetorical strategies you used, and why you used them; also discuss your assumptions about the typical audience for your school newspaper, and the effects you hoped to create among your audience through your choices (suggested length: 600 words).

B. Graphs and tables are an essential part of presenting data in chemistry. Do you think graphs and tables are equally important in all of the natural and applied sciences (for example, biology, astronomy, and physics)? If so, why do you think this is the case? How might the use of graphs and tables differ in the social sciences (for example, sociology, psychology, and political science)? Do you think graphs and tables are more crucial or play a more formal role in writing in the natural sciences? Do you find such elements helpful in understanding the data being presented? Authors sometimes include graphs and tables in an appendix following the article. When might a graph function best within the body of an article and when might it function best at the end?

 Using the questions above as a guide, **write an essay analyzing the uses and functions of graphs and tables** in one article from this volume and two articles from this week's *New York Times* or other credible national newspaper. Suggested length: 1200–1500 words.

C. Having read and considered social science essays in this section, do you think there is a relationship between various social science perspectives and the ways these authors use evidence?

 Research an issue of interest to you in the social sciences by locating three current journal articles. Be sure to use credible academic databases, like J-Stor or ProQuest; your instructor or a librarian are excellent resources if you're not sure how to access such databases, or are feeling a little rusty on using them. Take a close look at how the information in the articles is organized and presented. **Prepare a 5-minute talk**

1. introducing your topic of interest to a general audience (be sure to explain any jargon or technical terms you might use in discussing your topic);

2. presenting your findings, following generally the organizational patterns you found in the three articles. Of course, you're speaking, not writing, so you'll need to consider what kinds of revisions to those patterns you'll employ so that your audience can follow you.

D. Decide, for the meanwhile, to be a geologist, a cultural studies critic, an educational administrator, a chemist, or a nutritionist. Do some initial research, and find a complex, controversial, or unpopular but important idea in your field. As you further your research, be sure to use credible academic databases for your research; the databases indexing current journal articles will be your best sources.

Create a multimedia narrative that will run as a 4- to 5-minute long Power Point presentation, in which you present the complex, controversial, or unpopular idea you discovered through your research. Your goal is to argue your idea such that you educate, convince, or win over a skeptical audience. Cite, and integrate appropriately into the structure of your argument, a minimum of 6 sources.

WHEN MOTIVES COLLIDE

The essays in this section explore what happens when individual motives, corporate motives, and governmental motives collide. The authors identify the needs and desires motivating particular courses of action and explore the outcomes of motives at odds.

Amy Wysocker considers collision between the nursing profession and governmental health care policy-makers. Nurses' decisions, she writes, have real-world, weighty implications for both the nurses themselves and the people with whom they work. In decision-making, nurses must balance personal, professional, and civic motives, which will sometimes be in concert and sometimes be at odds. In "Profession and Policy in Collision: Nursing, Risk, and Responsibility," Wysoker recounts the post-9/11 terrorism-related smallpox scare, the U.S. government's call for health care professionals to put themselves on the "front-line" by receiving smallpox vaccinations, and nursing's professional response to a policy that put its membership at grave personal risk.

The hero's journey; the comedy; the tragedy; the epic: these are some familiar narrative models. In "Profit Motives and Public Interest: Colliding Forces in Broadcast News," Barbara Fowles suggests that viewers should become similarly familiar with some of the structures and forms that package TV news stories. Through a close reading of television news stories that promise to educate viewers about imminent health and safety risks, Fowles shows that viewers' critical attention to narrative tactics—particularly *backpedaling* and *bait and switch*—may be critical to their ability to identify credible, pertinent information about health and safety risks, as opposed to being misinformed and frightened by misleading, corporate profit-driven "news" stories.

In "Restriction, Circumvention, Innovation: The Daughters of Charity and the French Catholic Reformation Church," Susan Dinan uses primary historical documents to show how the Daughters of Charity triumphed over the Church's attempt to put them, literally, behind walls. Dinan shows that, in this case, colliding motives did more than simply "hit" or "miss"; instead, the energy reflected in collision was generative: the Daughters of Charity not only maintained their mission of service, but also expanded it.

Political punditry in the U.S. is almost never-ending: 24/7, we can read, hear, or view "talking heads" commentary. What happens, though, here or elsewhere, when the "experts" are wrong? In "The Unexpected Collision: Why the Dutch Rejected the Draft European Constitution," Anke Grosskopf offers a close reading of a political situation the experts read wrong. A political scientist, Grosskopf uses quantitative and qualitative methods to investigate the collisions among social, cultural, economic, personal, and national beliefs and motives that led to this surprising outcome, and also frames the outcome in terms of its significance for our connected, global, 21st century.

Pink elephants? Flying elephants? False elephants? Choose two of these three correctly, and you'll be squarely in the fantasist research of Todd Zimmerman. With a wink, a nudge, and a subtitle ("A fictional study"), Zimmerman writes up the results of "Natural history, food preference, and competitive interactions among three species of Pteroelaphas *(Hyracoides, Pseudoelaphidae)*. At the same time, Zimmerman's theoretical investigation into competition among species sharing a single motive—to survive and reproduce—is formally accurate, and has much to teach us about the patterns and process of biology, as well as writing for biology. As well, it connects to the simulated collision in the previous section, and raises the interesting question: Why might a scientist prefer a "fantastic" experiment over a "real" one?

PROFESSION AND POLICY IN COLLISION: NURSING, RISK, AND RESPONSIBILITY

Amy Wysoker, Nursing

INTRODUCTION

The nursing profession is the largest provider of health care in this country with approximately 2.7 million registered nurses (ANA, 2003b). As a profession, nursing has a social responsibility to be at the forefront of issues confronting our society and the health of its citizens. The 1995 document *Nursing: A Social Policy Statement* addressed nursing's societal commitment, stating, "The aim of nursing actions is to assist patients, families, and communities to improve, correct, or adjust to physical, emotional, psychosocial, spiritual, cultural, and environmental conditions for which they seek help" (ANA, 1995, p. 9). In addition to the profession's social responsibilities, the *Code of Ethics for Nurses with Interpretive Statement* outlines the profession's ethical responsibilities. One noted ethical responsibility states:

> Nurses, individually and collectively, have a responsibility to be knowledgeable about the health status of the community and existing threats to health and safety. Through support of and participation in community organizations and groups, the nurse assists in efforts to educate the public, facilitates informed choice, identifies conditions and circumstances that contribute to illness, injury and disease, fosters healthy life styles, and participates in institutional and legislative efforts to promote health and meet national health objectives. (ANA, 2001 p. 24)

As these statements suggest, nurses are taught the importance of not only becoming skilled clinicians but also becoming very active in the political and legislative arena. Nurses are asked to be advocates for the patients they serve, to promote public health issues, and to partake in the development of healthcare policy. However, in doing so the profession needs to protect its members and to remain committed to its social and ethical dictates. How one balances these issues is at times a struggle of opposing views and compromises. This struggle often results in a collision of motives between the nursing profession and the healthcare policy makers.

A PROFESSIONAL CONFLICT

A recent collision between the nursing profession and public healthcare policy occurred over President George W. Bush's Smallpox Response Plan. Following the terrorists' acts of September 11, 2001, President Bush initiated a number of anti-bioterrorist programs. One such program was the Smallpox Response Plan. The threat of smallpox as a potential health problem demanded the immediate attention of nurses throughout the country to fulfill their social and ethical obligations. As the nursing profession acknowledged, it was indeed its responsibility to the public to participate in President Bush's smallpox program. However, the response program did not address many issues pertinent to the welfare of the nurses volunteering, their families or the public they serve. The government's plan is an example of how health professionals found social and ethical responsibilities, personal concerns, and governmental health policy in conflict. The Plan also shows why nurses need to become politically involved, how they accomplish involvement, the importance of professional associations, and the commitment of all nurses.

SMALLPOX RESPONSE PLAN

Throughout the centuries, millions of people have died because of this deadly disease. There is no treatment for smallpox. Vaccination is the only intervention to protect one from getting the disease. In 1967 The World Health Organization (WHO) began a worldwide vaccination effort to eliminate this disease (UCLA). In 1980, the disease was deemed eradicated by the World Health Organization (CDC, 2002a; UCLA).

Despite the belief that the disease was eliminated and there was no known remaining health concern, samples of the virus were saved for research purposes in both the United States and the former Soviet Union. It was believed that terrorist groups might have obtained some of the remaining virus to be used for bioterrorist activities (NYSNA; CDC, 2002a; Webber, 2002; Breman, Arita, & Fenner, 2003; Gellman, 2002; Henderson, et al, 1999). If such an attack occurred, the Department of Health and Human Services (HHS) would coordinate with state and local government volunteer smallpox response teams to provide firsthand health services. Healthcare workers and other designated critical personnel would be asked to volunteer to receive the vaccine and become "first responders." It is felt that providing the vaccine to healthcare workers would facilitate inoculated people to administer the vaccination to the general public if a smallpox attack did occur and care for those affected. The President also included in the Smallpox Response Plan the vaccination of certain military personnel who might be deployed to vaccinate certain overseas personnel. The government did not deem it necessary to vaccinate the general public because there was no information indicating an imminent attack and because "there are significant side effects and risks associated with the vaccine" (CDC, 2002c).

POLITICAL ACTION TO RESOLVE CONFLICT

The President's Smallpox Response Plan was not seen as a response to an immediate threat but rather as preparation for that possibility. Preparation vs. Emergency Response can be seen very differently. If nurses had been placed in an emergency situation, they would have responded. However, it would have been quite different to prepare for a smallpox outbreak, which may never occur, for vaccination may have a negative impact on the nurse in preparation for that possible threat.

Why is this the case with smallpox vaccination? Many people are not candidates for the vaccine because of the potential adverse reactions. In some cases nurses would know the vaccine is contraindicated for them; however, in many cases, they may not know unless they are properly screened. On the other hand, even if there are no known contraindications, the vaccine may cause adverse side effects after administration.

Also, how do the nurses protect family members, close contacts and patients they treat after inoculation? Since the vaccine is a live virus, the utmost care needs to take place to prevent accidental transmission to an unvaccinated person. If a nurse is working with a high-risk population or has close contacts that are at risk of adverse effects then the nurse may not want to be a volunteer.

The nursing associations and various unions representing nurses in the workforce thus raised many questions. Are adequate screening procedures in place to ascertain who may not be a candidate and who will bear the costs? Who will pay for their loss of income and who will pay for the nurses' medical bills if there is an adverse reaction? What about the accompanying pain and suffering and possible death? Will employers discriminate against nurses who refuse to be vaccinated? The government formulated the Smallpox Response Plan without taking these issues into consideration. Certainly nurses want to help in an emergency. However, they have a right to be protected and to adhere to their ethical and social responsibilities.

WHEN MOTIVES COLLIDE

Interestingly, legal protections were put into place to protect the manufacturers of the vaccine from lawsuits if adverse reactions resulted (CDC, n.d.e). Protections were also put in place to protect those administering the vaccine from lawsuits if adverse events occurred (Scheld, n.d.). However, what about the nurses who were volunteering to serve their profession and their country by being vaccinated? Didn't they have the same right? A letter from the president of the Infectious Disease Society Association (IDSA) whose members contributed to President Bush's national vaccination program did comment on this concern:

> The plan in its current form provides no compensation for health care workers, their families or others who may become ill due to the vaccine. IDSA urges health care workers to make sure prior to being vaccinated that their health and disability insurers will cover such illnesses and to determine what workers' compensation coverage will be provided by their states due to loss of time at work should they become ill. IDSA hopes to obtain further clarification about liability coverage and compensation as these issues affect members both personally and professionally in terms of how well prepared they feel to discuss the vaccination program. (Scheld, n.d. p. 4)

Moreover, since the consequences of the potential use of smallpox in a bioterrorist attack were not clear, the relative risk of contracting the disease was not known. Since the vaccination may be administered from three days to one week after exposure to the disease, the public can receive the vaccine in a timely way when the risks of adverse reactions certainly outweigh not receiving it. However, in the case of nurses putting themselves in a situation of risk to the vaccine when there is not an outbreak is a different situation. Therefore, if the government wants health professionals to be ready if the disease became a reality, then it is imperative that the government provides a level of protection for health professionals who assume the risks in a non-emergency situation. Nurses could then meet their social obligations and be protected as well.

In response to the smallpox program, the American Nurses Association (ANA), its constituent state associations, and the various unions representing nurses in the workplace voiced concern and began to ask for public policy to ensure protections. In November 2002, the American Nurses Association had begun working with the current administration to create a beneficial smallpox vaccination program that would provide protection and facilitate nurses' participation in the President's program (ANA, 2002; ANA, 2003b). In December 2002 ANA raised forth important questions and concerns regarding the President's plan to vaccinate nurses and other health care workers (ANA, 2003b). Later in the same month the association offered testimony to the Institute of Medicine Committee on Smallpox Vaccination Program Implementation sharing these concerns (ANA, 2002). On January 16, 2003, the president of the ANA wrote a letter to the Bush administration asking the President to delay his plans to vaccinate healthcare workers (Blakeney, 2003). The following issues were raised:

- the potential transmission of the vaccinia virus to patients and family members;
- the right of coverage of medical costs associated with receiving the vaccine;
- the utilization of safer bifurcated needles;
- the critical need to establish an adequate prescreening and education program;
- maintaining sufficient staffing during the voluntary, pre-event vaccination program;
- compensation for lost time at work due to adverse effects of the vaccination program; and
- protection from job discrimination or retaliation for refusing to be vaccinated. (p. 2)

Ms. Blakeney concluded, "Without resolution of these concerns, ANA cannot fully support the smallpox vaccination program at this time" (Blakeney, 2003).

Early in 2003 the New York State Nurses Association and other groups representing nursing shared similar concerns both nationally and statewide (Webber, 2003). As a result of their opposition and input, the United States Congress in an effort to promote healthcare professionals to volunteer considered legislation that would compensate healthcare workers. Unfortunately, the various pieces of proposed legislation did not meet the concerns voiced by nursing representation, and the collision between the government and providers continued. In an alert to its membership in March 2003, ANA encouraged its members to contact their congressional representatives and urge them to vote No on the Smallpox Emergency Personnel Protection Act, for it did not provide "adequate education, prescreening, surveillance, and compensation—and it will not result in increased vaccinations" (Dexter, 2003). Also in March 2003 the American Federation of State, County and Municipal employees, AFL-CIO (AFSCME), representing over 360,000 healthcare workers, wrote to legislators urging them to vote No to the Smallpox Compensation Bill. They too felt there were many flaws in the bill, citing specific examples of one nurse who died and another on life support following vaccination (Loveless, 2003). The Service Employee International Union (SEIU), the country's largest healthcare union, also responded with similar concerns (SEIU, 2003).

Congress and the White House Administration continued to work at various compromise bills. Input from nursing and other sources continued, and legislation was passed on April 11, 2003 and signed into law by President Bush on April 16, 2003. ANA stated:

> ANA and nurses nationwide scored a victory by successfully advocating for a federal smallpox compensation package that better meets the needs of RNs and other health care professionals who suffer adverse effects after receiving the vaccine.
>
> Following intense lobbying from ANA, The White House and key congressional leaders hammered out an agreement that the association called "a positive step" toward protecting health care providers harmed by the vaccine. ANA, however, is concerned that the "Smallpox Emergency Personnel Protection Act" fails to mandate adequate injury prevention activities. (ANA, 2003, p. 6)

This statement indicates success; however, it also reveals continuing concerns. In June 2003 a *New York Times* article noted that government officials had reported that the smallpox vaccination programs "have virtually come to a halt" because few people volunteered for vaccination and because the military program had vaccinated all that it could (NcNeil, 2003).

The President's smallpox program is an example of why and how nurses need to be actively involved in the healthcare decision-making process in this country. Conflict can only be negotiated through membership in professional associations and individual commitment from the individual nurse. Without this involvement nurses are not adhering to their social and ethical mandates.

References

American Nurses Association (ANA). (1995). *Social policy statement.* Washington, DC: Author.

American Nurses Association (ANA). (2001). *Code of ethics for nurses with interpretive statements.* Washington, DC: Author.

American Nurses Association (ANA). (2002a). *Immunization News & Resources.* Retrieved April 9, 2003, from http//nursingworld.org/innpower/archive02.htm

American Nurses Association (ANA). (2002b, December 12). *Press Releases. American Nurses Association raises concerns about smallpox vaccination plans. Bush administration has not answered key questions.* Retrieved April 9, 2003, from http://nursingworld.org/pressrel/2002/pr1213.htm

American Nurses Association (ANA). (2003, May/June). Smallpox legislation signed by Bush. *The American Nurse. The Official Publication of the American Nurses Association,* 6.

Blakeny, B. (2003, January 16). *Letter to Bush administration. American Nurses Association asks President to delay smallpox vaccination plans.* Retrieved April 11, 2003, from http://www.nursingworld.org/pressrel/2003/1tr0116.htm

Breman, J., Arita, I., & Fenner, F. (2003). Preventing the return of smallpox. *New England Journal of Medicine, 348*(5), 463–466.

Centers for Disease Control and Prevention (CDC). (2002a, October). *Notice to readers: 25th anniversary of the last case of naturally acquired smallpox, 51*(42), 952. Retrieved July 5, 2003, from http://doc.gov/mmwr/preview/mmwrhtml/mm5142a5.htm

Centers for Disease Control and Prevention (CDC). (2002b, December 13). *Public health emergency preparedness & response. Protecting Americans: smallpox vaccination program.* Retrieved March 31, 2003, from http://www.bt.cd.gov/smallpox/vaccination-program-statement.asp

Centers for Disease Control and Prevention (CDC). (2003a, January 16). *Smallpox Vaccine, what you need to know. Vaccine Information Statement (VIS),* p.1 of 3, version 1.

Centers for Disease Control and Prevention (CDC). (n.d.). *Questions and Answers: Smallpox Program Implementation. Liability Issues.* Retrieved July 8, 2003, from http://www.bt.cdc/agent/smallpox/vaccination/vaccination program/qa.asp??type=cat&cat=Smallpox=Program=Implementation&subCat1=Lial

Dexter, S. (2003, March 31). *Action alert: smallpox vote today.* Retrieved March 31, 2003, from http://webmail.aol.com/fmsgview.adp?folder=SU5CT1g=&uid=612470

Gellman, B. (2002, November 4). Four nations thought to possess smallpox: Iraq, N. Korea named, two officials say. *Washington Post,* p.4, A1, A4.

Henderson, D.A., Inglesby, T.V., Bartlett, J.G., Ascher, M.S., Eitzen, H., Jahrling, Hauer, et al. (1999). Smallpox as a biological weapon: medical and public health management. *Journal of the American Medical Association, 281,* 2127–2137.

Loveless, C.M. (2003, March 26). *AFSCME. Letter to representatives opposing smallpox compensation legislation introduced by Representative Richard Burr.* Retrieved March 31, 2003, from http://www.afscme.org/action/103036.htm

McNeil Jr., D.G. (2003, June, 19). After the war: biological defenses; 2 programs to vaccinate for smallpox come to a halt. *New York Times,* Late Edition, p. A13.

New York State Nurses Association (NYSNA). *Position Statement. Pre-Event Smallpox Vaccination of Registered Nurses*. Retrieved April 11, 2003, from http://www.nysna.com/programs/nps/positions/smallpox.htm

Scheld, M. (n.d.) *Letter from IDSA president regarding smallpox*. Retrieved July 4, 2003, from http://nursingworld.org/innpower/idsa.htm

Service Employee International Union (SEIU). (2003). What's *at stake! Tell congress: make smallpox vaccination plan safer*. Retrieved March 31, 2003, from http://www.unionvoice.org/campaign/smallpoxplan/explanation

UCLA Louise M. Darling Biomedical Library. History and Special Collections. (2002). Smallpox, inoculation, vaccination, eradication, an online exhibit. Retrieved June 25, 2003, from http://www.library.ucla.edu/libraries/biomed/smallpox/jerrner.html

Webber, N. (2002, December). Smallpox vaccinations are coming. *NYSNA Report*.

Webber, N. (2003, January). Smallpox vaccinations: weighing the risks. NYSNA urges protections for nurses who volunteer. *NYSNA Report*.

AMY WYSOKER, REFLECTIVE PIECE

Writing this essay was indeed a challenge. I am a registered professional nurse. Nurses specialize in a specific aspect of nursing. It may be psychiatry, pediatrics, intensive care, home care, the operating room, or the like. Nurses are not only skilled practitioners; they are also patient advocates, educators, leaders, researchers, and consultants. In these numerous roles, nurses adhere to the profession's standards of care, code of ethics, and social policy statement.

When asked to contribute a chapter in a textbook that would be used to teach English composition, I was stunned. I questioned why I was invited to write a chapter. The editors of the collection seemed to assume that just because I am an advanced practice nurse with a master's degree and a Ph.D., I must also be an advanced writer. Writing, however, is not my expertise. My expertise is in the field of psychiatric/mental nursing. Why ask me? I can't write like English majors. English is their specialty. After all, the editors of this book are not expected to do psychotherapy or treat a mentally ill person.

Why is it expected that nurses be both writers and clinicians? The fact is that in the profession of nursing, this is an expectation. In academia professors do require proficient writing skills. I do demand that my students learn how to write well. Nurses need to contribute to the knowledge base of nursing. As leaders, researchers, clinicians, advocates, nurses need to publish. Politically it is also important to communicate to legislators and to be part of the development of healthcare policy. Being expert clinicians is not sufficient.

Interestingly enough, nurses write daily. Everything that is done for a patient must be documented in the patient's chart. However, providing both the documentation and the patient care is often a struggle. Obviously, patient care is the priority, but documentation is a necessity. However, nurses' writing ability can become impaired. In order to accomplish safe, competent nursing care, one needs to figure out how to document in a timely manner. As a result nurses write abbreviated sentences. For example, nurses frequently write sentences like "Patient reports . . ." Using articles "the" and "a" before "patient" tend to be eliminated from a nurse's language. Nurses tend to incorporate this new sentence structure in other writings as well.

Despite this struggle, I regularly publish in my specialty field, I have written chapters in books and articles in journals. How do I accomplish this, if in fact writing is a challenge for me? The same way I wrote this essay. My approach is to "free associate," meaning I just write my thoughts down without being concerned

WHEN MOTIVES COLLIDE

with grammar and writing style. Once I do so, I go back and correct the grammar and writing style the best I can at that time. I then need to go away from my work for a few days and later come back to it. Upon return, I realize that I typically need to reorganize my thoughts by moving paragraphs and sentences around to have the piece flow better. Then, once again, I correct grammar and sentence structure. It is amazing how much this improves my writing.

Receiving feedback from others and not being defensive or offended by the feedback is extremely important. In this chapter, the editors of the book provided me with extremely valuable feedback. Rather than looking at the numerous comments in the negative, I was very impressed by the feedback, which made a lot of sense. By making the changes, the piece was significantly improved. It is important to utilize the assistance available.

The topic I chose to address in this essay has great significance to the nursing profession and to individual nurses. If nurses do not engage in debate about health policy issues, they are not adhering to the profession's social policy statement and standards of care. Without a commitment to these principles, the profession lacks power and autonomy and will no longer be an independent profession. If nurses do not get involved, others will dictate what nurses should do and how they should do it. Smallpox identification is an example of the importance of involvement. When something personally affects you, the impact of your message is more powerful. I thus chose this particular dilemma, for I knew nurses could personally identify with smallpox, thereby making action possible. By extension, I hope that in the future nurses will get involved in issues that may not directly impact them but are important to society and to the nursing profession.

"THINK. WRITE. ASK."

1. What kind of organizational pattern (definition, narration, cause-effect, classification, comparison and contrast, problem-solution) does Amy Wysoker use to develop her essay? How do the section headings assist with the organization?
2. Wysoker identifies herself as a nurse. Does knowing this have any effect on your interpretation of her argument? In what ways might this enhance both the objectivity and subjectivity of her argument?

3. Wysoker combines evidence from primary sources (such as reports from the ANA, CDC, NYSNA) with evidence from her own experience as a nurse to support her argument. What elements of Wysoker's experience allow her to argue through her own voice, supported by these primary sources? How does her experience differentiate her from other nurses and perhaps give her the authority to speak on this particular subject?

4. Wysoker uses primary sources, while Mark Pires and Estelle Kamler rely on secondary sources. What do you think are the important differences between these two types of sources, and the types of essays that result from their use? Are there any situations (or specific disciplines) where one type would be preferred over the other?

5. One purpose of a conclusion is to bring closure to an essay. How does Wysoker achieve closure in her essay? How does her conclusion compare with Tognoli's?

WHEN MOTIVES COLLIDE

PROFIT MOTIVES AND PUBLIC INTEREST: COLLIDING FORCES IN BROADCAST NEWS

Barbara Fowles, Media Arts

INTRODUCTION

News is a uniquely important part of the flood of media content that comes to us each day. It is that part of media content that we look to tell us what is real, immediate, and important in our world (Schudson, 2003). In a media environment offering numerous "all-news" cable channels as well as print, on-line, and radio news services, it is surprising that broadcast television is still the primary source of news for the majority of Americans (Downie & Kaiser, 2002, p. 159). While we as viewers may think of news programming as a helpful public service, in fact, news programming has become an important profit center for television networks and the media conglomerates that own them. As a result, newscasts, in addition to providing a service to viewers, are increasingly expected to compete actively for large audiences and the high Nielsen ratings that go with them. Television news is thus the product of journalistic judgments about audience needs and expectations on the one hand and corporate economic and operational realities on the other (Cohen, Adoni, & Bantz, 1990).

When viewers tune in to their favorite network evening news program, most want to be provided with credible and timely information about the day's events. They expect at least some of this information to be useful and relevant to their own lives and communities (Altheide, 2002). They expect news to contribute to decision-making and to impose some logic on the often complex and messy events of the day (Bennett, 1996, p. 24). Nevertheless, because news programs are consumed in the context of a television diet that consists primarily of entertainment, viewers (though most would probably not admit it) expect news to be entertaining as well. They want news stories to be "both news and a story" (Hartley, 1996, p. 177). They are inclined to change the channel when the stories do not deliver both elements.

Media owners, on the other hand, expect that news programming will make money. Today, these owners are often huge conglomerates (Bagdikian, 1992), each owning many television stations and other media properties around the United States and the world. While in television's early years news programming was considered to be a "write-off" to satisfy government regulators' demands that the public interest be served, today news programming's success is measured by the degree to which it can attract large audiences and thus contribute to the corporate bottom line. Finally, and still with profits in mind, news content is chosen to minimize the effort and manpower required in the newsgathering process (Downie & Kaiser, 2002), while making optimal use of costly new technologies such as mobile satellite units. In short, news in this view is "a manufactured product" (Schudson, 2003, p. 82).

Television news, then, far from being a straightforward picture of reality, is a complex artifact built on diverse needs that often seem to work at cross-purposes. Television news programs organize the day's events for the viewer by actively constructing a series of non-fiction narratives (Murray, Schwartz, & Lichter, 2001, p. 77) and arranging them in a carefully planned order interspersed with commercials. Judgments about what is and what is not news are governed by a complex set of variables, many of which have very little to do with "importance and newsworthiness" (Bennett, 1996, p. 129). Instead, advertisers' demands as well as the need for efficient allocation of resources, time, and personnel often govern producers' decisions about news content. Yet these choices determine what we learn about the world.

One frequent criticism of news programming is that these influences often result in stories that are highly formulaic; the facts of the story are plugged into an established frame or format (Bennett, 1996; Slovik, 1997). These familiar narrative structures make the reporters' work easier by enabling them to select and organize facts quickly (Potter, 2002). It also demands less mental effort from the viewer who is processing the story, because he or she, as a "media literate" (Meyrowitz, 1998) person, finds the formula familiar. Different ways of "packaging" the story will result in different interpretations by the news consumer (Slovik, 1997, p. 44.), so the strategies that are used in structuring the individual narratives are of more than stylistic interests.

NEWS STORIES

The fact that we call the separate, usually self-contained items in a newscast *stories* is revealing. Human beings love stories because they organize complex realities and provide a coherent structure for events. A story also has inherent drama. The narrative moves forward to a satisfying conclusion. Over the course of our lives, we learn a great deal about the structures (plots) of stories, and we learn that there are only a few basic plots that fit most sets of circumstances, fictional or non-fictional, including news. For most of us, much of this knowledge (the rules of storytelling) remains implicit unless someone asks us to reflect deliberately on it.

The inherent drama of stories makes news entertaining but at the same time necessarily limits content and controls the degree of complexity (Stocking, 1999). This is especially true since news stories tend to be quite short. The separate, independent stories that make up newscasts "by definition encapsulate events" (Bennett, 1996, p. 159).

The purpose of this study is to look at the question of whether the colliding demands of media corporations and news consumers can influence the narrative strategies of individual news stories. The stories are drawn from network news because it is still watched by over half of news viewers (Bennett, 1996). Stories concerned with health and safety risks were chosen as the content of this study because they are a staple of television journalism (Dean & Brady, 2002; Klaidman, 1991). Scholarly interest in such stories and their influence on audiences has grown steadily as we have become a society that collectively demands a risk-free life (Slovik, 1997; Alcabes, 2003).

For example, Altheide (2002) tracks journalists' use of the key word "fear," which he equates with perceived risk, in order to determine how media emphasis compares to the actual degree of danger to the public. Singer and Endreny (1993) similarly examine the evolution of the use of the word "risk" in reporting. Slovik (1997) analyzes the role played by media coverage in shaping the public's understanding of public health risks.

The news stories examined for this study were gathered using a search of the LexisNexis database. The search was limited to the daily evening newscasts of three major television networks, ABC, CBS, and NBC, for a six-month period. The search terms used were health or safety and risk. Complete transcripts of 16 stories, six from ABC, seven from CBS, and three from NBC, resulted. Most of these stories concerned medical matters. Because CBS had the most health-related stories, I chose to focus on this network.

Close reading of this small sample of stories led to the identification of two recurrent narrative strategies. Between them, they characterize 11 of the 16 stories and were employed by all three networks sampled. Both of the narrative strategies illustrated below offer preliminary support of the claim that the viewers' need for information and the news organizations' need for profit are played out in the construction of individual news stories. This is not an indication of how prevalent these strategies may prove to be in a larger sample of news stories or in a broader spectrum of subject matter.

STRATEGY ONE: BACKPEDALING

The first strategy is quite simple: news stories begin with powerful, dramatically worded statements, designed to grab the viewer's attention. This statement is followed by the body of the story, which introduces more qualified language and adds more nuance and detail in order to meet the viewer's expectation for credible information. We can think of this strategy as *backpedaling*, since such stories confront the viewer with a bold statement and then temper it with less dramatic, often more equivocal information.

The following story from "The CBS Evening News" for Thursday, December 12, 2002, illustrates this strategy:

DAN RATHER, anchor:

It has enormous implications for public health and the battle against bioterror. President Bush is putting into motion a controversial plan to offer smallpox vaccine to any American that wants it to defend against possible attack with smallpox weapons. Before smallpox was officially re-eradicated a few day—decades ago, it killed hundreds of millions of people. Now the vaccine itself can cause horrid side-effects, even death. CBS' John Roberts reports the President's plan, the benefits and the risks.

JOHN ROBERTS reporting:

The first wave of vaccinations will be mandatory and will begin in early January, a half a million US troops who could be on the front lines of any bioweapons attack. Next will come voluntary vaccination of up to 10 million health-care workers, first-responders, police and firemen, the first line of defense in any outbreak. The public will have access to the vaccine in two ways. Americans can immediately ask to be inoculated with the existing stocks of old smallpox vaccine, or they can wait until late next year when new vaccine production comes online. White House officials said today that if someone really wants the vaccine in the coming weeks, they can get it.

President Bush wrestled with the decision of who to vaccinate for months. The reason: As infectious disease specialist Dr. Paul Offit told Dan Rather, the smallpox vaccine can be dangerous.

DR. PAUL OFFIT [Children's Hospital Philadelphia]:

We know that if we immunize a million people, that there will be fifteen people that will suffer a severe permanent adverse outcome and one person may die from—from the vaccine.

ROBERTS:

The White House felt the threat of a bioterror attack from Iraq, which is rumored to possess smallpox, or Al-Qaida was great enough to chance vaccinating millions of people. But Jonathan Tucker, author of "Scourge: The Once and Future Threat of Smallpox," says there's only circumstantial evidence that Iraq has smallpox, and at present the risk far outweighs the benefit.

MR. JONATHAN TUCKER [Biological Weapons Expert]:

It is a potential concern, but I don't see it as an imminent threat, and we need to weigh that against the known risks associated with mass vaccination.

ROBERTS:

Critics of the White House program say since a person can be effectively vaccinated up to three days after they've been exposed to smallpox, there's no need to do it preventively. But President Bush knew, politically, they had to offer the vaccine to anyone who wants it.

The White House will point out tomorrow that there are millions of Americans who should not be inoculated, people with certain medical conditions that put them at higher risk for severe reactions. But the decision to vaccinate will more likely be left between a patient and their physician. Dan.

This story begins with a statement by the anchor, which establishes a highly dramatic situation. It tells us the story has "enormous implications for public health," suggesting that the effects will extend to all of us, the viewers. This demands our close attention. It goes on to invoke "*the* battle against bioterror" (emphasis mine). This choice of words, which might more accurately have been "any potential battle," implies the existence of an ongoing battle against bioterrorism. The suggested immediacy of bioterrorism is likely to wake up the inattentive viewer.

The second sentence continues the drama in a similar way. It tells us that the President is "putting into motion a controversial plan," suggesting that the plan will unfold right away. Further, any controversy is inherently dramatic, especially when we are told it can affect "*any* American" (emphasis mine). Causing the individual viewer to feel imperiled adds to the drama and excitement of the story.

In his second statement, Rather envisions an attack that would use "smallpox weapons." Though here the attack itself has already been deescalated through use of the qualifier "possible," the implication is that there are "smallpox weapons" available to be deployed. In television, it is particularly easy to make these logical leaps, since audiovisual messages fly by. We can't go back and double check the reporter's reasoning. We tend to "go along" with the apparent implications of the story.

The reporter goes on from this point to add details to the story, details which serve the audience's expectation for news to be credible information. We are told which groups will be inoculated and how many individuals are included. The story is connected directly to us by noting that the public can ask for vaccine "immediately." Giving the viewer an action to carry out is likely to increase her investment in the story.

Statistics are introduced by an infectious disease specialist. Comments from an expert add an authoritative tone (Slovik, 1997). His choice of words to describe the danger ("severe permanent adverse outcome") contrasts with Dan Rather's earlier "horrid side-effects." While Dr. Offit's descriptive language is cool and clinical, Rather's language is alarming, though neither is actually particularly informative.

The reporter John Roberts continues to tone down the drama in the message by telling us that Iraq is actually only *rumored* to possess smallpox; that there are many questions about whether the benefits justify the risks; that there are a large number of people who will be excluded; and that, finally, there is no reason to inoculate people before exposure at all.

This news item exemplifies a strategy of grabbing and keeping viewer attention by conjuring alarming scenarios and then stepping back from the overstatement through use of details and statistics, qualifying language and authoritative opinions. The story is constructed as a compromise between the "hype" that will keep viewers tuned in and the informative function that is the ostensible purpose for a newscast. If the informative function alone were dictating the narrative structure of this story, the information featured in the lead might be that "a person can be effectively vaccinated up to three days after they've been exposed to smallpox." Instead, this information, which calls the whole dramatic inoculation campaign into question and is crucial information for anyone making a decision about personal inoculation, is buried in the reporter's concluding remarks.

This strategy can be found even in some very brief news stories. For example, a story broadcast on ABC "World News Now" on September 4, 2002 begins with the statement: "The Environmental Protection Agency says there's persuasive evidence that diesel exhaust can cause lung cancer." The very next statement says something that could be seen as contradictory: "The EPA acknowledges there are some doubts about the long-term health effects of exposure to diesel exhaust."

Here again, the dramatic opener is followed by a significantly qualified elaboration. That the dramatic function and the informational function are juxtaposed, creating a direct collision of meanings, demonstrates another feature of television newscasts: time pressure. Many stories are allotted less than a minute, leaving no opportunity for the subtler backpedaling evidenced in the first example.

STRATEGY TWO: BAIT AND SWITCH

While the first strategy described is simple and straightforward, the second strategy is more subtle and more intriguing. This strategy involves transforming a story about one thing into a story about something else that is more dramatic and framed as more relevant to the viewer. The information is there, but only the most critical viewer is likely to identify the kernel of real news that is couched in a more "user friendly" story frame. Most stories that exemplify this strategy also feature dramatic introductory statements, but their overall narrative strategy is more complex than backpedaling.

Two examples illustrate this strategy. The first is a story presented on December 17, 2002, on CBS Evening News, reported by Bob Orr.

DAN RATHER, anchor:

Driving in bad weather can be risky in any vehicle, but whatever the weather, some vehicles are more prone to rollovers than others—SUVs, for instance. The government is trying now to come up with some accurate measure of rollover risk. CBS's Bob Orr gives you the first look at how some experts are going about it in tonight's "Eye on America."

WHEN MOTIVES COLLIDE

BOB ORR reporting:

On a closed test track, a professional driver is about to perform an emergency steering maneuver, simulating what can happen when a car drifts off the pavement and onto the shoulder of a road. The abrupt overcorrection causes the Honda sport utility vehicle to tip at a speed of just 45 miles an hour. On an actual highway, that would have resulted in a rollover accident and possibly a fatality.

Rollover crashes kill more than 10,000 people each year across America. Rollover deaths are climbing as more people trade in their cars for high-riding, less stable pickup trucks and SUVs.

MR. CLARENCE DITLOW [Center for Auto Safety]:

It's the fastest-growing form of fatalities in motor vehicles today, and it's because we have sport utility vehicles that handle differently. And we need a real-world test that distinguishes how they do in the real world.

ORR:

That's precisely what's happening here at the Vehicle Research and Test Center in Ohio. CBS News got a rare look at federal regulators developing a test that will ultimately be used to compare and rate the stability of all vehicles.

Currently, cars and SUVs are rated for rollover risk based on mathematical calculations. Narrow vehicles that sit high off the ground are rated more likely to roll, but these tests may prove to be more precise than measuring how cars can actually perform in real driving maneuvers.

DR. JEFFREY RUNGE [National Highway Safety Administration]:

We're all watching this very closely to see how these vehicles will perform in these motion tests.

ORR:

Jeff Runge, who heads the National Highway Safety Administration, says the tests will not trigger new regulations, but publicizing rollover ratings will pressure carmakers to improve stability.

DR. RUNGE:

If they make vehicles that are prone to roll over, my hope is that people will not buy them. And they won't be able to sell them, and so they'll have to make changes. This is the basic market forces at work.

ORR:

The testing is expensive and painstakingly tedious.

MR. RILEY GARROTT [National Highway Traffic Safety Administration]:

We'll bring it down a little bit and see what happens.

ORR:

You're looking for maybe a threshold where this thing becomes unstable.

MR. GARROTT:

Yeah, threshold, mm-hmmm. That's right.

ORR:

And it could be model year 2005 before consumers have the real-world ratings.

MR. DITLOW:

The public needs the numbers because more people are being killed. We're getting more vehicles out there on the road with higher rollover characteristics, and we don't know which are the good performers and which are the bad performers.

ORR:

Regulators admit that real-world testing is overdue, but say automakers don't have to wait to make safety changes. And people can greatly improve their chances of surviving a rollover by simply buckling their seat belts. In East Liberty, Ohio, I'm Bob Orr for "Eye on America."

What is this story actually about? As viewers see it unfold, the story appears to be about the dangers of driving SUVs, and the increased numbers of fatalities that result from drivers being unfamiliar with the handling of this type of vehicle. Since millions of people drive SUVs, or share the roadway with them every day, this is a compelling story to many viewers. The next several statements elaborate on the connection between SUVs and traffic deaths.

However, the actual reason for this story is more prosaic: the development of a new test by the Vehicle Research and Test Center to measure the stability of "all vehicles." The reporter returns repeatedly to the SUV theme because it is more dramatic, concrete, and clear. In contrast, Orr's explanation of the testing procedure and its significance is fuzzy. He says that while current risks are calculated on the basis of mathematical formulae, "These tests ultimately may prove to be more precise than measuring how cars actually perform in real driving maneuvers." It's hard to tell from this statement which test we should trust. It is clear, though, that the test and its application are not this reporter's priority. The focus quickly returns to the deadly SUVs, where it remains.

A second story, also from CBS, illustrates this strategy equally well:

SCOTT PELLY, anchor:

Smokers trying to quit with the help of patches and other nicotine-replacement aids have potential health risk to think about tonight. On the *CBS Health Watch*, Elizabeth Kaledin tells us that aside from being highly addictive, nicotine may also be a deadly promoter of lung cancer.

ELIZABETH KALEDIN, reporting:

Nicotine is being looked at in a new light tonight. Once considered only addictive, now scientists say it may be more harmful, sharing the blame with its partner, tar, in contributing to lung cancer. In research done by the National Cancer Institute, the effect of nicotine was compared to the effect of the known carcinogens, or cancer-causing chemicals, in tobacco. Both the nicotine and the carcinogens interfered with the body's natural process of killing off the unhealthy cells that could eventually develop into tumors.

DR. PHILLIP DENNIS [National Cancer Institute]:

We feel this may be an early and important event that may allow the other events necessary for cancer formation to take place.

KALEDIN:

Dr. Phillip Dennis, who led the study, hopes the findings can lead to new drugs to block nicotine's effects. But this new look at nicotine is also raising questions about the safety of nicotine replacement therapy, the patches, gums and nasal sprays that Americans have come to rely upon to help them kick the habit. Nicotine replacement therapy is prescribed to be used temporarily, generally for about three months. Lirio Covey, who runs a smoking cessation program in New York City, thinks for the short term it's OK.

MS. LIRIO COVEY (New York State Psychiatric Institute):

The harm that we know from smoking is far greater than the possible low levels of nicotine that is delivered in the replacements.

KALEDIN:

Kirsty Guster, who just quit with the help of nicotine patches, would agree.

MS. KRISTY GUSTER (former smoker):

Two months on nicotine patches, you know, far better than—than smoking for six years, you know.

KALEDIN:

It may not be harmless and should be used wisely.

DR. DENNIS:

Ex-smokers should not indiscriminately remain on nicotine replacement for months or years.

KALEDIN:

But the consensus is anything is better than smoking. Elizabeth Kaledin, CBS News, New York.

WHEN MOTIVES COLLIDE

This story begins with a dramatic statement about nicotine-replacement therapy. We are told that nicotine is "highly addictive" and "may also be a deadly promoter of lung cancer." This statement implies that nicotine-replacement therapy is the same as smoking nicotine, so everyone thinking of using this therapy is in danger. This grabs our interest. While details are provided which back away from the alarming claim in the first statement as the story unfolds, close reading of the story reveals that the news being reported is not about nicotine replacement therapy at all. The news concerns a research finding on the chemical nature of nicotine, which is described cautiously and equivocally by the scientist interviewed in the story. Its applicability to nicotine therapy is not addressed in the research and is, therefore, not clear. The news writer has chosen to shift the focus of the story from the research to a widespread practice: using nicotine patches, gum, etc., to help us quit smoking. In the process, the story has probably misdirected the viewer by emphasizing more straightforward applicability to the therapy than the research suggests.

In both of these stories, it has been decided that scientific information must be dressed up in a dramatic narrative in order to hold viewers' attention, even though the relationship between the science and the story is tenuous.

Conclusion

This study deals with only two narrative strategies and a small number of news stories. The purpose of this exercise is to show, through close reading of news stories, how such stories reflect the larger struggle within news media organizations to attract the audiences that bring advertisers, and hence profits, while at the same time providing content that meets the viewers' expectations for what news should be.

Analysis of these stories can offer only preliminary ideas about how television news is written. These examples suggest that the imperatives of drama, rather than informative functions, are often the determining forces in television news. The reality is that commercial news stories often fall short in informing the public about ideas and events. If news stories were written to convey information, which is their ostensible reason for being, it is easy to imagine how different their construction might be. But would anyone be watching?

References

Alcabes, P. (2003, May 23). The epidemiologist's need to shatter the myth of a risk-free life. *Chronicle of Higher Education*, B11–12.

Altheide, D. (2002). *Creating fear: News and the construction of crisis*. NY: Walter de Gruyter.

Bagdikian, B. (1992). *The media monopoly* (4th ed.). Boston: Beacon Press.

Bennett, W. L. (1996). *News: The politics of illusion* (3rd. ed.). White Plains, NY: Longman.

Butler, J. (2002). *Television: Critical methods and applications* (2nd ed.). Mahwah, NJ: Lawrence Erlbaum.

Cohen, A., Adoni, H., & Bantz, C. (1990). *Social conflict and television news*. NY: Vintage.

Dean, W., & Brady, L. (2002, November/December). After 9/11 has anything changed? *Columbia Journalism Review*/Project for Excellence in Journalism, 94–95.

Downie, L., & Kaiser, R. (2002). *The news about the news*. NY: Vintage.

Hartley, J. (1996). *Popular reality journalism, modernity and popular culture*. London: Arnold.

Klaidman, S. (1991). *Health in the headlines; The stories behind the stories*. NY: Oxford University Press.

Meyrowitz, J. (1998). Multiple media literacies. *Journal of Communications, 48* (1), 96–108.

Murray, D., Schwartz, J., & Lichter, S. (2001). *It ain't necessarily so: How media make and unmake the scientific picture of reality*. Lanham, MD: Rowman & Littlefield.

Potter, D. (2002, November/December). Pessimism rules in TV newsrooms. *Columbia Journalism Review*/Project for Excellence in Journalism, 90.

Schudson, M. (2003). *The sociology of news*. NY: W. W. Norton.

Singer, E., & Endreny, P. (1993). *Reporting on Risk*. NY: Russell Sage.

Slovik, P. (1997). Public perception of risk. *Journal of Environmental Health, 59* (9), 22–25.

Stocking, S. H. (1999). How journalists deal with scientific uncertainty. In S. Freidman, S. Dunwoody, & C. Rogers (Eds.). *Communicating uncertainty: Media coverage of new and controversial science* (pp. 23–42). Mahwah, NJ: Erlbaum.

WHEN MOTIVES COLLIDE

BARBARA FOWLES, REFLECTIVE PIECE

Media Arts is a field that draws upon several disciplines and traditions in both the Humanities and the Social Sciences. The field is broadly concerned with the complex interactions between mass media and culture. This essay draws upon ideas about the nature and importance of story-form from the humanities but sits more squarely within the social sciences in terms of its structure. The essay is presented in the form of a research report that examines a sample of data, in this case transcripts of news programs, in order to answer a question about the strategies used to write them. The essay uses a small sample and is therefore exploratory in nature. The style of the essay is consistent with writing for an academic journal in the social sciences, though the technical jargon has been, I hope, kept to a minimum. Unfortunately, social science writing normally precludes humor and irony, so I have written in a serious, impersonal tone— although it is tempting to use sarcasm in discussing some of the more melodramatic statements in the news stories.

My original interest in undertaking this research was to determine how blame or responsibility is assigned within news stories about risk and how this might be related to an apparent rejection in our society of the notion of acceptable risk. I used the opportunity presented by the theme "collide" to examine a variation on this theme.

I begin the essay by presenting a simple idea: television news serves two purposes—profit and information. I refer to a substantial body of scholarship on this subject in order to show the broad acceptance among media scholars of the existence of this conflict between profit motives and journalistic purposes. I also cite pertinent scholarship in order to define where this particular piece of research might fit into the puzzle. Following the review of literature, I assert the purpose of my essay: to analyze individual news stories and to look for evidence of this collision of motives at the "micro" level.

The next segment of my essay deals with the special attributes of the story-form. I suggest that these attributes lay the groundwork for both the strengths and the weaknesses of communicating news in story-form. This section introduces some ideas about narrative, format, frame, and media literacy.

The body of my piece is an analysis of actual transcripts of news stories. Three of the transcripts are complete, and one is a partial transcript. I quote from these lengthy transcripts because my argument depends on the reader paying close attention to the way the story is developed in each case. Because of the small number of stories used, they should be viewed as case studies: we can learn from them and think about their implications, but we cannot draw general conclusions about television news based on them. I have not used a systematic theoretical approach to deconstructing these stories, a typical methodology used in the social sciences. Instead, I describe my method as close reading. This method would not be appropriate for a definitive survey of news strategies, but it is useful for a preliminary study like this one.

My conclusion is very brief, since the analysis of the transcripts themselves afforded me the opportunity to introduce critical comments. These comments, I hope, reveal the complex motives involved in commercial news-writing and suggest that news stories require our critical attention as viewers. The conclusion is primarily a summary of the evidence that news narratives reflect colliding forces. My intention is to leave the reader with questions about whether the news we watch every day is as clear and accurate as it could be. Finally, I try to suggest that the reality might be that we viewers do get what we want from television news. I hope to leave the reader with many questions about what goes on in television newsrooms and about whether significant changes are called for.

Looking at this collision of profit motive and public interest is significant because it demands that informed consumers of mass media content be aware of its dual nature as both business and culture. These impulses collide not only in news, as this essay demonstrates, but also in every product of commercial media from *Pokemon* to *Sex and the City*. "Bottom-line" imperatives inform every decision made by the creators of television, radio, film, and other mass media output. The success of a television series, for example, is not defined exclusively by its artistic merit or social impact, but rather by those attributes in combination with the show's ability to bring in advertising dollars. These factors are not necessarily in direct conflict; rather, they are inextricably linked. The various ways these forces interact always dictate content outcomes for mass media.

"THINK. WRITE. ASK."

1. What is Barbara Fowles's thesis? In what section of the essay does she state it? Is this where you expect a thesis to be?
2. Even though Fowles uses transcripts of news stories to support her argument, she warns us of the dangers of making such conclusions based on a few case studies. What importance can we reasonably attach to her findings, and what further evidence would be needed to turn her findings into definitive statements about the reality of television newscasts?

3. Fowles's intention in the essay is to leave the reader asking whether there should be significant changes to the way the news is presented to viewers. Based on the content of her analysis, do you think Fowles would ultimately advocate changes? If so, how can you tell?

4. Fowles tells us that she was tempted to use sarcasm in discussing the melodramic elements of news stories. How might using humor or sarcasm alter the impact of the essay? Think about the way tone affects an author's overall credibility. Would Fowles still have seemed credible to you if she had used humor?

5. While Erica Frouman-Smith uses MLA author-page parenthetical citation style, Fowles uses the APA author-date citation style. Why would the author-date style be more appropriate for Fowles, a social scientist, than for Frouman-Smith, a humanist? Does this APA citation style lend credibility to Fowles's argument?

6. In the second section of her essay, Fowles details her method of research and analysis. Why do you think Fowles chooses to outline her methods of research while Amy Wysoker and Jerome Tognoli do not?

WHEN *WORKING MOTHER* COLLIDES WITH *GENDER & SOCIETY*

Lori McNeil, Sociology

ABSTRACT

This content analysis is a juxtaposition of popular women's magazines and feminist academic journals in order to evaluate the objective and subjective nature of how the issue of childcare has been portrayed. The subject matter under study included three popular magazines—*Ladies Home Journal, Good Housekeeping* and *Working Mother* and three feminist/academic publications—*Signs, Gender & Society* and *The Journal of Marriage and the Family*. First, a quantitative analysis was employed that examined the extent to which the issue of childcare was addressed. Next, a qualitative analysis of how childcare references differed between these two styles of print media was undertaken. This research revealed two significant findings. First, in 2002/3, approximately 50% fewer references to childcare generally were made than had been made in 1996. Second, significant differences were noted between how childcare was addressed in popular magazines when compared to feminist/academic journals.

"All young families but the super rich are grappling with America's daycare crisis . . . of poor availability, affordability and quality" (Coplan, 2002).

As one evaluates the daycare crisis, it's evident that these above-cited issues have been part of family's daily stressors for some time. Stories of securing daycare slots as soon as a child is conceived are not unusual (Coplan, 2002). In a New York preschool, waiting lists have extended to 40–50 thousand names. Finding daycare does not necessarily mean that the difficulty is over. One vignette focusing on the daycare issue presents the story of a child who has had seven different childcare arrangements in her short three-and-a-half years (Ferguson, 2002).

Two nationally representative surveys collected data on childcare. A Roper public opinion poll (Women's Voices '96 Survey, 1996) found that 30% of respondents felt that finding affordable and dependable childcare caused them to be either very worried or somewhat worried. In 2000, respondents in another popular opinion poll reported issues related to childcare, leadership ability and foreign policy as equally important relative to the 2000 presidential election (Women and Voting Survey, 2000). Another question on this survey asked about the biggest challenge faced in people's daily lives; equal percentages of respondents reported their biggest challenges as childcare, pay equity and finding employment.

While the general public has seemingly identified childcare as a major issue, what is unclear is whether feminist researchers have taken up this cause as a legitimate and worthy research issue. In fact, the claim has been made that feminist researchers, while agreeing that childcare is problematic, have paid little attention to childcare as a research issue (Angelique & Culley, 2000; Henry & Sorrel, 1990). As a feminist researcher who has spent over eight years focusing on childcare research (McNeil, 2003; McNeil, 2002; McNeil, 2000; McNeil, 1999; McNeil, 1998) I have often been surprised how little research literature is readily available. Thus, this essay explores the claim that feminist research has tended to ignore childcare as a scholarly issue. In order to address this claim, content analysis was employed.

RESEARCH METHOD

Content analysis falls under the rubric of unobtrusive research, meaning that the social behavior under study is not affected (Babbie, 2001; Berg, 2001). Content analysis analyzes data which already exists, albeit the data tends to have been produced for reasons other than the research itself. Using an objective coding scheme, content analysis seeks a systematic comparison based on "criteria of selection" (Berg, 2001; Schutt, 2001). Criteria of selection, a deductive approach, is characterized by specific rules the researcher develops prior to data collection.

When employing content analysis, all human activity is considered text—a collection of symbols that convey meaning—for potential examination (Babbie, 2001; Berg, 2001). For example, text can consist of facial expressions, the firmness of a handshake or a specific ordering of letters which form words. Text also can include visual images, such as personal photographs and magazine and television images. Ideally, content analysis examines communication typologies that seek to understand better the perspective of the producer and audience of these original texts. It is these perspectives that will be scrutinized in this research project.

Prior to my undertaking this study, several limitations of this research design were noted. First, because the sample size of publications was small the results cannot be taken to represent *all* feminist journals and popular magazines. Secondly, the publications chosen to represent the categories of "general public" and "feminist research" were chosen using a purposeful sampling strategy. Random sampling was not employed, meaning that the results cannot be generalized or inferred beyond the actual publications sampled. Still, these publications do serve as quasi-indicators of the categories as one begins the initial exploration of these domains. Thus, while acknowledging these limitations, the results should be construed as a potential beginning point attempting to understand how childcare may be viewed generally as compared to how feminist researchers address the issue.

DATA COLLECTION

In order to examine how both the "general public" and "feminist research" publications address childcare, a content analysis of the two styles of publications was undertaken; the unit of analysis was magazine/journal articles. Data were collected in two waves of research activity.

In the initial wave of data collection, two traditional women's magazines were sampled: *Ladies Home Journal* and *Good Housekeeping*. It is argued that these magazines' content reflects the opinions, interests, and concerns of their readers and serves as a quasi-indicator of the general public's interest in the issue of childcare. In addition, these two publications address women's issues,[1] are marketed as women's magazines and have relatively high readership rates and broad circulation (Malkin, Wornian, & Chrisler, 1999; Schlenker, Caron, & Halteman, 1998; Pierce, 1997). *Ladies Home Journal* and *Good Housekeeping* tend to cover categories such as home, fashion, health, food, celebrities, fiction, relationships, and family.

The second publication style included feminist academic journals because this is where contemporary feminist research is likely to be published. In the first wave of data collection, two journals were chosen to represent this category. *Signs: Journal of Women in Culture and Society* and *Gender & Society: Official Publication of Sociologists for Women in Society* are leading feminist journals with reputations of being on the cutting edge of women's issues and feminist methods and theoretical formulations (Journal Citation Reports, 2000). *Signs* and *Gender & Society* include research articles, interviews, perspectives, and book reviews.

---

1. Women's issues are those that include "lifestyles, workforce participation, care of dependent family members, health and reproduction, poverty and homelessness, violence, and minority status" (Angelique & Culley, 2000).

The systematic analysis of these magazines was constructed by utilizing the criteria of selection referred to earlier. When assessing data for analysis, words, phrases, sentences and paragraphs can be sampled (Berg, 2001). In this case, initially the criteria examined included the surface content of articles where childcare was the primary focus (Babbie, 2001). This manifest coding style was augmented with a latent coding style for these four publications. Latent coding examines clusters of ideas and groupings of words that convey meaning or address an issue without actually referring to the issue by name (Berg, 2001).

Two years of each journal were first examined manually by searching each article title and corresponding abstracts where applicable (Angelinque & Culley, 2000). Articles including childcare content, either manifest or latent, were examined in order to evaluate the extent to which the articles refer to the issue. Whenever the words "daycare," "childcare/child care," or "babysitting" were found, coding reflected these as manifest examples of childcare. Latent references to childcare were also collected. Examples of latent childcare coding included difficulty keeping jobs due to the need to supervise children, caregiving by non-parents, working parents' guilt regarding inflexible work schedules, dissatisfaction with the quality of family life, and working too much to care for one's children.

First, all issues of all four journals were examined for the year of 1996. This year was chosen because the public opinion poll referred to earlier was conducted in 1996 and childcare was reported as being a major issue for families at that time. The content analysis was undertaken in July 2003; the preceding twelve months, July 2002 through June 2003, of each publication was examined in order to assess the presence of this issue in women's magazines versus feminist academic journals relative to 1996.

FINDINGS AND ANALYSIS

Two popular monthly magazines, *Ladies Home Journal* and *Good House-keeping*, were sampled in order to examine the extent to which the issue of childcare was represented. Twenty-four issues of each publication represented approximately 11,000 pages of printed text. More than half of each issue, however, is devoted to advertising, leaving fewer than 5000 pages of text devoted to articles.

Academic journals sampled included *Signs* and *Gender & Society*. *Signs* is a quarterly journal which publishes approximately 1150 pages per year for an estimated total of 2300 pages for the years 1996 and 2002/3. Only a few pages tend to be used for advertising in academic journals; therefore, the issue of advertising is not relevant for the journals sampled. *Gender & Society* is a bimonthly publication that publishes, on average, just under 1000 pages per year. Printed pages for the academic journals for both years represented approximately 4500 pages as compared to 5000 pages of the popular magazines. Thus, the amount of text examined in the popular magazines and academic journals is roughly equivalent.

Three main categories emerged based on manifest and latent coding styles. Manifest coding was represented through the actual words "childcare," "daycare" or "babysitting," and articles were also categorized as primary and secondary. The primary manifest category included those articles whose main focus was childcare whereas the manifest-secondary category referred to childcare directly but the article's main focus was something other than childcare. Manifest-secondary articles dealt with issues such as extended families or single parenting. Latent coding was represented by text which conveyed ideas of childcare, daycare or babysitting but did not use those exact words. A tabled representation of the results is presented below.

Childcare Content in 1996

	Manifest Primary	Manifest Secondary	Latent	Total
Ladies Home Journal	0	20	1	21
Good Housekeeping	0	0	0	0
Signs	0	6	2	8
Gender & Society	592	29	1	622

Childcare Content in 2002/3

	Manifest Primary	Manifest Secondary	Latent	Total
Ladies Home Journal	1	5	5	11
Good Housekeeping	0	5	1	6
Signs	0	0	0	0
Gender & Society	144	26	33	203

Upon examination of the research results, several initial observations are significant. First, it is particularly surprising that childcare content in popular magazines and in academic journals was significantly less in 2002/3 than in 1996. *Ladies Home Journal* childcare content was less by 48%, *Gender & Society* childcare content was less by 67%, and *Signs* had no childcare content in 2002/3.

This difference may be explained in part by the passage of the 1996 Personal Responsibility Act, commonly referred to as "welfare reform" (Public Law 104-103, 1996). Because welfare mothers were required to enter or reenter the workforce based on this federal legislation, childcare became a major obstacle and garnered a great deal of popular and research attention.

Only one of the four publications, *Good Housekeeping*, had increased in childcare content. *Good Housekeeping* had no childcare content, either latent or manifest, in 1996, but had six references in 2002/3. It is important to note that this content was categorized only as latent and manifest-secondary. None of the content was characterized as manifest-primary, meaning that none of the articles' main focus was childcare.

In addition to the decline of the magazine/journal childcare content generally, several other findings are noteworthy. First, it is important to note that the most prestigious feminist academic journal, *Signs* (Watson, 1990), contained very little childcare content based on the examination of year 1996 and year 2002/3. Although *Signs* is an interdisciplinary journal, meaning that its focus is not exclusively on the social sciences but may deal with other disciplines such as literature and medicine, it is nonetheless surprising that little attention has been paid to childcare. A similar pattern was evidenced relative to *Good Housekeeping*.

In sharp contrast to *Signs* and *Good Housekeeping*, *Gender & Society*, a leading feminist research journal (Journal Citation Reports, 2000), significantly addressed childcare. In 1996 alone, the publication contained 622 references to childcare. Part of this discrepancy between *Signs* and *Gender & Society* may be because *Signs* is geared to an interdisciplinary audience whereas *Gender & Society* is geared toward sociologists and social practitioners. Thus, its content would likely more explicitly relate to social issues and action.

These initial findings did quantify childcare content in two popular magazines compared to two feminist journals. The findings, however, do not provide enough data relative to the stated research aim. Thus, a second wave of data collection was undertaken in order to further examine the prevalence of childcare representations in popular women's magazines and feminist academic journals.

The unit of analysis sampling criteria was altered slightly in the second wave of data collection; the integrity of the original research design was maintained. That is, popular women's magazines and academic journals were examined, but publication selection was based on those publications where one would expect to find childcare content. Whereas the subject matter of the original four publications sampled might be, but would not necessarily be, geared toward issues of combining family and work life, the last two journals sampled deal explicitly with the combination of these two contemporary issues. One would anticipate finding the same patterns in these publications as in the first wave of data collection, although more overall references would be expected.

The two publications chosen in the second wave of data collection were *Working Mother* and *The Journal of Marriage and the Family*. *Working Mother*, a popular women's magazine, is published ten times a year and on average comprises roughly 900 pages per year; at least half of the magazine is devoted to advertising. *Working Mother* includes article categories such as "life and style," "children," "food and nutrition," and "on the job." *The Journal of Marriage and the Family* publishes roughly 1150 pages per year, is organized in a quarterly format and devotes very few pages to advertising. *The Journal of Marriage and the Family* included article categories such as work and family, policy issues, caregiving, family violence and book reviews. The following results were noted and are represented below in tabled form.

Childcare Content

	Manifest Primary	Manifest Secondary	Latent	Total
1996				
Working Mother	946	105	355	1406
Journal of Marriage and the Family	269	201	239	709
2002/3				
Working Mother	315	41	85	441
Journal of Marriage and the Family	25	55	147	221

Working Mother magazine referenced childcare in either manifest or latent forms 1406 times in 1996 but only 441 times in 2002/3. A similar ratio was evidenced in the first wave of data collection and analysis. The change between 1996 and 2002/3 represents a 69% decrease between the years examined. These data also suggest that when childcare is referenced in *Working Mother*, it is in articles specifically mentioning childcare. In 1996, primary manifest coding represented 90% of all manifest childcare references; in 2002/3, 88%.

When examining the academic journal *The Journal of Marriage and the Family*, the same relative decline in childcare references was noted as with *Working Mother*; however, the rate was lower at 50% as compared to 69%. Interestingly, the decrease of 69% for *The Journal of Marriage and the Family* is similar to that of *Gender & Society* with a decrease of 67%, and *Working Mother*'s decrease of 50% is similar to that of *Ladies Home Journal*, whose rate was 48%.

What is equally compelling about the above tabled data is that in both years sampled, 1996 and 2002/3, the popular magazine referenced childcare twice as often as did the academic journal.[2] *Working Mother* referenced childcare 1406 times in 1996 whereas *The Journal of Marriage and the Family* referred to childcare 709 times. In 2002/3, *Working Mother* referred to this issue 441 times as compared to 221 references in *The Journal of Marriage and the Family*.

Beyond the quantitative examination, it was critical to examine how childcare was represented in the six different publications. The following served to address that goal.

Although *Ladies Home Journal* did make reference to childcare as a "top women's issue" (October 2002, p. 60) on one occasion, the journal most often addressed childcare by expressing it as a personal or individual issue. In a sociological context, C.W. Mills differentiates between social issues and "personal troubles" (Giddens & Duneier, 2000). A personal trouble is not construed as a large-scale social issue in need of addressing, but as an issue concerning only the individual who experiences the problem. Other examples of categorizing the issue as "personal trouble" include suggesting that families "blend" so that more adults are available to pick up parenting "slack," offering tips on how to best work productively at home, and pointing out that flextime work arrangements are amenable with family life.

The few childcare references in *Good Housekeeping* dealt with issues such as getting a sitter on occasion for one's emotional health, or as an avenue to adding spice to one's marriage. Other childcare instances tended to be superficial and framed as afterthoughts. These references were often presented in such a casual fashion that the representation itself was obscured. For example, one author reported that she needed to drop her son at a sitter as she simultaneously envisioned the outfit she might wear to work.

Gender & Society tended to address childcare by examining the issue through the lens of race, class and gender. Thus, *Gender & Society* employed what is commonly referred to as a macro-level analysis. A macro orientation critiques and examines society through large-scale social structures. These structures may include the struggles of economic classes, or conflicts and constructions of institutions (e.g., family and government) as units of analysis (Babbie, 2001). References included arguments about childcare as unpaid and unrecognized labor in a traditionally male construction of work. A male construction of work defines

---

2. It is acknowledged that *The Journal of Marriage and the Family* is not normally referred to as a feminist journal but instead as an academic journal that deals with issues typically defined as women's issues, such as domestic violence and caregiving.

work primarily as that which receives monetary remuneration and secondarily as activity that occurs outside of the home. Gendered references were directed toward childcare as "women's work," and class references dealt with childcare as work that tends to be performed by those who are the most economically vulnerable, such as migrant workers. When examining childcare based on race and/or ethnicity, *Gender & Society* evaluated childcare practices between countries such as Spain and Taiwan. Examinations of childcare formulations such as shared mothering and differing conceptions of how childcare was defined based on race/ethnicity were also undertaken in *Gender & Society*.

Beyond the connections of childcare to race, class and gender, *Gender & Society* focused on childcare at a political level. For example, this journal published research on California's childcare system as a pivotal maternalistic social movement. Other political material published dealt with the role of the state in the general provision and regulation of childcare. References also included the examination of childcare public policy and women's employment status and how these are constructed and treated as separate from motherhood generally.

As noted earlier, *Signs* tended not to publish research that addressed childcare directly, or even indirectly. Instead, *Signs* published a great deal of information that related directly to feminist philosophy. It focused on critiques of positivism, including an examination of the construction of knowledge and how these constructions operate as a hegemonic discourse. In fact, the entire Spring 2003 volume was devoted to gender and science, publishing research in archeology, physics and biology. Other examples of *Signs* content included examinations of classical literature and film. This analysis of the now cult classic *Thelma and Louise* served as an example of an initial female gaze within popular culture. Other popular culture examinations included the television show *Sex and the City* illustrating the prevalence of women's issues demanding space within the public domain. Finally, *Signs* examined feminism internationally, presenting, for example, a comparison of Latin American and Caribbean feminisms as well as descriptions of how feminism is constructed in other nations.

In some cases, *The Journal of Marriage and the Family*, as did *Ladies Home Journal*, tended to address childcare on a personal level. For example, one article focused on how a mother's children may live elsewhere, perhaps even in another country, so that the mother is able to work without the added pressure of obtaining childcare. Most often, however, *The Journal of Marriage and the Family* addressed childcare on a macro level. Example studies included how childcare duties are divided among mothers, fathers and non-paternal caregivers, and the pattern of number of hours worked by mothers as an indicator of wage

rates. Other articles presented the increasing pattern of grandparent participation in childcare and how this pattern differs among people of different ethnic
backgrounds. The most recent articles reviewed presented research on changes
in women's satisfaction and stress at work and at home.

In contrast to *The Journal of Marriage and the Family*, *Working Mother*
addressed childcare at personal and political levels. For example, it offered solutions to the problem of having a babysitter called for jury duty. Some articles
focused on emotions and guilt connected with leaving a child in daycare after a
maternity leave. Most of the content was political. Articles explored the Family
and Medical Leave Act, addressed the inadequacy of back-up childcare and childcare for moderately ill children. Perhaps the most compelling references to childcare were embedded within the yearly accounting of the "100 Best Companies"
relative to mothers' employment. These references are imbued with both personal
and political overtones. The idea that a mother needs to find a company that
offers a family-friendly policy is constructed as personal. However, the very public and positive portrayal of these companies gives other companies direction
and models to follow. The following section presents an overview of this research
as well as additional analysis of the publications reviewed.

Summary and Conclusions

An examination of popular magazines and feminist research journals relative
to childcare references and representations was the main focus of this study. The
rationale for this content analysis is that the publications reviewed reflect the
perspective both of the producer and of the audience. Childcare references in
three traditional women's magazines, *Ladies Home Journal*, *Good Housekeeping*
and *Working Mother*, and three academic research journals, *Signs, Gender & Society* and *The Journal of Marriage and the Family*, served as indicators of discrep-
ancies between how the general public perceives childcare and how feminist
researchers may perceive this issue. While the charge that feminist journals ignore
childcare was explored, the findings do not fully support this claim.

Ladies Home Journal did address the issue but only in a limited fashion; *Good
Housekeeping* made little reference to childcare. *Working Mother* significantly
referred to childcare, as one would expect given that the magazine focuses mainly
on the combination of motherhood and employment. *Signs* made little reference to childcare. This is problematic since *Signs* is likely the most important and
prestigious journal in feminist circles. Conversely, *Gender & Society* referenced

childcare on numerous occasions, with numbers similar to that of *The Journal of Marriage and the Family.*

Interpreting research data is often a delicate and sometimes messy task. This is so because many times interpretation is a subjective practice, making it both difficult and exciting. The first wave of analysis centered on a quantitative accounting exploring to what extent childcare was represented in the six publications analyzed. The second wave of analysis centered on how childcare was represented in print media, specifically those sampled.

The concepts of "personal" and "political" offers a useful framework for the continued analysis of childcare. I reported that *Good Housekeeping* and *Signs* tended to depict childcare sparingly, never as an integral or central focus. In contrast, *Ladies Home Journal* referenced childcare more often, and primarily on a personal or individual level. This classification is important because identifying childcare as only a personal issue provides no movement toward any type of social consciousness or public awareness of childcare as a large-scale social problem. The "personal trouble" classification suggests that childcare is a problem for one person or another, but not for most people. Individual or personal problems invite individual solutions, not larger structural solutions. *The Journal of Marriage and the Family* often referred to childcare, as evidenced by the quantitative accounting presented earlier. Although the journal dedicated a great deal of research to childcare, again, the references were not addressed at a political level. This treatment stymies large-scale social change.

The overarching concerns, of course, are both *how* and *how often* childcare is depicted in the media and ultimately in society. Two journals, *Gender & Society* and *Working Mother*, made myriad references to childcare, oftentimes at both personal and political levels. These publications are embracing and addressing both the personal and the political domains. This practice is critical because both individual analysis and political accountability reframe childcare as a legitimate social issue. Moreover, the representation of any social concern is critical because social consciousness (i.e., public awareness) of an issue's existence or reality is often a direct avenue to developing an agenda to address it. What is talked about, and how it is framed or constructed, are valid social concerns (Barad, 2003; Harding, 1987; Bourdieu, 1977; Lukes, 1974). In other words, if discursive practices surrounding childcare are not actively engaged beyond a personal level, the issue begins to become less visible and eventually will fade from the universe of discourse, or what is discussed or is defined as meaningful social concerns (Bourdieu, 1977). Based on this formulation, a macro/political orientation promotes a national agenda for addressing the issue of childcare, an issue that is such a struggle for so many American families.

Since I also argue that continued and increased childcare research and public awareness is necessary, I suggest that this exploratory study be reformulated to include a larger sampling of popular women's magazines and feminist journals. An examination of additional publication years would also be helpful, especially in light of 2002/3's decline in childcare references relative to 1996. This decline pattern is a dangerous trend and must be better understood and researched. Other media types should also be sampled and could serve as indicators of research agendas or a general public concern over childcare. For example, a content analysis of popular television programs may be useful in understanding how the issue of childcare is portrayed and represented generally. An active research agenda relative to childcare is necessary because "all young families but the super rich are grappling with America's daycare crisis" (Coplan, 2002).

References

Angelique, H., & Culley, M. (2000, December). Searching for feminism: an analysis of community psychology literature relevant to women's concerns. *American Journal of Community Psychology, 28*(6), 793–808.

Babbie, E. (2001). *The practice of social research* (9th ed.). Belmont, CA: Wadsworth.

Barad, K. (2003, Spring). Posthumanist performativity toward an understanding of how matter comes to matter. *Signs, 28*(3), 801–832.

Berg, B. (2001). *Qualitative research methods for the social sciences* (4th ed.). Needham Heights, MA: Allyn Bacon.

Bourdieu, P. (1997). *Outline of a theory of practice.* Cambridge, MA: Cambridge University Press.

Coplan, J. (2002, April). Why good daycare is hard to find, and what you can do about it. *Baby Talk, 67*(3), 46–52.

Ferguson, S. (2002, April). The daycare dilemma. *Maclean's, 115*(14), 58–61.

Harding, S. (1987). Epistemological questions. In S. Harding (Ed.), *Feminism and methodology.* Bloomington, IN: Indiana University Press.

Henry, A., & Sorrel, L., (1990, February). Child care—who cares? *Off Our Backs, 20*(1), 12–22.

Giddens, A., & Duneier, M. (2000). *Introduction to sociology* (3rd ed.). New York: W.W. Norton.

Journal Citation Reports. (2000). Philadelphia: Institute for Scientific Information.

Lukes, L. (1974). *Power, a radical view.* London: Macmillan.

Malkin, A., Wornian, K., & Joan Chrisler. (1999, April). Women and weight: Gendered messages on magazine covers. *Sex Roles: A Journal of Research, 40*(7-8), 647–655.

McNeil, L. (2003). *Working mothers' uses of childcare routines: An ethnomethodological study of status integration.* Unpublished manuscript.

McNeil, L. (2002). *Understanding childcare through experiential knowledge*. Unpublished manuscript.

McNeil, L. (2000). *Childcare and experiential knowledge: Expanding definitions of childcare*. Unpublished doctoral dissertation, Western Michigan University.

McNeil, L. (1999, Spring). Assessing child care need under welfare reform. *Journal of Children & Poverty, 5*(3), 5–19.

McNeil, L. (1998). *Assessing childcare need in Niles, Michigan*. Unpublished master's thesis, Western Michigan University.

Pierce, K. (1997, October). Women's magazine fiction: a content analysis of the roles, attributes, and occupations of main characters. *Sex Roles: A Journal of Research, 37*(7-8), 581–592.

Public law, 104-193. (August 22, 1996). (H.R. 3734, 110 stat, 2105). Washington DC: U.S. Government Printing Office.

Schlenker, J., Caron, S., & W. Halteman. (1998, January). A feminist analysis of Seventeen magazine: Content analysis from 1945 to 1995. *Sex Roles: A Journal of Research, 38*(1-2), 135–149.

Schutt, R. (2001). *Investigating the social world: The process and practice of social research*. Thousand Oaks, CA: Pine Forge Press.

Watson, G. (1990). *Feminism and women's issues: An annotated bibliography and research guide*. New York: Garland Publishing.

Women & Voting Survey. (2000, February). Roper Center for Public Opinion. No. 353261.

Women's Voices '96 Survey. (1996, August). Roper Center for Public Opinion. No. 299708.

WHEN MOTIVES COLLIDE

Writing about one's writing process is a compelling task. An individual's writing process is a unique one, developed and honed over time but also guided by a discipline's conventions.

Feminist ideology directs much of my research activity, including topic selection. Feminist researchers tend to address issues that are central in their lives; for me, the issue of childcare is something I experience on a daily basis. In this case, experience offers direction and focus for this research topic. Relative to this essay, I had speculated, based on prior research, that a difference existed between how the general public regards childcare and how feminist researchers address the issue. Identifying this gap provided me with a research topic and focus. My topic selection and research aim was formulated somewhat simultaneously based on feminist ideology, prior research on the issue and personal experience.

When a research topic piques my interest, I often will not write for several weeks. Since feminist researchers often identify individual personal experiences as valid knowledge or ways of knowing about the social world, I might instead introduce the topic to different groups or individuals. Because my subject matter is sociological, it tends to include issues that people are engaged in on an everyday basis. For example, during a social engagement, I might introduce the topic of "childcare" in order to receive feedback about the issue. I may also employ this same technique in one of my classes in order to get a sense of what different groups of people feel and experience regarding childcare. This initial strategy enables me to receive differing perspectives on a potential research topic prior to beginning my writing.

Still, I may not yet be ready to write. Since I developed a prediction prior to data collection—a deductive approach—I wanted to choose a research design that would allow me to explore the relationship based on my observed differences between feminist researchers and the general public. I also wanted to choose a research design that can motivate action, another tenet of feminist research. The action I wished to motivate was an awareness of, and possibly a change in, how feminist research addresses the issue of childcare. Based on my research aim, the exploratory nature of my study and the action orientation, a content analysis seemed to offer what I required in a research design. I settled on a content analysis of popular women's magazines and feminist academic journals to test the supposed discrepancy about which I had speculated.

After this initial background work, I began a relatively conventional research process that included a literature review and data collection plans. The literature did suggest that feminists have not wholly immersed themselves in the childcare issue, whereas popular opinion polls suggested that women were concerned about the issue. This finding cemented my decision to proceed with my research using content analysis as my research design.

Since my literature review included the collection of information on content analysis, a plan regarding data collection using content analysis began to form. The literature identified the two popular magazines used in this study as important magazines to examine. I knew from my background in feminist issues that the other two academic journals I chose to use would reflect current academic research on women's issues. I also found in my literature review the coding styles and methods I would employ using content analysis as my research design.

At this point, I have spent a great deal of time learning about my topic and how my research would be constructed. I was finally ready to begin writing. I wrote approximately half of the paper in a proposed, future-tense style which introduced my topic, research aim, design selection and data gathering techniques, including data coding schemes. With this written work in a rough draft form, I was ready for the data collection step of the traditional research cycle.

As I collected the research data by combing through thousands of published pages of text, analysis was already beginning. But I soon realized that I needed to organize my data to aid my analysis. I found that tabling the findings allowed me to organize the patterns I was discerning. After organizing all my data into the tabled form later used in this essay, I began interpreting what I found.

The interpretation of the findings took me back to writing and to my literature review. Because there was such a discrepancy between the two years of publication I had examined, I knew that I must offer a feasible explanation in my interpretation. This finding took me back to reviewing additional literature to address the issue. The welfare reform legislation seemed to be a likely answer for such a difference. I also needed to address whether or to what extent my initial research prediction was supported, a consideration which is a typical exercise in my field as in most other disciplines. Thus, my interpretation focused on these two areas as being most significant.

I also found that my original research collection design was not adequate and that I needed to add additional publications for eventual analysis. Although it seemed that a difference did exist between academic feminist researchers and how individuals generally perceived the issue of childcare, the difference was not simply patterned and easily explained. Thus, additional data collection was necessary in order to better understand these differences.

Finally, I was ready to summarize and conclude this research paper incorporating the literature review, research question, research design, data collection and findings. The summary addressed those items referred to in the prior sentence. I also, however, needed to comment on the action orientation as well as construct a compelling argument explaining why childcare and research relating to childcare are critical. A return to literature on knowledge, power and discourse helped frame this paper theoretically as well as prove the action orientation I desired. The final component included in this paper was suggestions for further research, a customary part of a conclusion in my field. This template on how research is undertaken and supported is a fairly conventional one in my field. It utilizes the traditional research cycle/process in order to support my statements and findings about the social world.

In sum, topic selection is always an important aspect of any research, but to sociology it is critical. This is so because the sociological discipline is rooted in theorizing (i.e., trying to explain the world, including any social phenomenon). Thus research topics must reflect those daily experiences patterned in society. That is, the social phenomenon must collide with research in order for sociology to be sustained, relevant and necessary. If the discipline ignores things that are occurring in the world, the discipline will cease to exist as it will no longer be a useful science.

"THINK. WRITE. ASK."

1. Lori McNeil begins her essay with an abstract. What did you learn from the abstract, and how exactly does it differ from her introduction? Are there any stylistic differences between McNeil's, Nick Ramer's, Anke Grosskopf's, and Barbara Shorter's abstracts?

2. McNeil spends several pages detailing her methods of analysis and data collection. Why do you think she includes her research methodologies as part of her essay? Does this inclusion strengthen her findings and conclusions for you?

3. McNeil writes that feminist ideology, particularly using personal experience as a valid source of knowledge, and designing research such that it can motivate action, directs much of her research and writing. Locate instances in her essay where she uses personal experience as evidence, and describe how this evidence affects her argument.

4. Find places in the essay that reflect McNeil's desire to motivate the reader to action. How do you respond? Do you agree that a lack of affordable childcare is a pressing issue?

5. Throughout the essay, McNeil uses primarily third-person voice to report her research findings. In her concluding remarks, however, she switches to first person. How does her use of voice affect your reading of each section of the essay?

RESTRICTION, CIRCUMVENTION, INNOVATION: THE DAUGHTERS OF CHARITY AND THE FRENCH CATHOLIC REFORMATION CHURCH

Susan Dinan, History

The Catholic Church of the sixteenth century was on the defensive. In 1517 Martin Luther had unwittingly launched the Protestant Reformation by posting his "Ninety-Five Theses" protesting the Church's sale of indulgences. The Renaissance Church had been plagued by corruption throughout its ranks, and although Luther was specifically criticizing the practices of the Dominican friars, he was in fact attacking an entire Church that he found ridden with greed and corruption. Indeed the Renaissance Church had an insatiable appetite for money, an appetite which the sale of indulgences helped to feed. The popes commissioned glorious works of art and architecture for Rome, most obviously Michelangelo's basilica to Saint Peter, while those in Luther's parish struggled. It was clear that the members of the Church hierarchy were not obeying their religious vows of poverty, chastity and obedience. The Church was a polluted institution with a lack of moral leadership. Martin Luther was only one of many critics of the Church, but his voice was the loudest.[1]

The Catholic Church's response to Luther and the Reformation was halting at first, and in 1518 Pope Leo X dismissed him as a "drunken German who will amend his ways when he sobers up."[2] However, by the 1520s war had broken out between Catholics and Protestants in the Holy Roman Empire, and the Lutheran threat could not be dismissed. By the late 1520s the Church was mounting a multi-faceted response to Luther that went beyond battling against the Lutherans.[3] Much of the Catholic response to the Protestant Reformation was formulated at a Church Council that met in the middle of the sixteenth century. Church Councils are a regular feature of Church history; the Emperor Constantine convened the first in 325, and such Councils typically address doctrinal disputes or other crises within the Church.[4] The council that met in response to the Protestant threat convened in Trent, an Italian-speaking city inside the Holy Roman Empire.[5]

This paper will examine the way that the Council of Trent strove to implement reforms, many of which restricted the freedoms of women in the Catholic Church in an effort to create a better-disciplined church. It is the goal of this paper to demonstrate that the conflicts that developed among the Church, groups of women and secular authorities forced the Church to become more flexible and to accept groups of women who sought to provide social services to France's poor.

THE COUNCIL OF TRENT

In the later Middle Ages some women religious lived in tightly cloistered convents whereas others chose convents that allowed them to see visitors or return home when they were needed—for instance, to assist an elderly or sick parent. Still others avoided enclosure altogether, like Third Order Franciscans, the *beatas* of Spain, and the *beguines* of the Netherlands—groups of women who demonstrated their religious calling by working among the poor in their neighborhoods.[6] Before the Council of Trent convened, women with a religious calling exemplified a multitude of sanctioned vocations; however, during the Council their options were considerably narrowed.

The Council of Trent initially met in December 1545 with the goal of articulating the doctrines of the Catholic Church and implementing behavioral regulations.[7] The Council convened in order to spur the Church to action and to give it a solid doctrinal foundation from which it could check the advance of the Protestant Reformation. From its start, however, the Council had its work cut out for it. According to Giuseppe Alberigo, "the bishops gathered at Trent were few and often bewildered, overwhelmed by a rupture in the religious unity of the West that they did not really understand. . . ."[8] Moreover, the Council was pulled in two directions. The Holy Roman Emperor, Charles V, wanted the Council to remedy the disciplinary problems within the Church, whereas the Pope wanted the Council to address the theological issues raised by Luther with the goal of condemning Protestant doctrinal dissent.[9] The Council bridged these competing visions as those in attendance alternated between disciplinary and doctrinal questions. In the end, the Council was successful in formulating systematic responses to issues of both discipline and theology, although the formulation was long in coming. The Council did not conclude its deliberations until 1563—some eighteen years after it commenced. Despite very difficult circumstances that included warring heads of states who sought to influence the Council, the reigns of fives popes (including Paul IV who was hostile to the gathering), and an outbreak of the plague at Trent, the Council managed to lay the foundation for reform of the Catholic Church.[10]

The Council of Trent published many dictates to shape the behavior of members of the Catholic Church. It issued its legislation regarding women in religious orders during its last session in 1563. Here, the Council issued directives stipulating that women be sixteen before taking formal religious vows and testify that they were joining religious orders out of their own volition.[11] This was in direct response to the problems caused by families who used convents to house "surplus" daughters, daughters whom they could not afford to dower sufficiently to make a good marriage or those with disabilities. In so doing, the Church attempted to filter out the entrance of women who had little spiritual calling and sought to address scurrilous rumors about the character of religious life.

Having addressed the problem of unqualified women entering religious orders, the Council then turned to regulating the conduct of women who did enter religious orders and who seemed to have legitimate callings to religious life. The Council's choice of disciplinary measures was distinct from those handed out to men and is illustrative of the Church's understanding of gender. In the decree, the Council sought to cloister all female religious: "Provision is made for the enclosure of nuns, especially those who reside outside the cities." Further, "the holy council . . . commands all bishops . . . make it their special care that in all monasteries subject to them . . . the enclosure of nuns be restored wherever it has been violated and that it be preserved where it has not been violated. . . ."[12]

With this statement the Council resurrected Pope Boniface VIII's 1298 bull "Periculoso," which required all members of female religious orders to live within convent walls.[13] If nuns had obeyed "Periculoso," there would have been no need for Trent's "Provision"; however, many nuns ventured beyond the walls of their Renaissance convents. It has been argued that "Periculoso" both demanded greater enclosure of all nuns and simultaneously fostered the development of alternatives to the cloister.[14] In early modern Europe scandals erupted over the ease with which nuns could leave convents and lay women and men could enter them. Indeed, St. Teresa of Avila, a model of sixteenth-century piety, began her life as a nun in a lax convent where nuns regularly traversed the convent's doors to return to their families and friends.[15]

OPPORTUNITIES FOR WOMEN AFTER THE COUNCIL OF TRENT

The legislation of the Council of Trent dramatically altered the position of women within the Church. In contrast to the multiple vocational options available to women before 1563, this decree eliminated problems of female discipline by eliminating the possibility that religious women would encounter secular society. Thus while the male priesthood was to be disciplined by scrutiny and training, women were regulated by removing them from society—placing them beyond the reach of sin.[16]

While the Church had attempted enclosure before Trent, those efforts had been largely abandoned and women religious could have a public role, especially in instances where they offered charity to the poor. "Provision is made for the enclosure of nuns . . ." did not recognize these precedents, however, and went on to provide that, "no nun shall after her profession be permitted to go out of the monastery, even for a brief period under any pretext whatever, except for a lawful reason to be approved by the bishop. . . ."[17] Under the new disciplinary regime, such reasons were few, and unless the convent was on fire or suffering from an outbreak of contagious disease, nuns were to remain inside. The councilors' goal was to remove religious women from public life, and Pius V echoed their intention in 1566 when he issued the papal Bull *Circa pastoralis* suppressing all women's congregations not practicing enclosure.[18] With this Bull the pope attempted to cloister or disband all religious women who still lived outside of enclosure, including members of all tertiary orders.

Like many of Trent's decrees, the enclosure of nuns dictated behavioral expectations. Ostensibly, the Council was acting to protect unenclosed women from what it called "the rapacity and other crimes of evil men," namely rapists who broke into the convents or homes to assault religious women, but it also strove to protect the women from less dubious characters.[19] Scandals occasionally arose in Renaissance convents with lax enclosure when nuns confessed to having consensual sexual relations with priests, laymen or other nuns.[20] The Council was clearly concerned about restoring enclosure where it had been "violated." The message to women religious was clear: if they violated the regulations of the church by refusing *clausura*, they themselves were vulnerable to violation. This conciliar and papal legislation is indisputably sexual, and there is considerable concern about sexually active nuns who would bring shame and dishonor to the convent, the Church and to their families, who were often important convent benefactors. Church officials, however, sought to control more than just the sexuality of nuns. Enclosed women were more easily watched than those living in society; all aspects of their daily behavior, private and communal, could be better disciplined within the convent walls.

The practical consequence of the rulings of the Council of Trent and Pius V was a restriction of the vocational choices available to religious women. After Trent, women interested in spiritual pursuits had only two avenues permitted to them: life within marriage or a religious life in a convent.[21] However, some women wanted to remain active in the world by remaining single, pledging themselves to God, and expressing their faith by helping the poor and sick, as the *beguines* and *beatas* had done.

In 1633, 70 years after the closing session of the Council of Trent, Louise de Marillac and Vincent de Paul founded the Company of the Daughters of Charity, Servants of the Sick Poor. The purpose of the Company was to send young single women from peasant and artisan families into Paris's parishes to work with the poor. They called their organization a company or a confraternity because they had to retain their lay status in order not to be cloistered.[22] Like nuns, the Daughters of Charity lived in small communities and wore simple habits, but they did not call themselves nuns. If they had called themselves nuns, bishops motivated by Tridentine reforms (reforms coming from the Council of Trent) could have cloistered them. Like members of former third orders, the Daughters had the freedom to carry out the obligations entailed by their profession while sharing a religious life of group prayer and habitation.[23] By cultivating places in which unmarried women could work by creating a mode of behavior acceptable to contemporaries, the Company of the Daughters of Charity provided women with opportunities that they would not have experienced as wives or as nuns.

Not only did the Daughters of Charity avoid enclosure simply by calling themselves a Company, but they also did works that were critically needed by society. Seventeenth-century France experienced recurrent war, famine and epidemic. It was a society in desperate need of social service providers, but the nuns and women religious who had traditionally worked in this capacity had been cloistered. The Church authorities who met at Trent had not predicted the many social consequences of their decision to restrict the vocations of women religious. The decrees pronounced by the Council of Trent display the conflict in priorities between the Church's need to better control the faithful and society's need for social service providers; as the Church closed the door on traditional forms of female activism, women and men committed to social service opened other doors. The Daughters of Charity met the need for nurses, teachers and social workers; they were well-trained professionals who were inexpensive to employ.

The Daughters of Charity could pursue their active vocation in neighborhoods and institutions because of their choice of work and because they developed a unique mode of behavior that separated them from laywomen and from nuns. The Daughters' labors were an extension of sanctioned women's work and generally earned them praise, not censure.[24] The Daughters of Charity nursed the sick in their homes and in hospitals and hospices.[25] According to Merry Wiesner, contemporaries recognized nursing, like instructing girls and caring for orphans, as within the acceptable realm of women's work.[26] Families expected women to provide food, medical services, and basic education to their family members.[27] For generations, spiritually motivated women had visited the poor in their parishes.[28] In Medieval and Renaissance religious orders, nuns had nursed the sick and educated the young prior to the Council of Trent, so this work was also a familiar vocation for unmarried religious women. Thus, the Daughters did create a new identity within Tridentine Catholicism. This identity, however, recalled earlier forms of women's service, even if that service was rendered in a new manner.

CIRCUMVENTING THE DECRESS OF THE COUNCIL OF TRENT

One of the striking characteristics of the position of women religious in the early modern era was their capacity to serve as agents of Tridentine reform while, at the same time, engaging in the process of reinterpreting Trent to advance their own agenda. The Daughters of Charity were very much a part of the Church, despite their defiance of some of its decrees. Women defied enclosure, sometimes because they wanted a more active life and sometimes because they lacked the resources, particularly a dowry, necessary for enclosure.

Viewed in the light of their overall contribution as teachers, nurses and "servants of the sick poor," the Daughters of Charity clearly sought to embody the spirit, if not the letter, of the Council of Trent. The Daughters served as witnesses to the faith of poor families, taught girls catechism, and urged the sick to make confessions. Viewed strictly within the light of the Tridentine decree on enclosure, however, the Daughters of Charity were not obedient. Their reinterpretation of Tridentine rules concerning enclosure was deliberate, calculating, and specifically designed to frustrate the goal of keeping women within the cloister.[29] Ultimately, their place in early modern Catholicism was complicated and carefully negotiated. Ironically, then, to bring the Tridentine message of reform to the poor of France, the Daughters of Charity had to transgress the rules of the Council of Trent and make a place for themselves outside the convent and in the world. In the case of the Daughters of Charity the collision between the priorities of the Church and of society did not lead to destruction, but rather to the creation of a new form of religious life.

The Daughters of Charity and contemporaries who formed similar active communities for religious women manipulated the spirit of the Catholic Reformation to expand the opportunities available to women of different social backgrounds. The example of the Daughters of Charity demonstrates how the Catholic Reformation actually increased the opportunities available to women of different social classes in France, despite the Tridentine promulgations that sought to restrict women's vocational options. Wealthy women used the spiritual message of the Catholic Reformation to gain physical mobility when they went to visit the sick and poor on behalf of their confraternities.

The Daughters of Charity also offered a unique opportunity to women of peasant and artisanal families who experienced even greater freedoms than their wealthy counterparts did. Unlike the wealthy, poorer women could rarely enter religious orders because they could not afford the dowries that the orders required. Some did manage to join orders as "lay sisters" without paying a dowry, but in these circumstances they never became fully professed nuns and remained the servants of the "choir sisters."[30] With the advent of active religious communities like the Daughters of Charity, the opportunities available to women of artisan and middling families increased when they became full participants in these religious communities. The Daughters of Charity did not require novices to bring dowries to the community; they merely needed enough funds to pay for their first habit or their fare home if they were not suited for life in the community. Women from middling and poorer homes could thus afford a vocation within a religious community, an option that provided them with a choice other than marriage or spinsterhood.

Ultimately, the Catholic Reformation proved more flexible than the decrees of the Council of Trent would indicate. The Catholic Church was never able to enclose all women religious as it had planned. Tellingly, parish priests and the French government recognized the value of the Daughters of Charity's professional work as nurses, teachers, social workers and hospital directors.[31] Not only did the Daughters of Charity and other French communities defy the prescriptions of Trent, but they also used their freedom from enclosure to perform a variety of works that the Council could not have anticipated and became important missionaries who brought the message of the Catholic Reformation to the poor and sick of France. Ultimately the conflict between the needs of the Church and those of society created a compromise in which women were permitted to engage in acts of charity outside the boundaries of a convent.

Endnotes

[1] The Lutheran Reformation is the subject of a great many books and articles. Some of the most important books include Roland Bainton, *Here I Stand* (NY: New American Library, 1968), Euan Cameron, *The European Reformation* (Oxford: Clarendon Press, 1991), R. Po-chia Hsia, ed. *The German People and the Reformation* (Ithaca, NY: Cornell University Press, 1988), Susan C. Karant-Nunn, *Reformation of Ritual: Interpretation of Early Modern Germany* (NY: Routledge, 1997), Richard Marius, *Martin Luther: The Christian between God and Death* (Cambridge,

WHEN MOTIVES COLLIDE

MA: Harvard University Press, 1999), Heiko Oberman, *Luther: Man between God and the Devil* (NY: Doubleday, 1992), Steven Ozment, *Protestants: The Birth of a Revolution* (NY: Doubleday, 1992), Lyndal Roper, *The Holy Household: Women and Morals in Reformation Augsburg* (Oxford: Oxford University Press, 1991), R. W. Scribner, *The German Reformation* (Atlantic Highlands, NJ: Humanities Press, 1986), Lewis Spitz, *The Protestant Reformation*, 1517–1559 (NY: Harper Torchbooks, 1985).

[2] De Lamar Jensen, *Reformation Europe: Age of Reform and Revolution* 2nd ed. (Lexington, MA: Heath, 1992), 60.

[3] Some of the more significant works on the Catholic Reformation include Jodi Bilinkoff, *The Avila of Saint Theresa: Religious Reform in a Sixteenth-Century City* (Ithaca, NY: Cornell University Press, 1989); John Bossy, "The Counter-Reformation and the People of Catholic Europe," in *The Counter-Reformation,* edited by David M. Luebke (Malden, MA: Blackwell Publishers, Inc., 1999), 85–104; Peter Burke, "How to Become a Counter-Reformation Saint" in *The Counter-Reformation,* edited by David M. Luebke (Malden, MA: Blackwell Publishers, Inc., 1999), 129–142; Jean Delumeau, *Catholicism between Luther and Voltaire* (Philadelphia, Westminster Press, 1977); Carlos Eire, *From Madrid to Purgatory* (Cambridge: Cambridge University Press, 1995); H.O. Evennett, *The Spirit of the Counter-Reformation* (South Bend, IN: University of Notre Dame Press, 1970); R. Po-chia Hsia, *The World of Catholic Renewal, 1540–1770* (NY: Cambridge University Press, 1998); Jedin, Hubert. "Catholic Reformation or Counter-Reformation?" in *The Counter-Reformation*, edited by David M. Luebke (Malden, MA: Blackwell Publishers, Inc., 1999), 19–46; John O'Malley, *The First Jesuits* (Cambridge, MA: Harvard University Press, 1995); Richard De Molen, ed. *Religious Orders of the Catholic Reformation,* (New York: Fordham University Press, 1994); Michael A. Mullett, *The Catholic Reformation* (NY: Routledge, 1999); A.D. Wright, *The Counter-Reformation* (NY: St. Martin's Press, 1984).

[4] See, Christopher Bellitto, *The General Councils: A History of Twenty-One General Councils from Nicaea to Vatican II* (New York: Paulist Press, 2002), and Hubert Jedin, *Ecumenical Councils of the Catholic Church: An Historical Survey* (New York: Paulist Press, 1960).

[5] Michael Mullett, *The Catholic Reformation* (New York: Routledge, 1999), 37.

[6] For a fuller discussion of Spanish *beatas* see Mary Elizabeth Perry, *Gender and Disorder in Early Modern Seville* (Princeton, NJ: Princeton University Press, 1990), and for a fuller discussion of Dutch *beguines* see Florence Koorn, "Women Without Vows: The Case of the Beguines and the Sisters of the Common Life in the Northern Netherlands," in *Women and Men in Spirited Culture XIV-XVII Centuries*, ed. Elisja Schulte van Kessel (The Hague: Netherlands Government Printing Office, 1986).

[7] Hubert Jedin, *A History of the Council of Trent*, 2 Volumes, trans. Ernest Graf (St. Louis: B. Herder Book, 1957).

[8] Guiseppe Alberigo, "The Council of Trent," in *Catholicism in Early Modern History: A Guide to Research* edited by John O'Malley (St. Louis, MO: Center for Reformation Research, 1988), 211.

[9] Alberigo, 212.

[10] De Lamar Jensen, *Reformation Europe: Age of Reform and Revolution* 2nd ed. (Lexington, MA: Heath, 1992), 214–217.

[11] H. J. Schroeder, *The Canons and Decrees of the Council of Trent* (Rockford, IL: Tan Books and Publishers, Inc., 1978), 226 and 228. See also Elizabeth Rapley, *The Dévotes: Women and Church in Seventeenth-Century France* (Buffalo, NY: McGill-Queen's University Press, 1990), 186.

[12] Schroeder, 220–221.

[13] The Council of Trent referred to the Bull "Periculoso" of Boniface VIII issued in the early 13th century.

[14] Elizabeth Makowski, *Canon Law and Cloistered Women: Periculoso and Its Commentators 1298–1545* (Washington, DC: Catholic University of America Press, 1997).

[15] See Bilinkoff and Alison Weber, *Teresa of Avila and the Rhetoric of Femininity* (Princeton, NJ: Princeton University Press, 1990).

[16] For a more complete discussion of seminary reform, see Kathleen Comerford, *Ordaining the Catholic Reformation: Priests and Seminary Pedagogy in Fiesole, 1575–1675*, Biblioteca della Rivista di Storia e Lettratura Religiosa (Firenze: Leo S. Olshiki, 2001). Comerford's conclusions about the failure of seminary reform in Fiesole contrast with the traditional view that seminaries were an important key to sixteenth-century reform.

[17] Schroeder, 220–221. Legitimate excuses for leaving the convent were fire, leprosy and contagious disease; see also Rapley, 27.

[18] William Monter, "Protestant Wives, Catholic Saints, and the Devil's Handmaid: Women in the Age of the Reformations," in *Becoming Visible: Women in European History*, eds. Renate Bridenthal, Claudia Koonz, and Susan Stuard (Boston, MA: Houghton Mifflin Company, 1987), 209.

[19] Schroeder, 221. For a description of men breaking into a convent dormitory, see Jo Ann Kay McNamara, *Sisters in Arms: Catholic Nuns through Two Millennia* (Cambridge, MA: Harvard University Press, 1996), 385.

[20] Particularly in times of severe inflation families would choose to dower one or a few daughters generously in order to provide them with the best marriage options and offer their sisters more modest convent dowries. Gabriella Zarri, "Gender, Religious Institutions and Social Discipline: The Reform of Regulars," in *Gender and Society in Renaissance Italy*, eds. Judith C. Brown and Robert C. Davis (New York: Longman, 1998). Zarri argues that in the fifteenth and sixteenth centuries "monasteries had not yet been defined as placed separate from the social body and the urban context, and their perimeters could be traversed in both directions." For the less documented issue of love affairs between nuns see Judith Brown, *Immodest Acts: The Life of a Lesbian Nun in Renaissance Italy* (New York: Oxford University Press, 1986).

[21] M. C. Gueudré, "La femme et la vie spirituelle," *XVIIe Siècle* 62–63 (1964): 50.

[22] Susan E. Dinan, "An Ambiguous Sphere: the Daughters of Charity between a Confraternity and a Religious Order," in *Confraternities and Catholic Reform in Italy, France and Spain*, ed. John Patrick Donnelly and Michael Maher (Kirksville, MO: Thomas Jefferson University Press, 1999), 191–214.

WHEN MOTIVES COLLIDE

[23] Pierre Coste, *Monsieur Vincent: Le grand saint du grand siècle*, Volumes I-III (Paris: Desclée de Brouer et cie Éditeurs, 1934), I: 378.

[24] For example, Frances Ryan and John E. Rybolt, *Vincent de Paul and Louise de Marillac: Rules, Conferences, and Writings* (New York: Paulist Press, 1995), 51: "as the work spread, so did the reputation for quality service of the young women trained by Louise. Vincent would rejoice that 'there are so many requests for them from everywhere' and, indeed, there soon would be." Although Ryan and Rybolt write in a hagiographic tone, this citation provides a sense of the excitement that accompanied the expansion of the Daughters of Charity.

[25] See, for example, Archives Nationales (AN), S 6160, Contrat d'Établissement d'Arras: Contrat d'Établissement de l'École de Saint-Jacque, Contrat d'Établissement des Invalides, and Contrat d'Établissement des Enfans-Trouvées.

[26] The Daughters' labors were an extension of sanctioned women's work and generally earned them praise, not censure. According to Merry Wiesner, contemporaries recognized nursing, like instructing girls and caring for orphans, as within the acceptable realm of women's work. Families expected women to provide food, medical services and basic education to their family members. "Women not only received charity in early modern cities, but they also dispensed it. The hospitals, orphanages, and infirmaries run by the Catholic Church were largely staffed by women. . . . There was never any attempt to shelter women from the danger and drudgery of working in these hospitals; however the women cooked, cleaned, and cared for the patients, and also did administrative work and book-keeping, led the patients in prayer, and carried out examinations of admission." Merry Wiesner, *Women and Gender in Early Modern Europe* (NY: Cambridge University Press, 1993), 94.

[27] For example see, A.N, S. 6161a. Contrat d'Établissement de Bellême: "The Daughters of Charity were contracted to serve the sick poor in the parish as well as to direct and staff a school for girls. "It is known that the superior and officers are obliged to supply three daughters from this Company perpetually for the service of the sick poor at this hospital. In the realm of the temporal service to the sick poor, the Daughters of Charity will be entirely under the authority of their directors and administrators of this hospital. One of these Daughters of Charity will instruct the girls of this village of Bellême and the parish of St. Martin of old Bellême in the principles of this Catholic religion, apostolic and Roman, and also will show them how to write."

[28] Barbara B. Diefendorf, "From Penitence to Charity: The Practice of Piety in Counter-Reformation Paris," *Vincentian Heritage* 14: 1 (1993), 37–56.

[29] Susan Dinan, "Spheres of Female Religious Expression in Catholic-Reformation France," *Women and Religion in Old and New Worlds*, ed. Susan Dinan and Debra Meyers (NY: Routledge, 2001), 82–85.

[30] McNamara, 389 and 396.

[31] According to Elizabeth Rapley, "if the appearance of the sisters on the street caused some uneasiness, at least their occupation offended no one." Rapley, 114.

SUSAN DINAN, REFLECTIVE PIECE

In composing "Restriction, Circumvention, Innovation: The Daughters of Charity and the French Catholic Reformation Church," I use a common historical writing style, which is the argumentative essay. In such essays authors provide evidence to back up the point made in the thesis statement.

When historians set out to write an essay, they do not merely set down a series of facts and construct a story or a narrative. Rather, historians set out to answer important and compelling questions of fact or interpretation. Hence, the first question that a historian asks is "What am I trying to prove here?" Phrased another way, the historian must decide what the main issue is that the paper is trying to resolve. This is actually much harder than most people assume. In fact, if you choose a poor question, your paper will turn out bad. For example, if you choose to resolve a problem that is not very compelling, is too broad, or is not really a problem, your paper will either be boring or unfocused. The first step, therefore, is to find a question and determine if it should be answered.

Of course, it is not sufficient merely to find a good question. You will not have much of a paper unless you find a question that you can answer. To this end historians are very careful to compare, repeatedly, the question they are trying to answer with the evidence that they can reasonably find. For example, in my essay I set out to determine how the Catholic Church restricted women, and how women tried to get around these restrictions. I could not have answered these questions if I had not gone to France to do research into letters, records, and writings that address this question. More importantly, if I had not found evidence to answer the question, I would have had to return to step one and scrap my question. Hence the author must be very careful to study her evidence constantly, and revise the question as necessary to accommodate that evidence.

At this point the author has two things in front of her: the question and the evidence. Customarily, historians open their papers with a summary of what they intend to prove. This summary is often known as a thesis statement because it is a concise statement of the goals of the paper. The thesis statement should appear early in the paper, and it is usually the last sentence of the first paragraph in short papers. The author should avoid placing the thesis statement too late in the paper as it can cause readers to feel lost if they are reading without knowing the point of the essay.

The paper's introductory paragraph should give a clear sense of the direction, and it should also draw the reader into the essay. Sometimes it is helpful to include a brief anecdote or gripping quotation, but keep in mind that introductory paragraphs should be relatively short. The introductory paragraph in the essay "Restriction, Circumvention, Innovation" provides background information for the paper. Since the topic of the paper is the Catholic Church's reaction to the Protestant Reformation, I felt that it was important to begin the paper by introducing the Protestant and Catholic Reformations. The paper's introduction ends with the thesis statement. The thesis statement not only articulates my argument, but it also provides an organizational structure for the paper. The body of a history paper is a compilation of evidence that supports the thesis statement. In the case of "Restriction, Circumvention, Innovation," the thesis statement is located in the third paragraph. It reads, "It is the goal of this paper to demonstrate that the conflicts that developed among the Church, groups of women and secular authorities forced the Church to become more flexible and to accept groups of women who sought to provide social services to France's poor." This sentence makes it clear to the reader that I will describe a conflict among three parties, the Church leaders who sought to impose the decrees of Trent, women who wanted to act as social service providers and lay leaders who benefited from the women's work. Ultimately this conflict forced the Church to be more flexible, and groups of women active in good works were able to form communities in cities, towns and villages.

I believe that the key to the body of a successful history paper is clear organization. The author must organize the evidence so that the ideas unfold clearly and the thesis statement is well defended. It is helpful to draft an outline of the body of the paper before writing. But different organizational schemas are viable for history papers. Evidence can be listed chronologically, which allows the author to detail a series of events and explain how they corroborate the thesis statement. Some papers are better organized thematically, permitting the author to organize the evidence around topics deemed most relevant to the paper.

This paper is organized chronologically and also thematically. Not only does it lay out the information in sequential order, but it also is arranged topically. First I examine the Church's policies, then the work of the women, and finally the compromise reached between the two groups.

Paper Outline
- Description of the Council of Trent
- Statement of the Tridentine decrees about nuns requiring enclosure
- Explanation of the opportunities for women after Trent
- Explanation that the goal of the Church's regulation on enclosure was to protect women and the Church from scandal
- Discussion of the Daughters of Charity founded in 1633
- Statement of the strategies employed by the Daughters to escape enclosure
- Assertion that, although the Daughters avoid Trent's insistence on enclosure, they support other elements of Tridentine legislation like teaching
- Statement that the Catholic Reformation was not as restrictive as historians have thought

The evidence in a history paper should be thoughtfully analyzed and not just listed. Evidence does not speak for itself! It is the responsibility of the author to make the evidence meaningful. Therefore, it is not sufficient to state that France suffered from a series of catastrophes in the seventeenth century, but it is necessary to show that disasters meant that society needed women like the Daughters of Charity to perform essential social services. Moreover, do not ignore evidence that challenges your thesis statement. Include this information, and explain to the reader how you analyzed it and what your rationale is for deciding that it is less compelling than supporting evidence.

The conclusion paragraph is the place to wrap up your paper. This is an important paragraph; do not simply reiterate the introductory paragraph, as it will bore your reader. You can use the conclusion to compare the evidence you have presented to other pieces of evidence. The conclusion is also a place where you can relate your conclusions to larger issues in a more speculative way. In "Restriction, Circumvention, Innovation," I used the concluding paragraph to show how the case of the Daughters of Charity is important because it requires that historians reconsider their assumption that the Catholic Reformation Church was an inflexible institution. In some ways the conclusion is the paragraph in which you have the most creative license; do not waste this by just reiterating your thesis statement.

WHEN MOTIVES COLLIDE

"THINK. WRITE. ASK."

1. Susan Dinan tells us that the first step a historian takes in designing a research project is to find a suitable question and then determine if it can be answered. What is the question Dinan is attempting to answer, and how does she justify the importance of asking that question?

2. Dinan advises writers not to ignore evidence that challenges their thesis statements; rather, they should include this information and explain why they discounted it. In her essay, Dinan argues that the Daughters of Charity challenge the commonly held assumption that the Catholic Reformation Church was an inflexible institution. How does Dinan address the evidence that is not in agreement with her own?

3. Dinan's essay is organized both chronologically and thematically. Why is this type of organization appropriate in this essay? Which paragraphs or sections reflect these organizational patterns?

4. Dinan uses extensive endnotes, which provide the reader with numerous facts and references to other scholarship. Did you read these notes as they appeared in the essay, or did you read them at the end? How did the endnotes help your understanding of the essay?

5. Compare Dinan's concluding paragraph with Erica Frouman-Smith's. Can you distinguish how these two conclusions are different? What is the purpose of each conclusion?

6. Dinan believes—as many others do—that the thesis statement should appear early on in the paper, frequently as the last sentence of the first paragraph in shorter essays. How might Mark Pires, Todd Zimmerman, or Edmund Miller respond to this idea of thesis placement?

THE UNEXPECTED COLLISION: WHY THE DUTCH REJECTED THE DRAFT EUROPEAN CONSTITUTION

Anke Grosskopf, Political Science

ABSTRACT

When the Netherlands held their first national referendum in modern history on June 1, 2005, the usually European-minded Dutch stunned their political elites by soundly rejecting the Draft European Constitution. This chapter analyzes why the Dutch so unexpectedly said 'nee' and thus collided directly not only with their national but also with European political elites. The example of the failed Dutch referendum is then used to illustrate both the benefits and the dangers of direct democracy everywhere.

INTRODUCTION

"The European Convention—Philadelphia it was not . . ." (Everts and Keohane 2003: 168)

In 1787, the Constitutional Convention in Philadelphia managed to produce in only five months a slim yet bold document that became the cherished foundation of the American political system. Even though the Convention overstepped its mandate, the draft it produced won ratification by the states and has survived almost unchanged for more than two hundred years. Fast forward 215 years. In 2002, a different assembly called the European Convention in Brussels, Belgium, deliberated for eighteen months, finally drafting a cautious yet massive Constitution for Europe that was designed to become the solid foundation for a brighter future. Even though the Convention faithfully stayed within its established mandate and even though the European governments who had created the Convention approved of the draft, this latter constitution now languishes near political death after the French and Dutch people rejected the draft in separate referenda[1] in 2005. Particularly in the Netherlands, the rejection of the Constitutional Draft came as a surprise to most. What is most ironic and unexpected,

---

[1] A referendum is a democratic process in which citizens vote "yes" or "no" on a proposed law.

though, is that the greater democratic openness of the European constitutional process allowed people and governments to collide, thus undoing the European Draft Constitution. This article will ask why and how the people the rejected this constitutional draft, as the story of this collision promises to raise important questions about the nature and limits of democracy itself.

The Dutch rejection of the Draft European Constitution is particularly interesting because it was a significant departure from ordinary and expected political processes, though one that is part of a larger trend towards what political scientists call "direct democracy." This trend can be observed in many places (c.f. Dalton, Bürklin et al. 2001), including Europe and the United States. What might at first appear to be an exclusively European topic holds valuable lessons for Americans—and many others.

Exploring the Theoretical Background: How Interests Collide in Different Types of Democracy

Though we may not regularly think about democracy as a series of collisions, collisions are at the heart of democratic political processes. As societies create sets of binding rules, or policies to regulate life, different groups within that society have conflicting views over which policies are best. In modern, representative democracies, most of these collisions of interest are resolved through pre-determined governmental processes in which the people's elected representatives, organized through political parties, negotiate policy proposals with each other. Final policies are determined through decision-making rules that require a majority of representatives to agree. Collisions of interest are delegated to the safe realm of political parties and elected representatives, who resolve those conflicts for the people and in their name. These types of democratic procedures are known as *indirect* or *representative* democracy, since policy decisions are controlled by the people only indirectly through their representatives. The main advantage of these processes is that conflict between educated, specialized political elites is less likely to undermine the stability of the political system overall than are conflicts between the people.

Much less common is a set of democratic processes that permits the people to make policy decisions *directly*, without the intervention of elected representatives. Ballot initiatives such as California's infamous "Proposition 187,"[2] or

---

[2] California's controversial "Proposition 187" was a 1994 ballot proposition to exclude illegal immigrants from a wide range of social services, such as public schools and health care. Playing on racism and fears that illegal immigrants had caused the state's economic woes, the measure passed, but was later overturned in court (see Calavita 1996, Tolbert and Hero 1996).

referenda such as the Dutch referendum on the Draft European Constitution are examples of *direct* or *participatory* democracy. In these types of democratic processes, the people's vote does not elect a political representative, but instead, determines the fate of a policy proposal. In most countries, until recently, such direct democratic elements were used rarely due to worries about the people's lack of information on political topics, and the accompanying potential for making poor choices (following the lead of a seductive but evil demagogue such as Hitler, for instance). Also, conflict between the people and the government at large might destabilize a political system overall. In the last two decades, however, increasing distrust of the government has led many countries to a growing reliance on direct democratic processes, setting the stage for direct collisions of interest. The Dutch rejection of the Draft European Constitution was a clash between the people and their elected representatives.

Until 2005, the Netherlands was the only European country that had never held a national referendum (Nijerboer 2005: 393); since then, it has joined the small circle of EU member states where the people have said "no" to a proposed treaty.[3] This "no" is all the more remarkable since both the Dutch elites and the Dutch people were considered very pro-European. Yet on June 1, 2005 a solid 62% majority of the Dutch electorate voted "nee;" a paltry 38% of voters marked their ballots "ja"[4] (Aarts and Van Der Eijk 2006: 243). The collision was both powerful and unexpected.

ANALYSIS

Understanding with *whom* exactly the Dutch people collided, and *why*, is more complicated than we might expect. We first need to understand why the Dutch held a referendum in the first place, as well as how European politics plays out— on more levels than Americans, and other non-Europeans, are used to. In many ways it is surprising that two separate countries, France and the Netherlands, would even be voting on the *same* Constitutional Draft.

---

[3] The Danish people rejected the Maastricht Treaty in 1992 (though it was passed in a re-vote in 1993); the French and Dutch rejected the Draft European Constitution in 2005.

[4] Referendum turnout was also high with of 63% of eligible voters. By comparison, turnout in modern U.S. Presidential elections has rarely topped this mark (see, for instance, Franklin and Hirczy 1998).

Exploring the Historical Background of the Collision: The European Union, the Draft European Constitution, and Dutch Politics

Traditionally, we think of states or national governments as the ultimate level at which political decisions are made. We expect the highest level of politics that creates American policies, for instance, to be the U.S. Federal Government in Washington, D.C. Before the end of World War II, European national governments used to be such ultimate political authorities. In the late 1940s and early 1950s, however, this slowly began to change as the European states—devastated from the effects of WWII and facing the threat of expanding Communism in what came to be called the Cold War—realized that rather than fight each other (as they had done for the previous centuries), they needed to work together.

European Integration and the European Union

In 1951/52, six European states (Belgium, France, West Germany, Italy, Luxemburg, and the Netherlands) acted upon this insight by signing a treaty that deliberately transferred some of their states' power, or sovereignty, to a set of common European institutions known as the European Coal and Steel Community. Unlike international organizations such as the United Nations, which cannot create laws and policies that apply *within* nation-states but merely attempt to coordinate actions *between* them, this new European political entity was given specific powers to make *binding* decisions, policies, and laws for all six member states. As a consequence, the European Coal and Steel Community and its many successor/sister organizations came to be known as *supra*national organizations, i.e., organizations that are *above* the nation-state.

This supranational integration of European nation-states proved so successful that over the course of the next five decades, the original six member states decided to integrate more deeply in the initial areas of co-operation, as well as to begin integration in further policy areas, ultimately creating what we know today as the European Union. The success of supranationalism also attracted other European countries, which chose to join the original six,[5] ultimately

---

[5] Denmark, Ireland, and the United Kingdom joined in 1973; Greece in 1981; Portugal and Spain in 1986; Austria, Finland, and Sweden in 1995; Cyprus, the Czech Republic, Estonia, Hungary, Latvia, Lithuania, Malta, Poland, Slovakia, and Slovenia in 2004; plans for Bulgaria and Romania to join in 2007; several other countries entertain hopes of membership. The most controversial candidate for membership today is Turkey, which would become not only one of the largest states to join, but also the first Muslim state to do so (both of which make its membership hopes very controversial).

swelling the ranks of the contemporary European Union to twenty-five member states in 2004, with more countries hoping to join.

It is important to note that the process of transferring sovereignty, i.e., binding decision-making power, to common European institutions was driven almost exclusively by political elites and elected representatives—not by the people themselves. We need to keep in mind that after two world wars within a few decades, many Europeans deeply mistrusted other countries (Germany, specifically) and were hesitant to give those countries any measure of influence over their domestic policies. However, the economic success of integration created a tacit "permissive consensus" (Lindberg and Scheingold 1970) among the European publics that gave political elites license to further pursue European integration. Until the 1990s, and particularly in the Netherlands, the public had few opportunities to participate in the ratification process; European integration was legitimized through indirect democratic processes.

The 1992/93 Maastricht Treaty, which created the European Union and a common European currency, is widely regarded as the end of the "permissive consensus" era (Franklin and Wlezien 1997). By abolishing national currencies and replacing them with the Euro, the Maastricht Treaty brought more integration than some European citizens were willing to tolerate. In Denmark, the Treaty was voted down; it did pass during a second vote. In France, the public approved the Treaty, but only barely. Clearly, after the end of the Cold War in 1989, the people were becoming more critical of further European integration. A serious gap emerged between the opinions of politicians and those of the people, which led to increasingly louder calls for more transparency and the use of referenda.

The Draft European Constitution

All treaties before the Draft Constitution had been negotiated by the member state governments in what are called intergovernmental conferences (or IGCs). This process, in which states bargain behind closed doors, is typical of international treaties. The Draft European Constitution, however, marked a departure from this intergovernmental approach, as the member states had deliberately chosen to create instead an *independent, representative,* and *public* body, commonly called the "European Convention," to draft the European Constitution. Nonetheless, they reserved the right to approve and alter the Convention's draft at an intergovernmental conference before putting the document through their various national ratification processes, which meant that the end product of the Convention's labor was almost as unwieldy as a typical treaty (c.f. Magnette and Nicolaïdis 2004).

Conscious of the importance of the document and the need for transparency, member states encouraged public debate on the Constitution. They did not manage, however, to stimulate a Europe-wide discussion about the constitution nor did they manage to increase at least Dutch awareness and involvement in European politics (Aarts and van der Kolk 2005: 4). Regardless, the Convention submitted its 265-page document to the Rome European Council, which adopted the draft in July 2003 (Norman 2005). The ratification process could now begin.

Dutch Politics and the Draft European Constitution

Initially, it appeared unlikely that the Dutch would ratify the Constitutional Draft by referendum. There had been several attempts to call national referenda in the Netherlands since the early 1990s. These calls had always come from small extremist parties hoping to profit from appealing to the people directly, which made it easy for the majority parties to reject their demands. It was not until 2002 that national referenda became a real possibility, when a small extremist party, the populist anti-immigrant List Pim Fortuyn,[6] won a significant number of seats in national elections and joined a coalition government (see Nijerboer 2005: 394). The success of this populist party helped increase the pressure on main-stream parties to listen more closely to the people, and to hold referenda.

Given this context, it is tempting to assume that the Dutch referendum was initiated by extremist opponents of the Constitution, but hose who initiated it, and most of those who then supported it, had few doubts that it would pass, and wanted the additional credibility and legitimacy a referendum would provide (Aarts and van der Kolk 2005: 2).

The process through which the Dutch people would for the first time collide directly with their government was thus set in motion. But with *which* part of government did they collide? The parties that called for the referendum? The

---

[6] Pim Fortuyn, the charismatic leader of this party, was a rightist-populist who was a Euro-skeptic and who favored strong measures against non-integrated immigrants. He led his party to electoral success even after (or maybe because of) his assassination in 2002. Fortuyn, who was accused by many of scapegoating Muslim immigrants, was murdered nine days before the election. His killer, the Dutch fanatic Volkert van der Graaf, committed the murder because he feared the effects of Fortuyn's politics. But even without their leader, Fortuyn's party became the second strongest in the Dutch parliament with 17% of the votes and 26 out of 150 seats in the upper chamber of Parliament (Van Holsteyn and Irwin 2003: 42). Aided by widespread dissatisfaction with the government and by cynical attitudes towards politics, List Pim Fortuyn managed to secure a short-lived participation (July 2002 – January 2003) in a coalition government with the Christian Democratic and Liberal Parties (Van Holsteyn and Irwin 2003: 61–63).

governing Christian Democratic coalition that opposed the referendum? The European Union itself? The future shape of the European Union, perhaps?

Exploring the Theoretical Background of the Collision: Why "nee"?

Referenda are not politics as usual. Voting on a specific policy proposal requires a lot of information, and has specific and limited consequences. Referenda also tend to bring to the attention of the public topics they would have otherwise thought obscure (see Hobolt 2005).

Political scientists studying European Union elections and referenda have proposed several different theories about what motivates citizens' vote choices. The literature proposes three main types of answers or models.

The Value-Based Model

The first and earliest school of thought suggests that election and referendum outcomes reflect *general value judgments about the European Union*. In this value-based analysis, the particular content of the referendum does not matter much; as with "permissive consensus" (Lindberg and Scheingold 1970), voters are expected to follow cues from their government or their respective political parties, which are assumed to reflect voter values.

According to this theory, Europeans' rejection of the constitution was driven mostly by their general attitudes towards European integration. The implications of "no" are quite worrisome: At the very least, politicians, having lost touch with popular opinion, are pressing for more integration than the people are ready to accept. At worst, voters no longer share the value basis upon which European integration was built. This value erosion would dangerously undermine future steps towards integration, and question the very foundation upon which the current European Union rests. In this analysis, voters collided mainly with the *current and future* EU, as well as with pro-EU elites.

The "True" Attitudes- Rational Choice Model

The second school of thought views referendum votes as *"true" expressions of citizens' attitudes towards the object of the referendum,* that are based upon *rational cost-benefit analyses.* Some of these theories assume that voters made a rational calculation based mainly upon *economic self-interest* (see, for instance, Gabel 1998a). Economic transformation processes always create losers and winners: citizens' referendum votes are interpreted as judgments about whether they will become winners or losers (c.f. Gabel 1998a, Gabel 1998b, 1998c, Gabel and Palmer 1995).

Other "true" attitude theories propose that voters' cost-benefit analyses are performed on the *less tangible costs and benefits* of European integration. The European Union may, for instance, be a welcome relief and escape route from national political inefficiency (Kritzinger 2003) or corruption (Sánchez-Cuenca 2000), or it may be unwelcome as a (perceived) threat to voters' national identity and culture (De Vreese 2004, McLaren 2002).

As far as the collision of interests we are trying to understand, if rational choice theories are correct, Dutch voters mainly collided with *European* elites because they do not think that *further* integration will be beneficial for themselves (in either economic, political, or cultural terms). The collision with the national elites who endorsed the Draft Constitution would be only secondary, with the implied rejection directed towards future integration projects but not towards the current European Union, nor the national elites themselves.

The Second-Order National Elections Model

The third school of thought on referendum outcomes proposes that due to low information levels about European matters, voters' vote decisions are "contaminated" by purely national considerations, i.e., matters such as the current national government's lack of popularity. Therefore, these vote choices are really "second-order national elections" (Franklin, Van Der Eijk et al. 1995). This might explain why so many Dutch voted no even though all of the major political parties were officially in favor of the Constitutional Draft (Toonen, Steunenberg et al. 2006).

If all the Constitutional Draft encountered in the Netherlands was an unpopular national government, then the collision of interests did not directly involve the European level at all. Instead, the collision reflects national dissatisfaction, making it likely that the constitution would pass if a more popular government called for a re-vote.

Testing the Hypotheses: With Whom Did the Dutch Collide?

Theories remain educated guesses and unsupported speculations until they are tested against empirical evidence. In public opinion research, this evidence typically comes in the form of representative public opinion surveys, which allow researchers to draw conclusions about an entire country based upon a sample of about a thousand citizens.[7] We need to investigate the reasons for voting "nee" that Dutch voters have offered in the various surveys conducted after the Dutch referendum.

Data

The analyses below are based upon the Flash Eurobarometer Survey 172, "The European Constitution: Post-Referendum in the Netherlands."[8] This survey, which consists of a nationally representative sample of 2000 Dutch citizens,[9] was conducted in the days after the Dutch referendum on the European Constitution on behalf of the European Commission in Brussels.[10]

Since the aim of this article is to explain why the Dutch rejected the European Constitution, the analysis is centered upon two open-ended survey questions that ask respondents to give all the reasons why they voted "yes" or "no" in the referendum. "Open-ended" questions do not force respondents to choose from pre-determined answers (as most survey questions do); they allow respondents to talk freely about their reasons

The reasons offered by respondents were grouped into three categories. To be considered a *value-based reason*, respondents needed to mention a general, diffuse feeling about European integration as a reason for their vote. "Yes" voters, for instance, referred to the constitution as "essential to pursue the European construction," or they explained that they had "always been in favour of the

---

[7] It is possible to draw valid and reliable conclusions about a population of almost 300 million from such a small sample due to a mathematic principle known as the "central limit theorem." The basic idea behind this theorem is the same one we use in our everyday lives. To find out whether your morning coffee is still too hot to drink, for instance, you do not need to drink the entire cup. Provided that you have stirred the coffee to ensure the temperature is equal throughout the cup, a sip is enough to determine the temperature of the entire cup of coffee (the survey equivalent would be to ensure we interview a truly *random* sample). Similarly, we need to ask only a relatively small sample of people what they think in order to draw sound conclusions about what *all* people think. Obtaining a good random sample is more complicated than you might think, as it involves stringent scientific principles. This is why we should only trust public opinion surveys that were conducted by reputable and professional survey organizations.

[8] The author would like to thank the European Commission for making this dataset available. Since the chapter is based upon the author's own analyses, she bears full responsibility for them, including any errors or omissions.

[9] The analyses below are based upon all respondents who reported voting either "yes" or "no" on the Constitutional Draft. Nonvoters, as well as those who cast an invalid vote, were excluded from the analysis. In addition, the data were weighted by a survey organization-supplied weight factor (wfact) in order to make them more representative.

[10] The fieldwork for this telephone survey was carried out by TNS NIPO, the Dutch partner organization of EOS Gallup Europe (European Commission 2005: 2).

European construction." No voters offered justifications such as "I am against Europe/the European construction/European integration," or simply, "Europe is evolving too fast."[11]

Answers that were categorized as *"true" attitudes-rational choice* included that the Constitution "strengthens the role of the Netherlands within the Union/in the world," or that it "strengthens the economic and social situation in the Netherlands." "No" voters who offered reasons such as fearing the "loss of national sovereignty" or who thought the constitution "will have negative effects on the employment situation in the Netherlands" were also included in this category, as were those who thought the constitution would lead to a "loss of Dutch identity."

Second-order national effects classifications included "yes" voters who cited "support for the government/certain political parties," disagreeing "with the 'no' supporters," or having "been led by politicians, people who know." "No" voters were included if they explained, for instance, that they "oppose the national government/certain political parties," if they "found the 'yes' campaign not convincing enough," or thought "the economic situation in the Netherlands is too weak."

Testing the Value-Based Model

First, we need to investigate how much of the referendum vote can be attributed to value-based voting. As argued above, those who voted based upon values should cite general attitudes towards European integration as at least one of their motivations. Analysis of the data demonstrates that value-based voting was quite frequent in the referendum: Overall, 28.6 % of all reasons given as explanations for the referendum vote fall into the value-based category.[12] A remarkable 17.5% of *all* respondents gave 100 % value-based reasons for their referendum vote. Without doubt, value-based voting was quite common in the Dutch referendum, but it does not explain the entire rejection.

Once these numbers are analyzed in more detail, it quickly becomes clear that the European Union need not worry too much that the value basis of European integration is eroding: Value-based voting was far more common among those *approving* of the constitution than among those *rejecting* it. Overall, 45 % of "yes" reasons given were value-based, with almost a third of "yes" voters (31.3 %) giving *exclusively* value-based reasons. Among "no" voters, on the other hand, 18.3 %

---

[11] A full list of questions for the three categories is available from the author.
[12] Note that voters were allowed to cite as many reasons for their vote as they liked. Yes voters cited an average of 1.69 reasons, while no voters averaged slightly more with 1.82 reasons. This means that one voter's answers might place her into several categories simultaneously.

of all reasons given were value-based, with a mere 8.7 % citing such reasons exclusively. The data show an erosion of European values among a small (but significant) segment of the Dutch population, but this is minor compared to the broad value-based support the European Union still enjoys there. Only a small fraction of Dutch collided with the current European Union, leaving us to find the main explanation for the rejection of the constitution elsewhere.

Testing the "True" Attitudes-Rational Choice Model

By far the most commonly offered reasons (37.7 %) fall into the "true" attitudes-rational choice category,[13] meaning the bulk of the Dutch collision was with the *future* European Union as embodied by the Draft Constitution.

Why did so many "no" voters fear that they would lose out if the Constitution were to pass? It is instructive to break down the reasons offered by respondents. Among the economic reasons given were fear of "negative effects on the employment situation in the Netherlands" and concerns that "economically speaking, the draft is too liberal" (i.e., too free market-oriented). Almost half (45.8 %) of all rational choice *voters* cited one or more economic reasons; almost one quarter cited economic reasons *exclusively*. Overall, one third (34.3 %) of all rational choice *reasons* were economic.

The prevalence of economic fears can be explained by the prominence of debates over whether or not the 2002 introduction of the Euro had financially hurt the Netherlands. The common currency took on important symbolic significance in the referendum debate, particularly after the director of the Dutch Central Bank argued that the Dutch Guilder (the old currency) had been significantly undervalued when the Euro was created. Dissatisfaction with the economic effects of previous integration steps helped fuel disapproval of the Constitutional Draft (Aarts and Van Der Eijk 2006: 244).

Democratic concerns played a smaller role among rational choice voters. Only 16.5 % of these "no" voters cited one or more concerns such as that the constitution is "not democratic enough" or that "there is nothing on Human Rights or on Animal Rights." Almost one fifth of rational choice "no" voters (19.5 %) gave *only* democratic reasons. Overall democratic concerns accounted for only 24.7 % of rational choice reasons.

Identity fears are by far the largest segment of the rational choice vote. Reasons such as a "loss of Dutch identity" or a "loss of national sovereignty" make

---

[13] Yes and no voters were citing roughly equal proportions of rational choice answers (37.2 % and 37.8 % respectively).

up about 41 % of all answers, with more than half (52.5 %) of rational choice voters citing one or more identity-based reasons for rejecting the constitution. Slightly less than a third (30.4 %) of all rational choice voters gave *only* identity-based reasons for their rejection.

Dutch "rational choice" voters collided mainly with the *future* European Union. The largest share of "no" votes can be explained by Dutch citizens' fear of losses, mostly economic and identity-related ones, that further European integration might bring. For these citizens, the tolerable limits of integration have been reached, and maybe even surpassed.

Testing the Second-Order National Elections Model

The third set of theories suggested that the referendum outcome really might have been a vote of "no confidence" in the Dutch political system. The data show clearly that the second-order national elections model explains the smallest segment of referendum votes overall: 15.5 % of all reasons given fall into this category. Nonetheless, the impact of second-order national effects should not be neglected, as they are considerably stronger for "no" voters, 32.4 % of whom cite at least one reason in this category (only 10.5 % for "yes" voters). Among the "no" voters, 10.3 % were disenchanted enough with their government to offer *only* second-order reasons.

The Last Piece of the Puzzle: Lack of Information and the "Nee"?

Of all the reasons Dutch citizens offered for their referendum vote, one did not fit neatly into the theoretical models suggested by the literature. A stunning 31.8% of "no" voters cited "lack of information" as at least one of their reasons for rejecting the Constitutional Draft. In addition, for a remarkable 10.4 % of "no" voters, this lack of information was the *exclusive* reason justifying their "nee." These statistics clearly reinforce the importance of information in referendum campaigns (c.f. Hobolt 2005). They may also support the impressionistic assessment given by the President of the European Parliament merely a week before the referendum: "The Dutch are afraid. Afraid of the unknown. This can be explained by the astonishing lack of knowledge. This why there is said so much nonsense about this constitution" (Josep Borrell as quoted in Aarts and van der Kolk 2005: 5).

The referendum on the European Constitution came before the Dutch just as they were beginning to question their domestic model of multiculturalism and integration. This introspection was not only due to the Fortuyn murder but even more so to the assassination of Theo van Gogh (a prominent Islam-critical filmmaker and descendant of the famous painter) by the son of a Muslim immigrant (Leiken 2005: 122). Yet these developments were driven by *domestic* policies, not the European Union.

When given an opportunity to decide the fate of the European Constitution, the Dutch seized the chance to send a loud "nee" to their national government, as well as to the present and the future European Union. Six months after the referendum, the national debate about Dutch hopes and roles in the European Union had already ended (c.f. Toonen, Steunenberg et al. 2006: 594).

Conclusion

The Dutch referendum on the Draft European Constitution produced not one, but many collisions of interest between the Dutch and their government(s). No single set of explanations can account for the referendum outcome, but most of those who rejected the draft did so because they feared economic or identity loss, or because they felt they lacked the necessary information to approve of what they considered a risky new project.

The democratic irony is that due to this lack of information and understanding, many Dutch were unable to comprehend that they might have actually gained *more* control and democratic accountability by *approving* of the Constitutional Draft than by rejecting it: A simplified European Union framework would have strengthened the role of the directly elected European parliament and increased the power of the people *independently from their national governments*. Admittedly, Brussels was no Philadelphia, but if approved, the Draft Constitution would still have been a step forward.

What are the implications of these findings for direct democracy? Despite the failure of the proposed constitution, the referendum produced some genuine democratic benefits. It exposed a significant opinion gap between the Dutch people and their elected representatives; it stimulated public discussions on the long-neglected topic of European integration. Yet many voters *still* did not feel well-enough informed; further, the public attention to European politics proved to be short-lived. The dangers here are that the likely "gut reflex" of voters will be to reject proposals, even though their implementation might actually give them *more* benefits *than they currently have*, and that despite the effect of public debate, the public will learn little about the complex political dilemma behind the object of a referendum.

Such fears also apply to the U.S., even though it lacks the supranational element that complicated the Dutch referendum vote. Here, too, a lack of public understanding of complicated political matters may leave people vulnerable to fear-mongers who exploit the public's worries. Such constellations tend to favor the status quo over any proposed changes, leading to the likely rejection of important legislation.

To illustrate the potential impact of these dynamics, consider the following scenario: If the United States' Constitution had required ratification by popular referendum, would it have managed to win a sufficient majority?

The American Founding Fathers seem to have been acutely aware of the vagaries of direct democracy. They deliberately chose the route of asking state-level political elites to ratify the constitution in order to prevent amendments or even the rejection of the entire document. In Rhode Island, the lone state that chose to hold a referendum anyway, the people promptly rejected the constitution (Edling 2003: 17). Direct democracy does have its perils.

The lesson here should not be to simply reject all calls for direct democratic processes. Direct democracy does have the clear benefits of increasing democratic transparency and accountability. We need to remember, however, that in order for direct democracy to work, citizens must be well-informed, about politics in general and about specific proposals. At the same time, political elites— people who have, and have access to, knowledge and political power— have the responsibility to communicate clearly with the public about complex political matters without oversimplifying them.

It is an unfortunate situation: Too often, political elites misguidedly take public support for granted. Too often, the public is all too happy to delegate the complex world of political decisions to their representatives without staying informed themselves. Collisions may be at the heart of all democratic political processes, but they need not be the kind that occurred over the Dutch referendum. If such unfortunate collisions are to be avoided in the future, both citizens *and* political elites must learn to take more seriously their respective political obligations.

References

Aarts, K. and C. Van Der Eijk (2006). "Understanding the Dutch 'No': The Euro, the East, and the Elite." *Political Science & Politics* 39 (2): 243–246.

Aarts, K. and H. van der Kolk (2005). "Campaign Trends and the Dutch Referendum on the European Constitutional Treaty." Paper presented at the University of Twente Institute for Governance Studies Spring Conference, Twente, Netherlands, June 16–17, 2005.

Calavita, K. (1996). "The New Politics of Immigration: 'Balanced-Budget Conservatism' and the Symbolism of Proposition 187." *Social Problems* 43 (3): 284–305.

Dalton, R. J., W. Bürklin, et al. (2001). "Public Opinion and Direct Democracy." *Journal of Democracy* 12 (4): 141–153.

De Vreese, C. H. (2004). "Why European Citizens Will Reject the EU Constitution." *Center for European Studies Working Paper Series No. 116*. Cambridge, MA: Harvard University.

Edling, M. M. (2003). *A Revolution in Favor of Government: Origins of the U. S. Constitution and the Making of the American State*, Oxford University Press.

European Commission, D. G. C. (2005). "The European Constitution: Post-Referendum Survey in the Netherlands." *Flash Eurobarometer No. 172*. Brussels, Belgium: European Commission, Directorate General Communication

Everts, S. and D. Keohane (2003). "The European Convention and EU Foreign Policy: Learning from Failure." *Survival* 45 (3): 167–186.

Franklin, M. N. and W. P. Hirczy (1998). "Separated Powers, Divided Government, and Turnout in US Presidential Elections." *American Journal of Political Science* 42 (1): 316–326.

Franklin, M. N., C. Van Der Eijk, et al. (1995). "Referendum Outcomes and Trust in Government: Public Support for Europe in the Wake of Maastricht." *West European Politics* 18 (3): 101–118.

Franklin, M. N. and C. Wlezien (1997). "The Responsive Public: Issue Salience, Policy Change, and Preferences for European Unification." *Journal of Theoretical Politics* 9 (3): 347–363.

Gabel, M. (1998a). "Public Support for European Integration: An Empirical Test of Five Theories." *Journal of Politics* 60 (2): 333–354.

Gabel, M. J. (1998b). "Economic Integration and Mass Politics: Market Liberalization and Public Attitudes in the European Union." *American Journal of Political Science* 42 (3): 936–953.

Gabel, M. J. (1998c). *Interests and Integration: Market Liberalization, Public Opinion, and European Union*, University of Michigan Press.

Gabel, M. J. and H. D. Palmer (1995). "Understanding Variation in Public Support for European Integration." *European Journal of Political Research* 27 (1): 3–19.

Hobolt, S. B. (2005). "When Europe matters: The impact of political information on voting behaviour in EU referendums." *Journal of Elections, Public Opinion, and Parties* 15 (1): 85–109.

Kritzinger, S. (2003). "The Influence of the Nation-State on Individual Support for the European Union." *European Union Politics* 4 (2): 219–241.

Leiken, R. S. (2005). "Europe's Angry Muslims." *Foreign Affairs* 84 (4): 120–135.

Lindberg, L. N. and S. A. Scheingold (1970). *Europe's Would-Be Polity: Patterns of Change in the European Community*, Prentice-Hall.

Magnette, P. and K. Nicolaïdis (2004). "The European Convention: Bargaining in the Shadow of Rhetoric." *West European Politics* 27 (3): 381–404.

McLaren, L. M. (2002). "Public Support for the European Union: Cost/Benefit Analysis or Perceived Cultural Threat?" *Journal of Politics* 64 (2): 551 566.

Nijerboer, A. (2005). "People's Vengeances—The Dutch Referendum." *European Constitutional Law Review* 1 (3): 393–405.

Norman, P. (2005). *The Accidental Constitution: The story of the European Convention*. Brussels, Belgium, Eurocomment.

Sánchez-Cuenca, I. (2000). "The Political Basis of Support for European Integration." *European Union Politics* 1 (2): 147–171.

Tolbert, C. J. and R. E. Hero (1996). "Race/Ethnicity and Direct Democracy: An Analysis of California's Illegal Immigration Initiative." *The Journal of Politics* 58 (3): 806–818.

Toonen, T. A. J., B. Steunenberg, et al. (2006). "Saying No to a European Constitution: Dutch Revolt, Enigma or Pragmatism?" *Zeitschrift für Staats- und Europawissenschaften* 3 (4): 594–619.

Van Holsteyn, J. J. M. and G. A. Irwin (2003). "Never a dull moment: Pim Fortuyn and the Dutch parliamentary election of 2002." *West European Politics* 26 (2): 41–66.

Finding a collision to write about is not at all challenging for a political scientist, as collisions are the very heart of politics. Given the abundance of collisions of interests, identities, and information, narrowing them down to just one was the lone initial difficulty I encountered. My personal research interests allowed me to clear this hurdle easily enough; however, given my particular choice of collision, I soon faced much more difficult obstacles.

For my contribution to *Collide* I chose early on to analyze a particular collision within my disciplinary subfield (Comparative European Politics), one that had recently captivated my research interest: the stunning Dutch rejection of the Draft European Constitution. This event, together with the French rejection of the same Draft a few days earlier, had thrown Europe into a political crisis and had forced the Constitutional Draft into a state of suspended animation. My choice of topic thus reflects the preoccupation of both my disciplinary subfield and of the European politicians who now have the task of deciding the future life or death of the Constitution.

I suspected that not everyone would be as enthusiastic as me about this subject, though. Actually, as I tried to view things from the point of view of the typical first-year college student who will be using this book, I realized my choice of topic must at best seem vaguely remote, and at worst rather esoteric and "out there." Furthermore, most of my readers might lack the necessary background information to understand the collision of interests I wanted to analyze. So my main challenges in writing this essay were twofold: First, I had to make my obscure topic as relevant as possible for my readers. Second, I had to ensure that I provided sufficient background information for my readers to understand and appreciate this particular collision of interests.

I could have avoided these problems entirely by choosing a topic that hits closer to home for most American college students: The resurrection of a general military draft requirement, perhaps? The ongoing U.S. military involvement in Iraq—or some other topical political debate? The easiest route, however, is not always the best. So I decided to instead pursue the more difficult European topic, as it would allow me to do two things I could not have otherwise achieved (or at least attempted—it is up to you to analyze my success): First, to stimulate critical thinking about the benefits and limits of direct democracy; and second, to help Americans learn more about—and from—the rest of the world.

To me, these two aims are intimately related. Through my classroom experience I am acutely aware of the inherent difficulties of asking students to *critique* their own political system (note that I am not using the term "criticize"!). Unfortunately, all too often we are too emotionally attached to our own ideas and stereotypes to look at, let alone analyze, national politics with an open enough mind. By looking at similar problems in other countries, however, not only can we learn something about the rest of the world; we can also study foreign counterparts of our domestic processes with which we have no emotional attachment. This makes it much easier to *critique*, rather than to *criticize*.

The process of scientifically analyzing and critiquing is what distinguishes Political Science as a discipline from its topic of inquiry, politics. So I chose to write a research-oriented piece, even though I would have to modify the classic research article format somewhat to make it accessible to my readers.

On the one hand, my piece is typical of Political Science research writing in that its structure is driven by the puzzling research question that I am trying to answer. It is also typical in that my research question is too big and complicated to be answered in one step (complexity is what makes research questions worthwhile, after all), which is why I needed to break the question down into more manageable sub-questions. Everything comes together in the end to answer the main research question: "Why did the Dutch reject the Draft European Constitution?"

On the other hand, my piece is markedly different from classic Political Science research writing in that it is intended for a non-specialist readership. This atypical audience necessitated several changes. I had to assume that my readers (most of them not Political Science majors, let alone researchers) wouldn't have historical and theoretical background necessary for understanding the text; I had to provide more of the "back-story" than I otherwise would have. For an audience of Comparative European Politics scholars, for instance, much of what I discuss in the section "Exploring the Historical Background of the Collision" would be unnecessary. The section "Exploring the Theoretical Background of the Collision" would be somewhat shorter if this were a traditional research article. Also, I chose to begin and end my paper with references to the U.S. constitution, which allowed me to argue that questions about direct democracy are relevant not just in the Netherlands but also in the United States.

Other sections needed to be modified more. Although you may (depending upon what you usually read) have felt confused by the numbers in "Testing the Hypotheses," here I simplified the classic research model most dramatically. In public opinion research, scholars rarely analyze simple breakdowns of survey results, because complex decisions depend on a multitude of factors acting simultaneously. Political scientists try to gauge the independent impact of one explanation (say, citing value-based reasons, rather than "true" attitudes-rational choice reasons), with all other possible explanations neutralized. Maybe only highly educated citizens are able to process all the information needed to engage in rational choice voting, while their less educated compatriots instead rely on value-based voting. Maybe gender has something to do with it? Or maybe income does? Unless we can control for all of these confounding explanations (unless we can "hold them constant," as political scientists say), we cannot be confident that we are finding accurate explanations.

If I wanted to submit this essay for publication in a peer-reviewed journal in my discipline, I would have to use more sophisticated, state-of-the-art, computer-based techniques for analyzing the surveys. The specific statistical method appropriate for the particular analysis I present is called *logistic regression*. However, the details of logistic regression are far too complicated to be of any use to non-specialists; even Political Science majors are unlikely to engage this statistical method unless they pursue a Ph.D. So although I conducted the full-blown analysis for a related, traditional research paper that I am writing for submission to a journal in my discipline, I present a simpler analysis here.

Without a consideration of audience, then, even classic models of writing will sometimes collide with the purpose they are trying to serve: The communication of ideas. Writers should not be afraid to modify these classic models in order to meet specific needs. After all, good writing should always be purpose-driven and tailored to the needs of the target audience. But it is also crucial that writers master models *before* they choose to abandon them, as these models are classic for a reason.

"THINK. WRITE. ASK."

1. Anke Grosskopf tells us that she was very much aware of her audience—first-year college students—when writing her article. Many passages reflect her consideration of audience. Identify a half-dozen phrases or sentences in the first several pages that signal her awareness of you as her audience.
2. Grosskopf's essay analyzes a particular historical moment in Dutch politics. How does her historical analysis differ from Susan Dinan's? Can any of the evidence the two researchers use be described as similar? Locate

evidence important to each researcher's argument, frame it as similar or different in terms of "type," and support your analysis.

3. Consider Steven Nathanson, Belinda Kremer, Edmund Miller, and Grosskopf as "storytellers." Locate each writer's use of narration, and describe each writer's storytelling techniques.

4. Grosskopf points out that she is careful to *critique*, not *criticize*, other countries'— especially the U.S.'s—political policies. Such care is reflected in her analysis of Dutch and American politics. Locate three explicit instances of this care. In Grosskopf's usage, what is the difference between *to critique* and *to criticize,* and why might a writer be wary of the latter?

5. Grosskopf tells us that in choosing her research topic she wanted to accomplish two things: to stimulate critical thinking about direct democracy, and to help Americans learn from the rest of the world. She shows an awareness of audience, again, when she leaves her success up to readers: ". . . it is up to you to analyze my success . . .". Would you take a risk like this in your own writing? In either or both of her goals, was she successful for you?

NATURAL HISTORY, FOOD PREFERENCE, AND COMPETITIVE INTERACTIONS AMONG THREE SPECIES OF *PTEROELAPHAS* (HYRACOIDES, PSEUDOELAPHIDAE): A FICTIONAL STUDY.

Todd L. Zimmerman, Biology

ABSTRACT

Three enigmatic and little known species of false elephants (*Pseudoelaphus liliputanus*, *P. longiotarus*, and *P. roseus*) were studied in the wild and in the lab. Video monitoring of ghost cactus patches in Roswell, New Mexico, Groom Lake, Nevada, and the Superstition Mountains, Arizona indicate the three species are mainly nocturnal and utilize ear gliding from nearby trees to enter the interior of cactus patches. Laboratory food choice experiments indicate that there are significant preference differences among foods within and between species, and that there is an interaction effect when individuals of different species are placed together.

INTRODUCTION

The three known species in the family Pseudoelaphidae (false elephants), the pink *Pteroelaphas roseus*, the miniature *Pteroelaphas liliputanus*, and the long eared *Pteroelaphas longiotarus*, have been a taxonomic enigma since their discovery near Roswell, New Mexico in 1998. For lack of better evidence they have been tentatively placed in the Order Hyracoidea, due to the lack of the first and fifth toe on the hind legs, presence of a grooming claw on the second digit of the hind foot, hoof-like nails, and glandular foot pad. However, a mid-dorsal gland is absent, and the general skull shape resembles the modern day true elephants (Proboscidae), as does the presence of pneumatic cavities (Zimmerman 1999), which lighten the skull and reinforce it. The skull morphology may be an adaptation for the attachment of the ear and proboscis musculature. The dentition appears to be modified hyracoid, and suggests that the species feed mostly on soft vegetable matter (Zimmerman 1999, Draud *et al.* 2003). The long bones of the limbs are hollow, with bird-like airspaces connected to the lungs, and the neck and forelimb structure is unique (Zimmerman 1999, Doe and Zimmerman 2000a, Doe and Zimmerman 2000b). Structural modeling suggests that these are modifications for gliding and or powered flight (Draud 2002). The long, prehensile proboscis, and the flap of skin that extends from the ears to the forearm, gives them the look of tiny elephants when the flap is folded, especially from a distance (Zimmerman, 1999) and may be a reason why the animals remained unknown to science for so long. The term "seeing the elephant," often used in connection with the California Gold Rush, possibly made untenable early reports by prospectors of these rare and reclusive animals (Jaques and Gillian 2005).

The animals are relatively small, ranging from 50g (maximum size, adult male *P. liliputanus*) to about 150g (maximum size for adult male *P. longiotarus* and adult *P. roseus*). *P. liliputanus* differs not only in size, but in having a scoop-shaped cornified tip to its proboscis, reminiscent to the egg tooth on birds and reptiles (Zimmerman 1999). No additional specimens were reported between 1998 and 2004, and evidence for controlled gliding (on which the generic name is based) has been sparse until now (during the initial captures of *Pteroelaphas longiotarus* in 1998 one escaping animal jumped off of a rock at the edge of an embankment, spread its skin flaps and appeared to glide to the ground some 3 meters below). Other possible functions have been proposed including heat radiation, as is seen in true elephants (Family Proboscidae), and heat absorption during the cool desert mornings, analogous to the function of the patch of dark underfeathers used by roadrunners (*Geococcyx californianus*) for that purpose (Todd, 2005). The function of the animal's prehensile proboscis has also been speculated upon, with suggested uses ranging from picking cactus fruits and flowers from amongst spines to aiding climbing upon spines and twigs (Zimmerman 1999, Doe *et al.* 2003, Jacques and Gillian 2005).

The three different species were collected within a few kilometers of each other within the same habitat, in a rocky area with vegetation consisting mainly of ghost cactus (*Opuntia imaginaria*), with creosote bush (*Larrea tridentata*) and mesquites (*Prosopis* spp.) interspersed throughout. The habitat type is uncharacteristic of the surrounding vegetation. All three species were trapped in the same area suggesting that interspecies contact has the potential to be frequent. As in most cases when several related species coexist, competition among them results in partitioning of available resources. Sometimes this is instinctive (often termed "hardwired"), while in most cases resources would be used to the same extent, or nearly so, by each in the absence of the others (Krumbs 1989). When several species can use a set of resources to the same extent the actual pattern of use may be determined by direct confrontational interaction with other species (aggression), or be the result of learned behavior developed to avoid confrontation (young offspring learning which food stuffs to eat by following their mothers (Craquer and Krumbs 1989). Sometimes the pattern of resource use itself is not hardwired, but avoidance behavior after detecting the presence of other species is. The detection of other species is usually through a chemical in urine or through scent glands used by the competitor to mark territory or signify its presence (Stinque 1983).

MATERIALS AND METHODS

In the spring of 2004 three field stations were used to observe and capture the three species of *Pteroelaphas*. The sites were at the type locality, Roswell, New Mexico (April 1—April 30), Lost Dutchman mine (Dutchman site), in the Superstition Mountains of Arizona (May 1—May 27), and at a site near Groom Lake, Nevada (well outside of the restricted area) (May 30—June 25). The latter two areas were chosen due to reports of possible sightings (Helene Shelley, personal communication).

At each site bullet cameras with infrared light sources were placed in and around possible feeding areas (cactus patches in bloom and fruit). The cameras were a part of a DVS digital video monitoring system running off of a bank of 15, 12-volt marine batteries. Batteries were periodically recharged at nearby homes, automobile service stations, or gasoline powered generators located at least 30 km away in hopes that the sound would not cause problems. The surveillance system recorded only when motion was detected. Files were backed up to several 200-gigabyte backup drives, and then transferred to DVDs for later analysis. Once activity patterns were established, observation blinds were set up and the animals were monitored by us using night vision equipment in addition to the monitoring system.

During the last two weeks of the study period in each locality animals were trapped for behavioral testing, which was done back in the lab. Two levels of mist netting were set up around the perimeter of likely feeding and/or travel areas other than those under surveillance. Sherman traps (XLF15) baited with a combination of raisins, fresh strawberries, and rolled oats were used on the ground. Hoop traps (1m diameter), usually used for trapping fish, were baited with the same mixture and set up near trees and shrubs both near to and at some distance from cactus patches. At this time pads, fruits, and flowers of the ghost cacti were collected and frozen for later use in feeding experiments (the video monitoring indicated that these were eaten by all three species).

In the lab, animals were housed in "sugar squirrel boxes" (Draud 1995). Testing was carried out in the LIU aviary (20x20x8ft) on the G.W. Past Campus.

WHEN MOTIVES COLLIDE

Animals were offered a variety of food stuffs: grapes (red seeded, and Thompson seedless), raisins, strawberries, green beans, snow peas, tofu; cactus pads, fruits, and flowers (from *Opuntia basilaris*), squash blossoms and fruits (zucchini), dandelion flowers and leaves, oats, bird mix (Wipple brand No. 3), mealworms, and crickets (*Achaeta domestica*). Oats and bird mix have been previously used to test resource partitioning among different species of Italian gladiator mice, which live in a similar habitat (Hepburn and Peck 1953).

Two experiments were conducted, one to test for differential resource use (food types) within and among species, and another to test for change in food preference/use when in the presence of the other species. Experiments were conducted in the LIU-GW Past animal observation room inside an octagonal chamber 2.5m high by 1.75m diameter. Eight infra-red/color digital cameras were placed around the test enclosure with only the lenses protruding through the plastic. Placements were as follows: one at the top facing down (2.5 meters), three placed halfway (1.25m) down, equidistant around the perimeter, and three slightly raised off of the bottom (0.25m), equidistant from each other but in between the upper cameras (Figure 1). Four foods were used: the cactus pads, fruits, and flowers col-

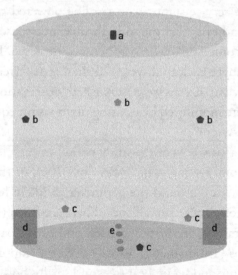

Figure 1.   Test chamber for feeding experiments conducted on three species of species of *Pteroelaphas*; *P.liliputanus*, *P.roseus*, and *P.longiotarus*. Height = 2.5m, diameter = approximately 1.75 m. Camera, food dish, and sleeping box placements as follows: a - top video camera at 2.5 m, **b** - three equidistant video cameras at 1.25m, **c** - three equidistant video cameras at 0.25m, **d** - sleeping boxes, **e** - food dishes. Walls consisted of 6 mil plastic sheeting stapled to an octagonal wooden frame made of 1"x 2" boards. Plastic sheeting was taped to a plywood floor. The ceiling was made of 1/4" hardware cloth.

lected at the study sites, and meal worms. Mealworms were eaten by all three species while in captivity prior to the experiments, and are similar to larvae of several species of beetle that occur in the study areas. Number of visits to each food bowl, and time spent at each, were recorded. Food was withheld for 24 hours before each animal was used. Same-sex animals were used in each case.

For food choice experiments, single animals were placed in the observation room and observed for 48 hours. Notes on the condition of remaining food stuffs were made in addition to the video data. Five animals were used in each case (two adult males, two adult females, and one subadult female). Results of both time spent at each bowl, and number of visits to each bowl were compared using a 2-way ANOVA to test for significance of differences among food types and among species. To test for competitive interaction the same five individuals of each species were tested against same-sex and -age individuals from each of the other two species. Results of pooled data for each species were tested using chi-squared analysis.

RESULTS

Field observations: At the Roswell site population density of all three species was lower than at the other two sites, and resulted in only three sightings of *P. liliputanus*, six of *P. roseus*, and eight of *P. longiotarus*, all in the evening within three hours after dark. Animals were seen on the ground, crawling through the cactus, and gliding from bushes to the ground near cactus. Data suggested no pattern other than the animals fed in the early night time hours until temperatures began to drop below 25°C. No animals were trapped at this site.

At the both the Dutchman site and the Groom Lake site densities of all three species were much higher than at the Roswell site. The two larger species were seen more often, but trapping indicated similar numbers at both sites (Table 1). Except for the morning captures of *P. roseus* the two larger species were trapped less frequently in the high mist nets and hoop traps than was *P. liliputanus*. This corresponded to our observations that *P. liliputanus* tended to glide into the cactus patches, most often landing on the spineless flowers or fruits, rather than glide to the ground before climbing up the plants, as was the norm for the other two species. Jumping points were usually on the outer twigs of mesquite trees for all three. *P. liliputanus* also showed more control in its gliding, and even utilized flapping to direct its descent and hover before landing. "Ear flapping" also enabled these animals to heighten and prolong leaps from position to position on top of cactus patches. Feeding generally took place in the evening and at night, while morning observations indicated that social interactions were taking place. Vocal-izations were heard, and skin flap displays were common when two animals (either of the same species or different species) were visible to each other. Both behaviors by all three species took place from high points on the cacti; however the animals tended not to fully expose themselves, remaining somewhat pro-tected by the large cactus spines. *P. roseus* tended to be seen in areas where the light pink cactus flowers and red fruits were sparse.

In the lab the three species ate a variety of both vegetal and insect foods, but unlike desert rodents, did not feed upon large or hard seeds. In feeding experi-

Table 1. Observational and trapping data for three species of *Pteroelaphus*: *P. liliputanus*, *P. roseus*, and *P. longiotarus* in 2004. Study sites are: Roswell, New Mexico (April 1 to April 30), Lost Dutchman Mine, Arizona (May 1–May 27), and near Groom Lake, Nevada (May 30–June 25). PM sightings occurred from just after sunset (at 1607h) to 0130. AM sightings occurred from about dawn (0538h) to 0931h. * All captures of *P. roseus* occurred in the morning.

Site-Species	P. liliputana	P. roseus	P. longiotarus
Roswell site			
Observed PM	3	6	8
Observed AM	0	0	0
Trapped—Sherman	0	0	0
Trapped—Fish Hoop	0	0	0
Trapped—High net	0	0	0
Trapped—Low net	0	0	0
Dutchman site			
Observed PM	35	48	49
Observed AM	12	32	20
Trapped—Sherman	1	4	7
Trapped—Fish Hoop	2	0	1
Trapped—High net	3	1	0
Trapped—Low net	5	3	5
Groom Lake site			
Observed PM	40	52	45
Observed AM	10	35	17
Trapped—Sherman	2	0	5
Trapped—Fish Hoop	5	2	0
Trapped—High net	4	5*	2
Trapped—Low net	1	3	6

ments there was a significant difference among species (α= 0.05), and among food choices. *P. liliputanus* tended to feed on a greater proportion of insects and cactus flowers, while the other two species visited each food more or less equally.

When in the presence of other species, food preference significantly changed for all three species. In the presence of both larger species *P. liliputanus* included a larger proportion of cactus fruits in its diet, but only after the larger species had fed on and exposed the softer inner tissue. The "tooth" on the end of the trunk of the smaller species was used to scrape at the soft inner part of the fruit. The feeding preferences of the two larger species shifted in the presence of each other. Each spent less time with food overall, and *P. roseus* increased its overall time and number of visits at the dishes of the cactus flowers and fruits, while *P. longiotarus* shifted its feeding towards cactus pads (Figure 2). In general the species showed little aggression towards each other except when both approached the dish of mealworms at the same time.

DISCUSSION

The low population density of all three species in the in the Roswell area may be real due to habitat restriction caused by the very large but widely dispersed stands of cactus, or may be an artifact due to the patch size limiting our trapping and observation. The amount of partially eaten foodstuffs and droppings found at Roswell suggests the former reason. At the other two sites cactus patches were smaller and interspersed with other vegetation such as mesquite trees that the animals could climb and use as takeoff points to glide from one patch to another. This would result in local metapopulation dynamics such that extinction in any one patch from causes such as fire or predation would be temporary and have little effect on the regional population.

Resource partitioning, evident from the laboratory results (Figure 2) helps explain how two species of similar size (*P. longiotarus* and *P. roseus*) can coexist in the cactus patches. *P. roseus* seems to be the more specialized animal due to its camouflage within the pink flowers and red fruits, but this is more likely a case of adaptation and divergent evolution with *P. longiotarus* due to competition. *P. roseus* did not exhibit feeding specialization unless in the presence of *P. longiotarus* (and vice versus). *P. liliputanus* was the most specialized species, being adapted towards dependence on flowers much the same as a New World hummingbird or African sunbird, although comparison with nocturnal pollen and nectar feeding bats may be more appropriate.

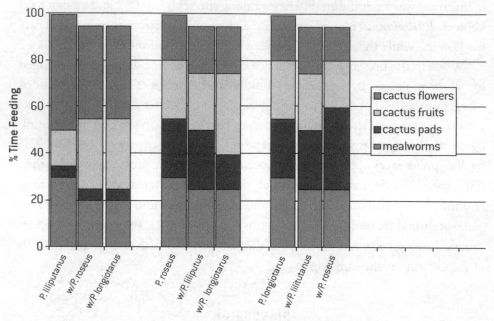

Figure 2   *Pseudoelaphus* spp. food preferences with and without each of the two other species. Summary data for all same sex same age pairings of two adult males, two adult females and one subadult female for each species observed for forty-eight hours after a 24 hour fasting period. Data for same species are means for the five test subjects observed individually.

The preference of all three species for mealworms is unusual for animals dependent on a primarily vegetarian diet, but is not surprising considering the protein limitations of such a diet. Insect foods are only seasonally abundant in desert regions and more so in certain years (Lee 1972) so that the animals remain adapted to the more reliable plant foods.

Although these three species are enigmatic in their evolutionary relationships and unusual in design, their ecology is not out of the ordinary. They exhibit adaptations reminiscent of what is found in several other animals. Arm-leg skin gliding has evolved independently in several groups; most notable are the flying squirrels, and the marsupial sugar gliders. True flight was achieved by bats and pterodactyls with skin extending from the hind legs to the digits of the hand, and the gliding snake flattens it ribs to form a wide, flat surface out of its entire body. It seems likely based upon skull architecture that the skin and musculature of the head and upper body that evolved in the larger ancestors of the false elephants for a different purpose lent itself to gliding small species. The ear flapping of the smallest species, *Pseudoelaphus liliputanus*, suggests that true flight could possibly evolve. The food resource partitioning is similar to that seen in the seed-eating species of

Galapagos finches, where competitive interaction is only evident during times of food shortage, and the cactus patch habitat partitioning is reminiscent of many bird assemblages inhabiting forest canopies.

ACKNOWLEDGEMENTS

I would like to thank Jane Doe, and the staff of the Roswell Wildlife Service, and G. Washington for guiding us in the Superstition Mts. This study was supported by grant AOB-254-7600 from Blue Peace.

Literature Cited

Craquer, U. and I. M. Krumbs. 1989. Confrontational resource competition in the Long Island weasel finch. Long Island Bulletin of Scientific Nature 65(4): 54–76.

Doe, J., T. L. Zimmerman, and M. Draud. 2003. Skeletal structure and muscle attachments for ear gliding in the species of *Pteroelaphas*. Journal of Hyrax and Manatee Research 1: 1–15.

Doe, J., and T. L. Zimmerman. 2000a. Convergent evolution between birds and flying elephants. Journal of Improbable Publications 5(1): 1–12.

Doe, J., and T. L. Zimmerman. 2000b. Review of flight adaptations found in small, large-eared mammals. Journal of Improbable Publications 5 (3): 291–307.

Draud, M. 1995. Sleeping boxes for the successful care of one-toothed sugar squirrels. Squirrel Amore 36(4): 1262–1278.

Draud, M. 2002. Structural modeling of the skeletons of pteroelaphids. Bulletin of Pseudoscience 13: 52–65.

Draud, M., T. L. Zimmerman, and J. Doe. 2003. Comparative form and function of the Pseudoelaphidae. Bulletin of Pseudoscience 14: 52–65.

Hepburn, A., and G. Peck. 1953. Some small animals endemic to the Coliseum of Rome: observations and experiments. Italian Journal of Animal Skepticism 2:324–331.

Jacques, B., and G. Gillian. 2005. The origins of mythical animals and animal myths. C.W. Past Press, Brookville. Pp 243.

Krumbs. Z. Y. 1989. Interspecies Behavior in the Modern World. Pergatory Press, London. Pp 324.

Lee, T. 1972. Population fluctuations of short grassjumpers (*Limutus propulso*) in the Mojave Desert. Proceedings of the Amboy Entomological Society 23(1): 786–794.

Stinque, R. 1983. Pheromone application systems in mammals. Quarterly Review of Olfactory Ecology 23(2): 34–58.

Todd, K. R. 2005. Morphological and behavioral adaptations for thermal regulation in reptiles, birds and mammals of the greater Roswell ghost cactus habitat. Journal of the Royal Biological Society of New Mexico 31(8): 12–22.

Zimmerman, T. L. 1999. Do flying pink elephants exist? Description of three species of hyrax-like animals from the American Southwest. Un-American Naturalist 12(3): 133–148.

WHEN MOTIVES COLLIDE

TODD ZIMMERMAN, REFLECTIVE PIECE

When I was thinking about what to write I considered the purpose of the article: to show a writing style of my discipline that would be useful to undergraduate biology students. Having taught scientific writing in the past, I know how difficult it is to find a real-life example that not only contains many of the writing basics, but also is readable. It is easy to become lost in the technical jargon and compact style of leading-edge publications. I know that I often have to read articles several times in order to sort out all that the author is trying to say. Most of us learn and apply by mimicking the many journal articles we read to keep current in our field, but students generally are not immersed in that kind of literature and it is difficult to see the style through the words when first starting out. A second consideration was from a research viewpoint. The worth of your findings from an original study are diminished if that information does not get first to other people in your field, so it should be come out first in a publication seen by many of the researchers in your field. My third consideration was student use of the information. I could have written up real data from simple observational studies and experiments common to biology lab classes, but there would be the chance of students lifting that information for their own lab reports.

To solve these problems I asked if I could write up a fictitious study. I gave the animals Latin names that reflect their characteristics to make reading a little easier, and for stylistic examples I included a basic table plus two types of figures—a diagram and a graph—multiple in-text reference citations with single and multiple authors, and proper usage and abbreviation of species names. I avoided common mistakes students make like putting in lists of raw data, and I only used the word "significant" when describing the outcome of a statistical test. The topic and details of the study are fairly simple (we videotaped some animals in the wild, and brought some back to the lab to find out what they eat) and could be something students would do in a behavior or ecology class; the stylistic examples (for instance, the citations, and table format) are appropriate for any field of biology.

The exact formatting of a biological study, whether it is of an organism or a molecular component of a cell, is dependent on the journal to which you plan to submit the manuscript for publication. Luckily, in all but a few cases scientific journals in the discipline of biology follow the same general pattern, with only minor deviations in the way headings and citations are formatted (fonts, abbreviations, use of commas, etc.). I use a general disciplinary style when I first write the manuscript, which can be easily reformatted later when the target journal is decided upon (or a second-choice journal if the manuscript is refused by the first). Every journal has a page of information to contributors detailing how it wants manuscripts formatted. (By the way: it is important for students to know that the format you see in a journal is not the way a manuscript gets submitted. It is the editor's and printer's job to do the sizing and placement of tables and figures, organize text into columns, put the title into the preferred font and format, etc. It is the author's job to submit a manuscript that can be easily read and upon which reviewers and the editor can fit written comments. A straightforward, double-spaced manuscript, with full-page figures and tables at the very end, is the norm. This is also the way I prefer to receive reports from students. Making a paper look "professional" is not going to improve a grade; it just makes it frustrating for me when I am trying to write down comments.) For professional manuscripts, I go through several personal drafts in order to submit the cleanest paper possible, then a draft or two addressing comments from reviewers and the publisher, and finally a galley proof, which is the work finally formatted as it will look when printed. That is a lot of red ink I see between my double spaced lines before the public sees anything!

Biology study/experiment papers are easy to write once you get used to the pattern and process; each section gives the author one type of information to concentrate on at a time. An eight-page lab report or professional manuscript reporting on a set of experiments is essentially four, two-page sections, with a specific format for the organization and flow ideas and information. However, we are not trained as writers to think this way, and if something is difficult in learning to write for biology, it's probably breaking the habit of blurting out everything you know and want to say about a specific topic (the five W's) in a well-structured opening paragraph.

The independent sections of a study/experiment manuscript are: Title, Abstract, Introduction, Materials & Methods, Results, Discussion, Literature Cited, and Tables & Figures. However, these sections are not thought about/organized in your mind in that order before you sit down to write. Materials and Methods are known before the study or experiment ends; thus, that section is, or can be, written first. Results are known next, after the raw data has been transformed to meaningful information via organization and/or statistical analysis. Working tables and figures are created from the data so that they can be used for writing the Results and Discussion sections. Legends and final labeling on the tables and figures can be done later. Once the Results section is written the Discussion section can be written, or formulated in your mind. In it the writer speculates on the meaning of the results, and ties them into what is previously known—information mainly provided in the Introduction, which is written *after* Results and Discussion, when you know what supporting information will be pertinent to the discussion of the results. (Most of the background information that appears in the Introduction, though, and much that will never be cited in the paper, will be known by you before the study begins.) The Abstract is the last "thought" section to be written. It needs to summarize the Introduction, Methods, Results, and Discussion in a few sentences.

The Literature Cited section is built during the writing process as each reference is put down. I was asked which standardized style and formatting was appropriate for the Literature Cited section of biological journals, so I pulled out articles from several journals, and although all of them had placement of names, year, title, journal, volume number and pages in the same order, each formatted the sections slightly differently. Some bolded names, some bolded volume number, some used small caps for names, some used italics for journal names. In all cases, common journals were abbreviated in a standardized form, but since my fictional journals are not common, and because graduate students are often required to list the full journal name in their theses (mainly to show that they looked up the actual articles rather than took the information from cited context in another paper), I have left these unabbreviated. Luckily, I found a couple of journals that kept to basic formatting, so that is what I have kept to here. The same is true of title and section fonts and placement. I have decided to follow the *Bulletin of the California Academy of Sciences* formatting not only because it is the most basic, but also because it is also a journal in which this type of study on desert animals might be published.

Each person interested in your study has his own agenda; some are interested in your methods, some in your results, and some in your background information. It is important that your study can be "found" by someone searching through the literature using published guides or web-based search engines. These depend on keywords and the title, so the title is very important, as is the abstract because that is the section that will be read to see if the entire article should be tracked down.

After pattern and process, brevity and tone are the next skills to master. During my formative education I was encouraged to develop the ability for clear, interesting, and entertaining writing, which usually meant that fewer words weren't necessarily better than more, and that opinions and ideas could be developed creatively. Writing up a scientific study goes against this training. Brevity is necessary because scientific journals charge a page cost ($50–$100 or more per page) if you want more than the set number of free pages they provide. The reporting must be as unbiased as possible, and opinion must clearly be shown as speculation. I must avoid the words "prove" or "fact" because they go against the scientific method. Results can not prove a hypothesis, only support or refute it, because there is always the possibility that there is an unknown background factor affecting the results. The red ink that I put on the first draft of a student's lab reports often consists of suggestions for clarity and brevity, not criticism of the worth of the paper. Clarity coupled with brevity is a difficult skill to develop. I often show students the red ink covering various drafts of papers I am working on with coauthors.

When writing an introduction, it can be difficult to get used to this: the entire introduction will contain almost no original thought from the author. This lack of original thought wasn't a value I was taught in high school, where I was generally told to use quotations and to make sure my own ideas were present. However, in high school I would have been writing mainly in the humanities, where the announcement of an original idea in the introduction is required. The proper use of citations makes writing the introduction of a biology manuscript very easy, though, because I don't need to develop my own ideas. I only have to organize the ideas from previous authors/studies to make a foundation for what follows. One of the main purposes of the introduction is to lead the reader to every other publication that has discussed or proposed an idea, or presented data, relevant to your work. It is not uncommon to cite, within one sentence of your text, four or five references to a single idea. Because of the importance of linking previous works with specific facts or ideas, citations are placed in the text as close as possible to the relevant phrase, before an unrelated idea begins; sometimes links to information are so specific that citations will be placed in the middle of a sentence. Other times several sentences will be related to only a single reference.

When I write up my Materials & Methods I have to make sure it is detailed enough so that someone else in the field can duplicate the study exactly. Science is about consistency, and the ability to disprove others to get at the truth.

The Results section is difficult to write because it is not the place to interpret the data; it is for presentation, description and clarification of the findings. Interpretation is left for the Discussion. I find Discussions both easy and difficult at the same time. I get to talk about what my results tell me, but I also have to fit that into what else is known, and the importance of my results within that context. It is easy to go overboard with unsupported opinion. I have a Post-It next to my desk that says "speculation" because this is where critics hit you the hardest if you word something the wrong way and say something your data does not support.

Other concerns: I prefer to concentrate on using third person because it seems less biased, and when first person is used it seems that "I" and "we" clutter the paper. With third person I still use "I" and "we" in specific cases when personal action must be pointed out. I avoid using the word "called" when describing or clarifying because it is pointing out the obvious. Using phrases like "Table 1 shows . . ." or "Figure 1 shows . . ." is bad form because it is not my/the author's prerogative to tell the reader how to interpret the data on a table or figure. Another thing I try to avoid is referencing another work by using direct quotation (or using the word "says") rather than simply using the work in a logical train of thought and citing it properly (which aids brevity). There are certain circumstances when direct quotation and "says" are appropriate, but in general these are red flags telling me to take a closer look and consider using different wording.

"THINK. WRITE. ASK."

1. The title of Todd Zimmerman's article begins with "Natural history, food preferences, and competitive interactions . . ."; it ends with "A fictional study." Based on your reading of both the article and Zimmerman's reflective piece, *why* is this study fictional?
2. Zimmerman is inventive and witty in his fictional references in the "Literature Cited" section of his article. Which offer the most cues to the fictional nature of the study? Why might Zimmerman have chosen to be funny here, as opposed to simply false?
3. Nicholas Ramer's article is titled "Simulating the Collision of β-Poly(vinylidene fluoride) with Infrared Light." How is "simulation" used in Ramer's research? How does Ramer's "simulation" relate to Zimmerman's "fictional study"?
4. Imagine that you need to come up with a fictional study of your own. Your fictional study must generate fictional data, such that you can present your findings seriously (if tongue-in-cheek), according to the conventions of the discipline, as Zimmerman does. What will you study? Where, when, and how will you collect data? Where in the write-up of your findings will your results appear? How will you organize your data: charts? graphs? tables? Your section might want to consider actually doing such fictional studies.

WRITING PROJECTS RELATED TO MOTIVES IN COLLISION

A. How have the authors in this section, "When Motives Collide," interpreted and applied the term *motive*? One thing is certain: differently. Draw up a short list defining *motive*—both what it is, and what it's in collision with—for the six essays in this section. Among which three essays does *motive* display the broadest range of difference in meaning?

Using the question above as your guide, **write a 5-minute monologue** discussing the definitions of *motive* and the collisions of *motives* in three essays from this section; also speak to how each author is connected to or participates in the collision(s) he or she names. Remember to try and make your choices so that the *motives* you're exploring are as different from each other as possible. Be sure to practice and time your monologue, and edit as necessary. Your goals include being a lively and interesting speaker, and hitting the time at 5 minutes on the nose.

B. Consider the essays in this section, and think about those you enjoyed the most, for whatever reasons.

Choose one essay on which to model an essay of your own; you're going to **engage in the ancient practice of copying or mimicking** as learning—a practice we apply in teaching people everything from music to swimming, but often shy away from in writing, at least in Western cultures. Because we are acknowledging and agreeing that copying and mimicking are not only appropriate but required here, and because you will not submit your "copycat" essay anywhere as original (that would constitute insufficient citation, a kind of plagiarism), we can all relax and enjoy the pleasure of learning from outstanding models. Suggested length: let the length of the essay you choose be your guide.

C. Time for some nuts and bolts: mechanics.

Identify the citation style of each essay in this section (MLA? Chicago? CBE? APA?). Choose an essay **in the citation style most unfamiliar to you**, or with which you've had the least practice, and *transcribe*—copy out, word for word, space for space, comma for comma—the first 15 sources cited. Using these citations as a guide, do a little research, and **find and correctly cite 6 new texts** that a reasonable human being would agree are relevant to the essay's topic. Integrate the full citations of the

6 new texts, in correct order and format, to your "short list" of 15, bringing your total to 21. (It's a lucky number.) Every time you practice these
formats, their difficulty and mystery recede.

D. Consider a situation on campus that reflects a collision of motives. For
   example, it's easy to imagine colliding motives in campus alcohol policies, or in the costs and types of meal plans available, or in various rules
   about extracurricular activities, or between some students and administrators or professors regarding academic policies, and so on.

   Write a 5- to 7-minute dialogue (that is a piece for two voices; think
   of it as an a scene from a television show, video, movie, or play) that
   makes clear the nature of the collision and what institutional, organizational, or individual bodies are involved. The goal of your dialogue is to
   educate listeners to what's at stake (what's the problem?), and to make real
   the conflicting or colliding motives, without resorting to irony or sarcasm, and without making one side seem ridiculous.

WHEN LANGUAGES COLLIDE

In this final section, authors explore what happens when languages collide. Each essay examines competing ways of talking about ideas, and then explores the impact of these discursive collisions on our perception of the ideas.

Consider, as Jerome Tognoli does, The Wizard of Oz. *When the tornado drops Dorothy, Toto, and the house in which they have been spinning, the house collides literally with the ground. In "A House Collides in the Land of Oz: The Search for Home and Identity," Tognoli suggests that the house collides, too, with itself. Using the languages of film, literature, psychology, trauma, and psychotherapy, Tognoli shows that the collision, and the subsequent repair and integration of "home" and "identity" in Oz, provide rich therapeutic ground for the integration of home and identity in individuals.*

"[I]mmobility is movement ceased recreated reinvented," writes poet Ann-Marie Alonzo, a former dancer confined in a wheelchair who refuses the language of "paralysis." In "Aesthetic Collisions: Dialogues in Dance and Poetry," Cara Gargano illuminates conversions in language: Alonzo's writing as dance, and Alonzo's collaborator Margie Gillis' dance as writing. Investigating diction—"static," "fixed," "feeling," "thinking," "rhetoric," "ductus"—and the evolution of "composition," Gargano traces the history of the body as a figure of language, and alerts us to a collaboration in two languages that gives birth to a third, new language.

Rosario Castellanos, argues Erica Frouman-Smith, uses language to redress her gender and her body, and, by extension, the female body. In "Rosario Castellanos: Charting a Course Toward Another Way to Be," Frouman-Smith shows that language expresses metaphor by finding tenors and vehicles that accurately express relationships between things. Too, though, she shows that metaphor might not merely connect a known thing to another known thing, but as with the collaboration between Alonzo and Gillis, above, make a new thing possible: Frouman-Smith traces Castellanos' work, life conditions, and iconic influences from de la

Cruz to Malinche, and argues that her innovative, feminine discourse actively created new possibilities for the female body.

In All Begin Guy Walks into a Bar, *Belinda Kremer and Angela Pisano collide multiple languages and genres: graphic arts, the written word, photography, poetry, the joke, narrative. Manifesting collision as a purely positive property, their text articulates each language or genre unto itself, and as part of a larger whole—not collage, not pastiche, not a sampler; cohesive, and energized by its supposedly disparate parts.*

In "What's She Talking About?: Post-Feminist Notes on Sexist Grammar," Edmund Miller describes not an energizing, but a destructive, collision. Investigating the forceful impact between some existing and some emergent ideas about gender in language, Miller makes the case that the use of gender-free language is unnecessary, illogical, and even harmful to language itself. Forthrightly and with certainty, in an argumentative style many readers relish, he argues that the use of gender-free language "arbitrarily and often awkwardly circumscribe[s] a writer's resources without addressing any real issues in sexual politics."

*Coincidentally—where to coincide is to happen at the same time, though not at all to share the same position (*Second college edition of the new american heritage dictionary*)—our final essayist, Steven Nathanson, exactly counters the preceding argument when he writes that reports by educational diagnosticians must be "rigorous, objectively transparent, and clinically appropriate" if they are to improve the lives of struggling learners. In "When Data and Perception Collide: Writing Educational and Diagnostic Reports," Nathanson argues forcefully, and from a deep well of reference, that the values of culture-free, bias-free, and technically transparent language not only are necessary and ethical, but also have the power to change lives.*

A HOUSE COLLIDES IN THE LAND OF OZ:
THE SEARCH FOR HOME AND IDENTITY

Jerome Tognoli, Psychology

One of the central concerns in *The Wizard of Oz* is the search for home and personal identity. The novel, written by Frank Baum in 1900, was published the same year as Freud's *The Interpretation of Dreams*. In 1938 the novel was made into the famous film version starring Judy Garland. The popularity of the story, especially with adults, might be due to its strong mythological and psychological underpinnings, and it is these aspects of the psychological that serve as the basis of this essay.

The main character in *The Wizard of Oz*, Dorothy Gale, is raised by her Aunt Em and Uncle Henry on a bleak farm in Kansas. When a tornado strikes, Dorothy and her dog, Toto, are whisked into the air, house and all, and when she awakes she steps out into a colorful world of Oz. What follows is Dorothy's dream, and this is made most clear in the film because her entire experience in Oz is portrayed in color, whereas the scenes in Kansas are depicted in black and white. In Oz, Dorothy embarks on a mythic journey in an attempt to return to her home in Kansas (a metaphor for self-identity). Along the way she meets a variety of characters (the lion, the scarecrow, and the tin man), who help one another overcome some enormous obstacles.

A variety of collisions occur throughout *The Wizard of Oz*. Initially, the house, carried away by a tornado, transports Dorothy and Toto out of Kansas and collides in Oz, landing (accidentally) on top of the Wicked Witch of the East, crushing her to death. Another prime set of collisions revolves around the frustrating attempts to return home—a metaphor for the search for a personal identity. These attempts involve encounters with obstacles that block the goals of Dorothy and her companions. Over the course of her journey, Dorothy develops enormous strength of character as she continues on her quest to help her friends the Lion, the Tin Man and the Scarecrow acquire fearlessness, a heart, and a brain. Through a variety of deeds, they are assured by the Wizard they already have these qualities, but the confrontation with the Wizard is disappointing because he is revealed to be very ordinary. However, the Good Witch Glinda informs Dorothy that she already possesses the ability to return home anytime she desires by clicking her heels three times.

The Wonderful Wizard of Oz, a quest novel, is essentially a myth concerned with the search for personal identity, triggered by the loss of and then the eventual gain of home (and sense of self). It is this aspect of the quest in which the Oz myth has been useful as a psychotherapeutic tool for helping clients acquire an enhanced sense of self, and it is one of the concerns of this essay to indicate instances of how the Oz myth has been put to this use. The story involves a search for home, personal identity and growth; it possesses deep psychological meaning and serves as a therapeutic tool for therapists. Each of these directions, with its "colliding" aspect, is explored below.

THE SEARCH FOR HOME AND SELF-IDENTITY

When *The Wonderful Wizard of Oz* was first published in 1900, the novel represented a huge departure from traditional children's literature and fairy tales, which tended to comprise cautionary tales, often involving attempts to subdue (kill) evil forces. For one thing, the novel was about seeking pleasure and exploring one's growth potential, and it conformed well to Frank Baum's interest in the nineteenth-century concern with "mind cure," which focused on individual enlightenment, empowerment, and overcoming adverse conditions. Baum also stressed that the pleasures in life were there for the taking and that the denial of pleasure was essentially a negation of the self (Leach, 1993).

The meaning that home has for individuals is both intense and complex and is affected by personal/historical experiences that are usually neither wholly good nor wholly bad. Its meaning is also affected by cultural imperatives, distortions, and exaggerated claims. In many cases, it is only when one experiences the loss of home that one begins to understand and appreciate its significance. In an extensive review of the literature on residential environments (Tognoli, 1987), I have noted that the concept of home could be grouped into at least five separate categories. These include centrality, rootedness and place attachment; continuity, unity and order; privacy, refuge, security and ownership; self-identity; and the sense of comfort derived from social, family and cultural attachments.

These concepts not only represent an ideal that residents maintain about dwelling spaces, but they also represent optimal conditions toward which individuals gravitate when disruption to and/or loss of home occurs or when the concepts of home and its absence collide. In a seminal article by Clare Cooper (1976), the concept of home is suggested as symbolic of the self. Cooper argues that until one feels secure in his or her own physical space one is not able to feel at home with oneself. In his article "Grieving for a lost home," Fried (1963) identifies the intense anguish experienced by individuals who were relocated in a Boston urban renewal project. Home meant more than housing to these residents: the underpinnings of neighborhood, community, and self had been destroyed.

The fact that Dorothy is concerned to return to Kansas (and home), even though she cannot articulate the reasons, suggests that there are underlying processes at work that maintain a sense of psychological connectedness—a concept explored extensively in Altman and Low's (1992) *Place attachment*. Considering the drab portrayal of the grayness of the Kansas landscape, it is probably not the physical place that draws Dorothy home, but rather the meaning construed through her attachment to Aunt Em. But her journey away from home has also empowered her with a sense of identity and character development that would not have been possible if she had never left in the first place. This concept of self-identity is explored in several articles regarding the Oz myth: as a feminist reading of the power of the female imagination (Paige, 1996), as a symbol of gay male individuation (Hopke, 1989), and as a statement of unfulfilled desire for independence and pleasure (Gilman, 1995). In each case, collision and conflict ultimately contribute to an enhanced or altered sense of self.

Lurie (2000) describes the character of Dorothy as having virtues of a "Victorian hero rather than a heroine: she is brave, active, independent, sensible, and willing to confront authority" (p. 17). Paige (1996), however, in her feminist reading of the Oz film, sees the overriding message to be much more complex—as a triumph of patriarchy. For instance, the red shoes are linked to the Wicked Witch of the East, and although they signify rebellion and imagination, they ultimately carry Dorothy back to Kansas as she recites the incantation three times: "There's no place like home." Paige further argues that the Good Witch Glinda is in fact an agent of patriarchy whose role is to insure Dorothy's return. The return to Kansas and the clash of two divergent worlds represents an emergence into adult responsibility—but in this case, unfortunately, with rather limiting and prescribed female roles.

Considering that the main character in *The Wizard of Oz* is female, it might seem strange to note Hopke's (1989) reading of the novel as a statement about gay male individuation. But Hopke claims that "*The Wizard of Oz* offers gay men a myth of masculine integration and feminine redemption" (p. 68). He argues that by default "in so far as gay men have internalized a feminine self-definition, they need to set out on the same journey as Dorothy toward the Wizard, a masculine source of power" (p. 69). The Lion, Scarecrow and Tin Man are grouped together under the term "Dorothy's friends," which has become a common euphemism for gay men. The term represents a collision of different images, and Hopke notes

In and of themselves, Dorothy's companions are inadequate male figures, but they are eventually the source of Dorothy's wholeness. The salvation and completion of inner masculinity through integration of such personal qualities as activity, intelligence, fearlessness, and discrimination—qualities identified in Western patriarchal societies with the heterosexual male—is as important a task for women as it is for gay men. (p. 70)

A second task that Hopke cites as critical for gay men involves the coming out process and the rejection of a compromising societal persona in favor of "a mediating persona that will reflect who they 'are'" (pp. 75–76). The Wizard represents disappointment and ineffectuality and therefore raises the need to redirect efforts toward "inner development rather than outer achievement."

Gilman (1995) introduces a psychoanalytic reading of the film/text. He sees Dorothy's desires as split into manifest and latent content reflecting a tension—a conflict between the ego, or self, and the repressed desires of the unconscious. Gilman views the film's Technicolor dream sequence as "an age-appropriate conflict between a childish need for security and dependence and an adolescent need for independence" (p. 165). Aunt Em and Miss Gulch are conflated as the Wicked Witch of the West—a character toward whom Dorothy expresses her hostility—and although the desire to leave Oz is depicted with ambivalence (witness Toto's delay of the departure), the ultimate message is one in which Dorothy is told that one need look no further than one's own backyard (i.e., that home will provide us with all that we need). In one sense, Dorothy's desires are ultimately thwarted.

The articles of Gilman (1995), Hopke (1989), and Paige (1996) typify the approach that many scholars have taken toward *The Wizard of Oz*—namely applying psychological (and often psychoanalytic) interpretation to the film and novel. These, and other articles, interface well with work to be described in the final section showing how the text (and conflict depicted in the text) is actually applied in therapeutic practice.

"THE WIZARD OF OZ" AS A THERAPEUTIC TOOL

In addition to those articles that have applied a psychological and/or psychoanalytic reading of the Oz myth, there has begun to emerge an array of articles suggesting that the myth itself could serve as a useful paradigm or framework for conducting psychotherapy or informing the therapeutic process. Ellis (1990) cites the Oz myth, among other stories such as *Peter Rabbit*, *Pinocchio* and *Robinson*

Crusoe, as illustrative of the anxiety, dangers and conflicts accompanying the leaving of home and the eventual search for or return to home and identifies ten criteria which appear in separation anxiety stories. Ellis describes several therapeutic cases that illustrate aspects of adult agoraphobia and childhood separation anxiety, and she notes *The Wizard of Oz* to be a prime example of separation anxiety and a rare case in children's literature: Dorothy journeys "to womanhood through assertiveness, courage and perseverance" (p. 436). Ellis contends that "[c]hildren's separation anxiety stories may serve an important purpose in children's lives in illustrating how they may acquire the skills needed or how they may implement the use of skills they already possess to surmount obstacles they encounter, and thus arrive 'back home' at a stage of safety and security" (p. 439).

Reiter (1988) makes use of a process referred to as bibliotherapy. Here, the therapist utilizes a particular story whose characters represent core qualities or "character essences." In the case of *The Wonderful Wizard of Oz*, clients are asked to discuss what the story has meant to them. In one case, Reiter cites the response of a 48-year-old woman with a diagnosis of schizo-affective borderline personality. She states, "I'm like Dorothy—I keep trying to get home, but I never seem to be able to get there" (p. 153). In another situation, a man who felt abandoned by his parents commented that his favorite character in the book was Toto. He said, "Toto was her only ever-faithful companion who never left Dorothy's side despite all her troubles. Even when life was at its worst, in the cyclone, that little dog stayed with her" (p. 154). In each case, Reiter mentions that the discussion about conflicts and collisions in the book opened up insights into the client's personality on his path of self-exploration.

Pancner and Pancner (1988) describe the Oz myth as analogous to the colliding experience of a mental breakdown, and the eventual achievement of a breakthrough toward "better mental health, constructive attitudes and balanced living" (p. 158). But, they also stress how patients often regard their therapists as "gurus, healers, shamans, or gods" (p. 158), as Dorothy and her friends are asked to regard the Wizard. As a result, patients often strive toward external solutions to their problems rather than focus on aspects of an inner spiritual journey (equated with Dorothy's "going home"). The authors recommend that patients become familiar with the Oz myth so that it can become a tool that will help them reframe their experiences and help them recognize the various stages they will need to encounter on their therapeutic journey. The Oz characters are regarded as parts of the whole person—the Scarecrow as the intellect, the Tin Man as emotion, the Lion as energy and drive, and Dorothy as spiritual quest.

WHEN LANGUAGES COLLIDE

McDargh (1994) describes his therapeutic work with a group of gay men who all had childhood experiences growing up in alcoholic families. All of the members in this group are seen to be on a spiritual journey attempting to find their way home, because they have been marginalized from their homes and families of origin. Their collisions within their families are viewed as analogous to various collisions occurring in Oz. One member of McDargh's group, contemplating leaving the group, described his situation as feeling like a "free fall" not dissimilar to Dorothy being swept away by the tornado and landing "with a great jolt in Oz." Another group member, discussing a psychic assault he experienced at his place of work compared himself to the Scarecrow who was "attacked in the haunted woods and . . . had the straw stuffing beaten out of him" (p. 295). The formation of the group itself is like the arrival in Oz. Dorothy is alone, but soon discovers the help of her friends (and Toto), and the group members garner support from one another in their attempt to make their lives "complete and worthwhile." McDargh speaks about his own role in the process, comparing himself to the Wizard, noting, "How many times I have sat in the group and succumbed to the fear that if I did not find the right lever to push (right words to say, correct interpretation to offer) . . . all would be lost. The circus would never find the park" (p. 296).

Perhaps the most practical application that is made of *The Wizard of Oz* story is provided by Carmichael (2000) in her description of the use of metaphor in working therapeutically with survivors of a tornado disaster who had lost their homes. The author contends that the clients were able to discuss difficult and painful material if they had the opportunity to reframe their problem in a less threatening way through the use of metaphor in the Oz myth. Carmichael claims that the metaphor helped the disaster victim normalize a terrifying emotional experience. This process also helped induce a feeling of commonality among the survivors of the disaster. A counselor working with the survivor group asked the members to begin telling the story of *The Wizard of Oz*. Once a group member mentioned that Dorothy realized she was no longer in Kansas, the group began to discuss what a different world they were now in after the disaster—that they felt lost and surreal. They disclosed "their personal sense of loss and helplessness." The process continued in this manner, touching on issues such as there being no magic solution for dealing with the grief resulting from such trauma, to needing permission from others to be less brave and to be able to express their fears and to be able to grieve. Ultimately, they also began to draw on the emotional strengths that each possessed.

Conclusions

It is unlikely that such attention to the book and film could have occurred without the therapeutic orientation that Frank Baum brought to his writing as a result of his interest in "mind cure" and the Theosophy movement. In his book on the history of psychotherapy in America, Philip Cushman (1995) notes the nineteenth-century "mind cure" movement laid the groundwork for the very individualistic orientation that psychotherapy was to take into the twenty-first century. Baum advocated the theory that people could reach their highest potential through self-directed efforts and a focus on the satisfaction of personal desires without recourse to guilt. However, Cushman feels that psychotherapy in American culture has become overly concerned with a consumer-oriented emphasis of the self, pursuing desire down the yellow brick road and moving recklessly toward an empty self. Even Baum seemed to recognize the emptiness of Oz-based life, where people barely had to work and where there was an abundance of material goods. The clash Dorothy experiences between the worlds of Oz and Kansas ultimately results in her choice to return home—presumably for the family she has lost. Dorothy, rather than the Wizard, has become the therapist for her friends by empowering them (and herself). Whereas "mind cure" places an emphasis on individualism, Baum seems to have recognized the healing importance that social connections with family and friends can offer. Thus as the worlds of Oz and Kansas collide, there arises a synthesis, mediated by the concept of home and based on personal growth in a social context.

References

Altman, I., & Low, S.M. (1992). *Place attachment.* New York: Plenum Press.

Baum, L.F. (1900). *The wonderful wizard of Oz.* Chicago: George M. Hill & Co.

Carmichael, K.D. (2000). Using a metaphor in working with disaster survivors. *Journal for Specialists in Group Work, 25*(1), 7–15.

Cooper, C. (1976). The house as symbol of the self. In H.M. Proshansky, W.H. Ittleson, & L.G. Rivlin (Eds.). *Environmental psychology: people and their physical settings* (pp. 435–448). New York: Holt, Rinehart & Winston.

Cushman, P. (1995). *Constructing the self, constructing America: A cultural history of psychotherapy.* Reading, MA: Addison-Wesley.

Ellis, E.M. (1990). Adult agoraphobia and childhood separation anxiety: Using children's literature to understand the link. *American Journal of Psychotherapy, 44*(3), 433–444.

Freud, S. (1900). *The interpretation of dreams.* In J. Strachey (Ed.), *The standard edition of the complete psychological works of Sigmund Freud: Vol. 8.* London: Hogarth Press.

WHEN LANGUAGES COLLIDE

Fried, M. (1963). Grieving for a lost home. In L.J. Duhl (Ed.), *The urban condition*. New York: Simon & Schuster.

Gilman, T.S. (1995). "Aunt Em: hate you! Hate Kansas! Taking the dog. Dorothy": Conscious and unconscious desire in *The Wizard of Oz*. *Children's Literature Association Quarterly, 20*(4), 161–167.

Hopke, R.H. (1989). Dorothy and her friends: Symbols of gay male individuation in *The Wizard of Oz*. *Quadrant, 22*(2), 65–77.

Leach, W. (1993). *Land of desire: Merchants, power, and the rise of a new American culture*. New York: Vintage Books.

Lurie, A. (2000). The oddness of Oz. *The New York Review of Books, 47*(20), 16–24.

McDargh, J. (1994). Group psychotherapy as spiritual discipline: from Oz to the kingdom of God. *Journal of Psychology and Theology, 22*(4), 290–299.

Paige, L.R. (1996). Wearing the red shoes: Dorothy and the power of the female imagination in *The Wizard of Oz*. *Journal of Popular Film and Television, 23*(4), 146–153.

Pancner, K.L., & Pancner, R.J. (1988). The quest, gurus, and the yellow brick road. *Individual Psychology: Journal of Adlerian Psychology, 44*(2), 158–166.

Reiter, S. (1988). *The Wizard of Oz* in the land of the id: a bibliotherapy approach. *Journal of Poetry Therapy, 1*(3), 149–156.

Ryman, G. (1992). *Was*. New York: Penguin Books.

Tognoli, J. (1987). Residential environments. In I. Altman & D. Stokols (Eds.), *Handbook of environmental psychology* (pp. 655–690). New York: John Wiley & Sons.

JEROME TOGNOLI, REFLECTIVE PIECE

This essay attempts to synthesize works of a psychological nature as they relate to *The Wizard of Oz*, the concept of self-identity and the meaning of home. Since the citations in the literature come from a variety of academic disciplines, they provide a challenge in terms of writing a coherent piece. Essentially, I was confronted by the collision of ideas and source material, and the essay went through multiple revisions. In the beginning there were too many themes, and these themes took me in too many directions—such as trying to include all the articles I came across that dealt with how psychotherapists used *The Wizard of Oz* in their work, or trying to include too much historical material about the life and work of Frank Baum. In the end I tried to restrict the articles I incorporated to those that emphasized the search for home (in the Oz myth) and the search for personal identity.

Initial attempts to narrow the focus to the essay were frustrating for me, although I found it helpful to have in mind the theme of the text, *Collide*, to guide me in a very general sense. As an environmental psychologist, I typically draw on research articles from a variety of disciplines to shape a particular research problem that I am investigating. These disciplines might often include social, environmental, personality, developmental and clinical psychology, gender studies, sociology, geography, and architecture, planning and design. In addition, my tendency as a research psychologist is to view human (and fictional) behavior as a cause and effect relationship. For example, the tornado causes Dorothy to lose her home and to land in Oz. Being in Oz sets off a chain reaction which assumes the shape of a quest. Each of Dorothy's companions then motivates her to solve his problems. The meeting with the Wizard establishes an awareness in her that she has the inner strength to return home.

The current essay includes academic disciplines that normally are not considered part of environmental psychology—namely literary criticism, history, film studies, and psychoanalytic theory—and I found myself more comfortable initially veering off in many different directions as the situation warranted. For example, I wanted to show how the life of Frank Baum was relevant to the work he created, which meant reading historical and biographical material. I also wanted to show that the film/novel had multiple meanings for discrepant subcultures, writers of fiction, clients of psychotherapy, academicians, gay men, and victims of tornadoes. Again, space devoted to each of these areas had to be limited, with more attention being devoted to common underlying themes of home and identity.

Initially, the essay was inspired by my long-standing research interest in the meaning of home and my reading of the novel *Was* by Geoff Ryman. I was fascinated with the multiple directions that that novel pursued: a pseudo-historical account of the life of the "real" Dorothy Gale, the parallel life of Frances Gumm—the "real" Judy Garland—and the life of the novel's main character, Jonathan, who is dying of AIDS and who searches frantically for home (Dorothy's and his own sense of place in the world). In the novel, Jonathan and his therapist discover that Dorothy has been abandoned by her mother and sent to live with her aunt and uncle in Zeandale, Kansas. We learn that Toto has been murdered by Aunt Em, and that Dorothy has been repeatedly sexually abused by Uncle Henry. She eventually runs away, enters a life of prostitution, and ends up in a mental hospital. It is no accident that Ryman chose a psychotherapist as one of the characters who joins Jonathan in his search (or quest).

There is significance in examining home and identity from a psychological perspective. I felt that many aspects of the novel possessed psychological meaning and resonated with my research interests about home—particularly those aspects of home as an extension of the self, the trauma of home loss, the quest for and return to home, and the concept of home as representing place attachment, continuity, refuge and comfort. While the "collide" theme was an overarching one, I also needed to pull together issues about home and loss and self-identity, connect them with aspects of *The Wizard of Oz* and with articles in the research literature that illustrated how psychotherapists have likewise made use of the material. A by-product of the various collisions was the synthesis that Dorothy had become a real wizard—empowered through hard work and confrontation with repeated obstacles in order to return back home (or return to her self) a stronger person with access to landscapes in her imagination (Oz) that went beyond the ordinariness of Kansas.

"THINK. WRITE. ASK."

1. Jerome Tognoli tells us that he often draws on research from a variety of different disciplines, not just psychology. For instance, in this essay he draws on gender studies, sociology, geography, and architecture. How does Tognoli connect all these disciplines? What, to you, are the most interesting connections Tognoli makes between these disparate fields?

2. Take a close look at the way Tognoli concludes his essay, and then describe it (for instance, he might restate his thesis, or make connections between various points, or leave readers with something new to consider). How might closely reading a number of conclusions help you strengthen the conclusions you write?

3. Pick a paragraph of medium length from Tognoli, Cara Gargano, and Nick Ramer, and compare the writers' sentence lengths and structural variety. What are some of the differences and similarities you found?

4. A thesis statement is often limited to one sentence, and is frequently placed in the first paragraph of an essay. Compare Tognoli's thesis statement with Steven Nathanson's and Edmund Miller's. How do the thesis statements differ in identifying the purpose of their essays?

5. "Tognoli's essay corresponds most closely, in this volume, with Simone Weil Davis' 'Crash: Collision and Contact,' Cara Gargano's 'Aesthetic Collisions: Dialogues in Dance and Poetry,' and Belinda Kremer & Angela Pisano's *All Begin Guy Walks into a Bar*." Explore this statement. What do you find you need to think about when asked to compare an interdisciplinary essay, a "wish," a *choreography*, and a graphic poem?

AESTHETIC COLLISIONS: DIALOGUES IN DANCE AND POETRY

Cara Gargano, Theatre, Film, and Dance

Poet Anne-Marie Alonzo wrote of dancer Margie Gillis:

> I dance for you and you
> read for me we will join one another (49)

In Alonzo's long poem *La danse des marches* (1993), writing and dance become creative force fields that literally and metaphorically collide with synergistic energy. Alonzo creates a world in which the two art forms literally reconstitute each other: the poet "dances" while the choreographer "writes." Alonzo, a former dancer, can dance today only through poetry. Confined to a wheelchair since a car collision as a teenager left her a quadriplegic, she can only access movement through the act of writing it. Because writing is physically challenging for her, she must consciously choreograph her movements to inscribe words on a page.

La danse des marches functions as a physical, emotional, and intellectual *pas de deux* between Alonzo and the well-known Canadian dancer and choreographer Margie Gillis. While Alonzo "dances" through her writing, Gillis, as a choreographer and performer, "writes" through dance. Gillis recognizes that dance, as an articulation of human experience, is too often relegated to the realm of "feeling" alone; to correct this she offers dance workshops specifically for the "thinking body." Her choreography is theatrically narrative and thick with imagery and metaphor; she considers dance not as a physical exercise alone but as a language, a way of "speaking" to her audience. Her dances describe the world around her by using movement as a manifestation of the intellect as well as of the body. While her inspiration is frequently literary or poetic, she seeks neither to appropriate nor to serve the work with which she dances. Rather, like Alonzo, she creates something new from her synergistic meetings with another artist, a fusion of cognitive and somatic communication: "Bless the continual stutter of the word being made flesh," she writes, describing her choreography and her dancing.[1]

---

[1] See Gillis's website, www.margiegilles.org, where she shares her thoughts on dance with the dance community.

I call attention to the collision between these two artists and their respective art forms because this interface between dance and writing may seem contradictory today. As dancer/anthropologist Cynthia Novack writes, "most Americans share a conception of the mind and body as separate and opposed" (183). Dancing and writing are often seen as antithetical in Western culture, with dance belonging solely to the body and writing to the mind alone. For the early Greeks no such split existed between mind and body. The goddess Technê (from whom we get the word technology) presided over both the arts and the sciences, over both written and felt communication. Indeed, the word choreography comes from the Greek and means "dance writing."

Dance, more than any of the other arts, perhaps, reflects the prevailing world view on the most basic level (i.e., how bodies, at rest and in motion, relate to each other in time and space). If later Classical Greek logicians promoted the world view that has come down to us today, we can find traces of the early connection in many of their legacies, from the harmonic dance of their mathematics and astronomy to the movement inherent in the art of rhetoric. It is within the art of rhetoric as practiced by Alonzo and Gillis that this collision between writing and dancing becomes artistically fruitful and provocative.

A brief, if necessarily simplified, sketch of the ongoing if uneasy relationship between dance and rhetoric may be appropriate here. Mary Carruthers shows how rhetoric, derived from the Greek word for speaking, first connected writing to movement. Even in medieval Europe, where early Christians condemned the body as the antithesis of mind and spirit, the rhetorical concept of *ductus* describing the flow or movement through a composition was essential to the medieval idea of rhetoric. Medieval rhetoric, according to Carruthers, is inherently movement-oriented, posting the rhetorical gesture as a journey, moving in time and space. She writes that "music and dance were fundamental parts of a rhetorical education" connected to *ductus*. She reminds us of the technically precise hand movements required to produce readable writing:

> . . . what to us is fixed or static—the shapes of a letter—in this culture was understood as inherently dynamic and full of movement, because letters were created from choreographed patterns of hand motions and not simply picked out from pre-fabricated shapes. (111)

Often copyists could not read the very texts they traced but relied on the choreography of the hand to make meaning. In one sense, this is not so dissimilar to Alonzo's poetry, where the very gesture of writing also becomes its content.

In the sixteenth century, as Mark Franko has shown, French court dance, generally considered to be the source of Western concert dance,

> was frequently likened to, and indeed contrived to suggest, a written text. . . . Dancing became identified with highly rhetorical forms of late Renaissance culture . . . where the choreographic figure presented bodies as physical metaphors of written characters or symbolic designs. (191)

According to Franko, these dances were still associated with classical notions of rhetoric; audiences were required to "read" choreography, deciphering language written on and by a moving body in space. Dancers could be seen "as a living alphabet" and "dancing bodies as letters," and "the body was used as a figure of language" (192). The capacity to "read" bodily writing was highly prized and indeed, as Franko notes, was considered a noble and kingly attribute.

The rhetorical power of the dancing body, however, became minimized during the Enlightenment, an era that privileged empirical observation and intellectual rigor over physical instinct. Power was located in the spectator, and dance became something to be viewed rather than read, a corporeal image not a rhetorical text, an aesthetic experience rather than a structured argument. The dancer was increasingly seen as merely a body to be manipulated by the teacher or the choreographer, who represented the "brains" of the system. The scientist became separate from the artist, and the scientific world was seen as the "real" one.

The separation between dance and rhetoric was completed by Cartesian science and by nineteenth-century colonial expansion, which gave birth to anthropology as a study of the "Other." Dance as an expression of cultural memory and communal purpose was seen as representative of a societal world view but was necessarily skewed by the association of bodily knowledge with the primitive or "natural." Dance was considered not as a highly sophisticated and culturally evolved art form but as an unregulated outpouring, a throwback to origins that "civilized" man had outgrown. These new dance scholars viewed but did not experience the movement. In other words, unlike Alonzo, they "wrote about" but did not "write" dance.

As the twentieth century progressed, rhetoric and dance resumed a closer relationship, as dancer/choreographers such as Martha Graham and Katherine Dunham addressed important social issues such as human conflict and racism and introduced their academic studies into their dances. In addition, Dunham and Pearl Primus changed the face of anthropology by participating in, as well as observing, indigenous dances. In the latter part of the century, dancer/choreographers such as David Parsons, Elizabeth Streb, Stephen

Petronio, and Maguy Marín have made dances about the very science that writes itself using metaphors of dance and movement. Choreographer/dancer Bill T. Jones refers to his work not in terms of collaboration but as collision: "I was forcing—just jamming—things together, and trusting, almost like action painting. We throw it together and there is a result. It will send off sparks. It will do something" (Daly 74).

In a broad sense, the movement in dance in the twentieth century corresponds to the emerging world view propounded by quantum science, which questions the Newtonian/Cartesian world view that was concretized in the eighteenth and nineteenth centuries. While collision in a Newtonian/Cartesian universe often results in destruction or damage, collision in the quantum world view offers creative possibilities of a synergetic nature; Gillis and Alonzo, each in her own way, are at the forefront of exploring these possibilities. The quantum world view suggests that there is a holistic flow between all things in the universe that is the result of continuous collisions that occur on the atomic level.[2] In the quantum world view, elements and concepts that we have always seen as antithetical seem to be crashing into each other to create new events, a universal web of relationships where all things are related in space and time. Such collisions are occurring daily in many disciplines and on many levels. I see the collision between Alonzo's poetry and Gillis's dance as an aesthetic version of such a collision, an explosive meeting between art forms and artists that goes beyond simple interdisciplinary exchange, but is synergetic, resulting in a cataclysmic transfer of energy and creating a larger and more important event, a third new object from the two colliding bodies.

The trope of collision is also fundamental to Alonzo's poetry and Gillis's choreography in a different and perhaps more profound way than the simple reiteration of the quantum metaphor.[3] As primarily a solo artist, Gillis rarely risks

---

[2] Dance became an important metaphor as scientists sought to describe this new universe. Larry Dossey calls the dynamism of life "the biodance," while physicist Richard Feynman refers to the "atomic dance" of the universe. Nobel prize-winning physicist David Bohm even proposes a new kind of language to speak of this new movement-oriented world, based on the action verb, which he calls *rheomode* (i.e., "moving mode"). Bohm's rheomode and Feynman's "dance" are very akin to understanding and explaining our reality. By moving language and writing into an active mode, Bohm brings us back full circle.

[3] Dancers traditionally avoid collision in a literal sense, and even contact improvisation, which is based on collision between two or more bodies, and where each body's trajectory is altered by that contact, is, as Susan Leigh Foster points out, a structured discipline, not unlike a jazz improvisation or an Indian raga. For the most part, dance performance is based on the excitement of potential collision and predicated upon an implicit trust that any physical encounter will be mediated by technical expertise and will be relatively safe.

collision with other bodies.[4] Gillis's collisions are uniquely aesthetic, asking how human beings, as thinking bodies that live within a cosmic *ductus*, can develop the physical and mental discipline to interact with the energy fields with which they are in constant collision. Like Alonzo in her encounters with the completed work of other artists, Gillis creates a third artistic object from her interaction. Her meeting James Joyce's character Molly Bloom transforms the character and gives her a central role in her own drama. Her celebrated dance to Tom Wait's rendition of "Waltzing Mathilda" is a heartbreaking solo about the human need to dance, juxtaposed against our ability to transcend our physical limitations. "Waltzing," in this dance, becomes a metaphor for the impossible ideal of human artistic expression as the dancer, her feet painfully twisted, is pathetically earthbound. The dreamed-of freedom of the waltz, juxtaposed against the character's reality, reminds us that as humans we may hope for flight but are never far from the exigencies of gravity.

In "Slipstream" (1985), one of Gillis's signature works, the dancer becomes caught up in a flow of repeated movement. At first the movement phrase is small, fully realized, contained and controlled by the artist. The dancer clearly initiates the motion, and her hip-length hair swings in response to her movement. Soon however, the dancer herself is caught up by the whirlwind that she has created; the force field she has entered carries her through the air, tossing her in all directions, lifting and suspending her body in space only to send it on a dizzying trajectory toward the floor. The movement becomes larger, literally expanding to fill the available space. The dancer, apparently out of control, has slipped into a motion stream; it is as if by entering the magnetic field of dance she has slipped sideways into another dimension where all is movement. For Gillis, "Slipstream" seems to represent the collision between human and environment and suggests that dance is a way of making that creative collision visible.

----

[4] In 2003 Gillis celebrated a 30-year career as a solo dancer. Her personal technique and unique style have evolved from her exploration of many dance forms; for her, "dance is a vital form of expression in our society." She speaks to her audiences directly through movement. It is this need to communicate that led her to introduce modern dance to China in 1979; she was the first performer, teacher, and lecturer in the arts to visit China since the Cultural Revolution. Gillis has also toured India, Europe, the Middle East, and throughout North and South America and has been named Cultural Ambassador for both Canada and Quebec. In 1988 she became the first modern dancer to be awarded the Order of Canada. In all her travels, she has sought to be open to aesthetic and cultural collisions of a positive, creative nature. Gillis writes: "My regard to the human condition—compassion for its failings and vulnerability, celebration of its hopes, achievements, wisdom, healing, inspiration, and honesty." Her work offers audiences an opportunity to encounter new ideas and, particularly, possible relationships in a synergetic way: we are changed by her dancing as she is changed by her dancing for us.

WHEN LANGUAGES COLLIDE

Given Gillis's propensity for aesthetic collision and for physical and artistic risk-taking, it is not surprising that she should be the focus of Alonzo's rhetorical dance. The trope of collision or colliding is also the very premise of Alonzo's poetry and is linked to dance from her earliest work. Her subject is her "physical state and its moral consequences," both of which arose out of the literal vehicular collision that nearly killed her (243). In her early work, she presents herself as a dancer who is mutilated by forces moving beyond her control in a piece of chaotic choreography gone terribly wrong. As if in dark parody of Gillis's "Slipstream," these forces throw her body into an endless twisting and breaking, jerking it into spasms of disjointed movement:

> broken propelled thrown over the head dances one two
> three four vertebrae unlinked dislocated displaced
> possessed i lose it all and the neck attach detach your
> seat belts forced failed landing i fly there are the seats the
> windshield holds me back i fall no one can fly you know that
> (*Geste*, my translation 21)

Her language also seems to be in free fall; she uses neither punctuation nor capitalization in a series of cascading verbs that relive a timeless moment of eternal collision, as beautiful as it is terrible.

In *La danse des marches*, however, Alonzo uses the figure of dancing in a new way and allows her poetic voice to collide with Gillis's choreo-dancing voice to create a virtual poetic dancing body. In this poem she suggests that synergetic collision can be both transformative and healing. Alonzo moves between French (her language of choice) and English (Gillis's language). Personal pronouns, too, are constantly shifting: "I," "you," "we," "us," "she," and "me" become interchangeable. The two artists meet within a physico-linguistic rheomode that not only flows between their works but connects them to what physicist David Bohm calls the "holoverse," where all is movement.

Through her meditations on her own immobility, Alonzo creates herself as a virtual dancer whose performance exists within the rhetorical collision of writing and dancing. Alonzo's immobility (she refuses the word "paralysis") becomes movement because

> immobility is movement ceased recreated reinvented
> by you (20)

If Alonzo's writing is a precious chance to find her own dancing again:

> . . . dance with me dance move
> around me carry me over lift me help me to fly (20)

Gillis's dance is never "only" dance but engages in a complex writing that assumes itself to be part of a literary and cultural discourse. She asks us to read her dances within the complex web of our social structures and to read other writers' writing by interrogating it. For both Gillis and Alonzo, collision with whatever force is encountered materially alters the artist who, as she absorbs the impact of the collision, allows that force to become part of the work of art being created and part of her own movement through life. The effect of the artist within that collision is equally important, because it has the capacity to change the world both materially and virtually.

Carruthers remarks that rhetoric "has no subject of its own, its method and categories can be applied to all that is human and that invokes conversations" (100). In this sense, dance can be said to align itself once again with rhetoric, since, at its most basic, it is both a dialogue with the world about the "physical and moral consequences" of the human condition and an attempt to alter them. Writing on dance and dancing on writing then offer a special kind of pleasure because they create sites of multiple creative collisions. The meeting between a composed work, an artist's performance, and an audience's reception is just the beginning. Each work is created anew in each performance/reception, and each "reading" depends as much on the audience's contribution as it does on the work itself. In the context of such collisions, there is no delineation between the performer and the receptor, and Gillis and Alonzo each act in both capacities. It is the written and somatic movement of spectators through the work that truly allows the work to exist, but it is the movement of the work itself that makes us feel alive and that challenges us to create. Our writing on dance should ideally be a conversation with the work: "from the dance the word emerges," writes Alonzo. Our dancing must reflect the collisions with writings that affect us. Gillis and Alonzo teach us to engage in an eternal *pas de deux* which is both a collision and a new birth.

Alonzo's purposeful collision with Gillis allows her to dance again through her choreo/graphy; her choice of Gillis highlights Gillis's own project as a choreographer (i.e., to write and think from a bodily perspective and to re-establish the dancing body as a cognitive as well as a somatic instrument). Together Gillis and Alonzo redefine choreography as dance-writing in a bodily and material way, connecting the physical with the metaphysical and the literal with the symbolic. This is, in many ways, the true task of the artist.

Works Cited

Alonzo, Ann-Marie. *Geste*. Laval: Editions du Trois, 1997.

———. *Margie Gillis: La Danse des Marches*. Montreal: Editions du Noroît, 1993.

Bohm, David. *Wholeness and the Implicate Order*. London: Routledge, 2000.

Carruthers, Mary. "Rhetorical *Ductus*, or, Moving through Composition." *Acting on the Past: Historical Performance Across the Disciplines*. Ed. Mark Franko and Annette Richards. Hanover: Wesleyan UP, 2000. 99–117.

Daly, Ann. *Critical Gestures: Writing on Dance and Culture*. Hanover: Wesleyan UP, 2002.

Dupré, Louise. "Ecrire comme vivre: dans l'hybridité. Entretien avec Anne-Marie Alonzo." *Voix et Images XIX* 2.56 (1994): 238–49.

Franko, Mark. "Writing Dancing, 1573." *Moving History/Dancing Culture*. Ed. Ann Dils and Ann Cooper Albright. Middletown: Wesleyan UP, 2001.

Gillis, Margie. www.margiegillis.org.

Novack, Cynthia. "The Body's Endeavors as Cultural Practices." *Choreographing History*. Ed. Susan Leigh Foster. Bloomington: Indiana UP, 1995. 177–84.

CARA GARGANO, REFLECTIVE PIECE

For me the process of writing and the reason for writing have their source in a series of what I think of as "aesthetic collisions." I find that my writing circles around the often surprising encounters among my diverse areas of interest. In the case of this article, I was initially struck by the way Ann-Marie Alonzo, a poet I admire, rewrites her "physical state and its moral consequences" through the metaphor of dance. Her focus on dancer Margie Gillis resonates with me because I have always admired Gillis's dancing and choreography. When I learned through my research that Gillis considers dance an articulation of our human need to "speak" about the human condition, I saw reciprocity between Gillis and Alonzo that seemed provocative.

This reciprocity between artists from two media that have often been seen as opposites brought me to reflect on the sources of this opposition and to seek the source of their surprising commonality. As a dancer/choreographer who has worked for over twenty years in a university setting, I have often asked myself why we so often see the mind and body as separate entities: why do we in the West believe that the mind must instruct the body and not vice versa? Why do academic institutions privilege "intellectual" endeavor over the somatic? Thus my purpose emerged as part of my ongoing project as a dancer and as a writer: to explore the ways that artists seek to transcend the Western world view that supports the separation of bodily and cognitive knowledge. Alonzo and Gillis seem to me to represent the best of this sort of interconnectedness because they do not "become" each other but rather, through collision not fusion, create a third aesthetic object.[5]

One of the pleasures of writing about dance is that, like rhetoric, as Mary Carruthers suggests, "its methods and categories can be applied to all that is human and invokes conversations." There are as many approaches to dance as there are scholarly fields of study; in a recent collection of articles about the practice of dance, these approaches included phenomenology feminism, gender studies, history, deconstruction, anthropology, and cultural studies. Professional conversations about dance, then, tend to be eclectic and to be the results of synergistic collisions between areas of writerly interest.

___

[5] I see the difference between collision and fusion as being the difference between retaining autonomy as an artist and sacrificing artistic identity. While Alonzo and Gillis collide, they never fuse.

WHEN LANGUAGES COLLIDE

My second phase is to find the supporting information through research that will serve as a foundation for the written or performed event. The third phase is to make the journey of the work accessible to the audience. Their journey will not necessarily parallel mine since mine has been longer and more complex, looping back on itself and returning to the nodal point many times over. In clarifying the reader/spectator journey, I often understand mine in a new way.

These three phases do not occur sequentially but overlap and collide. An article or a dance usually takes me quite a while. After an initial creative period I typically put the work aside for a while to give me distance and to reflect on what I have learned by committing words to a page or putting movement on dancers. The very fact of moving an idea to paper or giving movement to dancers transforms thought and feeling to action, crystallizing it. Finally what is left is to refine the work so that everyone can participate in it in some way; this is why I am such a fan of revision. In later stages I read my written work aloud to understand the flow of it and to discover gaps in the argument. In the case of choreography, I often video the work or perform it in an informal showcase so that I can see it as others might. These collisions between the "I" and the "Eye" help me shape the work into its final form.

For me, the most important elements in both writing and choreography are curiosity, an eagerness to explore, and a sense of responsibility. The artist is a powerful purveyor of values and assumptions and thus has a responsibility to learn and think and create critically about the human experience.

"THINK. WRITE. ASK."

1. In her reflective piece, Cara Gargano writes that she "tries to make the journey of the work accessible to the audience." In what ways does Gargano choreograph her journey of exploring the collisions between writing and dancing? Identify passages that are helpful in making this journey visible for you.

2. Gargano creates long, flowing sentences, connecting strings of clauses and phrases with commas and semicolons. Notice how the syntax of these sentences is part of what she's saying about writing *as* movement. For instance, the use of a semicolon as opposed to a period affects the feel of reading the following sentence: "Soon however, the dancer herself is caught up by the whirlwind that she has created; the force field she has entered carries her through the air, tossing her in all directions, lifting and suspending her

body in space only to send it on a dizzying trajectory toward the floor." Take some time to read back through her essay; find, and copy down, a half-dozen sentences that exhibit clearly the choreography described above.

3. "Aesthetic Collisions" argues that writing is a form of dancing. Can you identify any repeated movements in the text that correspond to repeated movements in dance?

4. When Gargano uses quotation marks, as here:

In other words, unlike Alonzo, they "wrote about" but did not "write" about dance.

—how is the meaning of the "quoted" words affected? Locate a few instances of this kind of "quoting," and try and describe the effect of the "quotes." What does Gargano accomplish by using them?

5. Erica Frouman-Smith also performs a close reading of a text. How do these close readings function in the essays? What similarities and differences do you find in the way each author uses these close readings to support her arguments?

ROSARIO CASTELLANOS: CHARTING A COURSE TOWARD ANOTHER WAY TO BE

Erica Frouman-Smith, Foreign Languages

When Rosario Castellanos died at age 49 in 1974, she had been living in Israel as Mexican ambassador, an honor bestowed in 1971. She was an established and respected writer who left behind an important body of work that included poetry, essays, fiction, and drama. Although her poetry and fiction had won important literary prizes during her lifetime, in traditional literary circles her work was discounted by those who were not yet equal to the task of seriously considering a woman as a writer of consequence (Ahern, "Castellanos" 146). Her state funeral provoked an outpouring of grief from those who greatly admired her for fearlessly chronicling and condemning the injustices she and other Mexican women faced in their daily lives. Her colleague, author José Emilio Pacheco, wrote the following in response to her passing: "When the commotion passes and people reread her work it will become evident that nobody in her time had as clear a consciousness as she did of the meaning of the two-fold condition of being both a woman and a Mexican. . . . Of course we didn't know how to read her" (qtd. in Ahern, "Castellanos" 147). It was not until the 1980s that scholars in Mexico and the United States began to appreciate the depth and originality of her work in both its content and its style. Only in recent years has Castellanos achieved the status she so richly deserves, as a seminal author whose life and writings have followed a pattern of colliding with the values of patriarchal culture, evident in the texts chosen for the discussion that follows.

Castellanos was born in 1925, the older of two children of landowning parents, in the southern region of Chiapas, an area heavily populated by the Chamula Indians. As a young child, she experienced the death of her seven-year-old younger brother Benjamín and her parents' subsequent rejection of her as the girl child, an event that left an indelible mark. Her parents' eventual move to Mexico City was necessitated by the loss of their land, a result of the reparations to the indigenous population instituted by the post-revolutionary Cárdenas regime (1941). Castellanos's concern for the marginalization of Indians and women in Mexican culture expressed in her writings are a reflection of her personal experiences. Her profound understanding of the barriers imposed on Mexican women within a traditional patriarchal culture exemplifies her own struggle to secure her place as a writer.

Castellanos's legacy as an innovative thinker and the foremost feminist of her time was shaped by her readings of Simone de Beauvoir, Simone Weil, and Virginia Wolf. Beauvoir's influence is evident in Castellanos's anticipation of the major ideas of the Woman's Movement of the 1970s. Similar to de Beauvoir, Castellanos rejected traditional notions of women as the "other" and viewed femininity as a cultural construction at a time when such notions were regarded as radical. Castellanos's perceptive portrayal of the oppression of the Indians of Chiapas was helped by her familiarity with the diaries of the French mystic Simone Weil. Virginia Woolf's fictional creation of remarkable female protagonists whose uniqueness was directly related to their gender and her discussion of societal constraints on women's opportunities resonated with Castellanos (Ahern, "Castellanos" 142). The Mexican writer's novel writing style in her female-centered works in which she inserts her self into the text and writes her body are the hallmarks of what French feminists years later will designate as *écriture féminine* or feminine discourse.

Not content to merely disclose the oppression of Mexican women, Castellanos repeatedly encourages women to take charge of their lives. In an important essay from 1971, Castellanos criticizes Mexican women's most notable virtue: "I insist that, if self-sacrifice is a virtue, it is one of those virtues that Chesterton says have gone mad. And for this madness, the only straitjacket we have is the law" ("Self-Sacrifice" 262). She concludes with an exhortation to her female compatriots: "If injustice still affects Mexican women, they have no right to complain. That is the choice they have made. They have scorned the legal recourses they have at hand" (263).

Castellanos's reading as a woman led her to reassess the past with fresh eyes and fill in the historical silences surrounding iconic Mexican women (Ahern, "Reading Castellanos" 6–7). In doing so, she pursued an important mission of illuminating and uncovering for her female public the reason for this void, something that could only be accomplished by a woman of Castellanos's intellectual depth and personal fortitude. In her essay "Once Again, Sor Juana," the author focuses on the silence that for many centuries greeted the work of the great seventeenth-century Baroque poet despite having produced some of the most important poetry within the Hispanic world of her time. Sor Juana Inés de la Cruz, in an important autobiographical letter written to defend herself against the constant attacks to which she was subjected for not devoting more time to her religious duties ("Letter in Reply to Sor Philotea," *A Woman of Genius*), revealed that her decision to enter the convent primarily for the opportunity to study and write rather than because of a true religious calling represented a realistic appraisal of the narrow opportunities available to women of that era.

Deemed to be too daring and provocative in her rejection of a traditional female destiny, Sor Juana eventually lost her battle and was silenced by the Church hierarchy. Resigned to her fate, Sor Juana divested herself of all that she held dear—her books, musical instruments, and scientific tools—and died five years later caring for her sisters during an epidemic in Mexico City. In her essay Castellanos states that of the three most important female icons in Mexican culture—the Virgin of Guadalupe, Malinche, and Sor Juana—the poet represented the most problematic case to her contemporaries because she was a *female* genius ("Once Again" 223).

Castellanos's insights into Sor Juana relate to the interesting parallels between the two women. Both were criticized in their lifetimes because they exceeded societal expectations of what was acceptable for women of their respective eras. Both died fairly young—Sor Juana at age 47, Castellanos at 49. Although Castellanos ultimately achieved great renown after her death—principally because of the recognition accorded her by feminists—it is ironic that three centuries after Sor Juana, Castellanos encountered the same kinds of obstacles for women within her milieu.

In addition to Sor Juana, Malinche was a past voice Castellanos sought to recover. Malinche, the Aztec woman who as a child was sold into slavery to the Maya, played a pivotal role as Hernán Cortés's interpreter during the Spaniards' conquest of the ferocious and imperialistic Aztec people in 1521. Admired for many years by the Spaniards for her loyalty, bravery, intelligence, and linguistic skills, Malinche was reviled by Mexicans as a traitor once the country achieved independence from Spain in the early part of the nineteenth century. Malinche's important legacy remained shrouded in silence until Castellanos recovered it and created a portrait that deconstructs the Malinche-as-traitor paradigm to reveal Malinche's own betrayal at the hands of her mother. The dramatic effect of Castellanos's eponymous poem derives from the use of Malinche as the narrating "I," essential to creating a more complete view of her. No longer silenced and objectified, Malinche speaks as an active subject who exposes the pain she endured in her relationship with her mother by casting the latter as the architect of betrayal. Like the evil stepmother in the fairy tale Snow White, the mother looks in the mirror and sees her daughter as her rival who must be destroyed: within the confines of a patriarchal culture, only one woman can be the fairest in the land.

Cast out, expelled
from the kingdom, the palace, and the warm belly,
of the woman who bore me in legitimate marriage bed
who hated me because I was her equal
in stature and in rank,
who saw herself in me and hating her image
dashed the mirror against the ground.
I advance toward destiny in chains
leaving behind all I can hear,
the funereal murmurs with which I am buried. (96)

In this poem Castellanos establishes a connection between herself and Malinche via the oppression she sustained in her problematic relationship with her own mother. As Castellanos chronicled in her first autobiographical novel, *Balún Canán*, she experienced grievous repudiation by her mother when her younger brother died. Castellanos's recourse for dealing with this rejection was to write her way out of a state of powerlessness into being an active agent of her destiny as well as the destiny of other women. In reasserting Malinche's literary voice, Castellanos simultaneously calls attention to her own struggles as a woman.

Castellanos's reading of her two most iconic female predecessors, Sor Juana de la Cruz and Malinche, led to a series of poems and stories that reflect her willingness to confront traditional female roles. "Meditation on the Brink" (1971) is one such poem where she rejects the extreme fates famous women of history and literature experienced at the hands of the dominant culture:

No, it's not a solution
To throw oneself under a train like Tolstoy's Anna
Or gulp down Madame Bovary's arsenic . . .

Nor to deduce geometric laws by counting the beams of one's solitary
    confinement cell
like Sor Juana did. It's not a solution
to write, while company arrives,
in the Austen family living room
or to shut oneself up in the attic
of some New England house
and dream with the Dickinsons' family Bible
under a spinster pillow.

Castellanos dismisses the traditional strategies of the past (i.e., suicide and isolation) as too high a price for women to pay in order to express themselves and, instead, issues a declaration of hope and a call to arms to find a new solution for women:

> There must be another way . . .
> Another way to be human and free
> Another way to be. (111)

Her message resonates with her readers and represents an important and daring clash with the status quo.

The short story "Cooking Lesson" belongs to Castellanos's mature period, a period in which her feminist concerns are most overt and therefore deserve more attention here. Part of the collection *Álbum de familia* (1972), published two years before her death, "Cooking Lesson" is among a series of short stories that center on women of the urban middle class. Although the story belongs to a particular period when women were on the "brink" of expanding their options, it can still be appreciated for being ahead of its time.

Written in a blunt, ironic, and humorous style, "Cooking Lesson" is a subversive lesson on what is wrong with the institution of marriage from a woman's perspective. It also exemplifies Castellanos's innovative use of domestic spaces— here, the kitchen—as a way to uncover new meanings regarding women's lives. It is in part a parody of traditional women's magazines in which a typical young newlywed, eager, yet anxious, reads a cookbook to help her prepare her husband's dinner. But in Castellanos's version, the newlywed is not so young nor does she have the requisite enthusiasm for her task. Instead, she is older, well-educated, and ready to subject to critical analysis conventional ideas about the roles automatically assigned to women whether or not these roles are appropriate for them.

By inserting her protagonist into the kitchen, Castellanos subverts traditional notions of it as a feminine space in order to create a radical message, as did her predecessor Sor Juana. In her biographical letter "Sor Philotea," Sor Juana comments on the kitchen, a place to which she retreated when not engaged with her books and in which she could not help but make interpretations of a scientific nature while cooking. Her statement suggesting that, if Aristotle had been a cook, he would have written much more, serves as an ironic commentary directed toward her critics who viewed certain tasks as inherently suitable to one gender rather than another (Cruz 62). In "Cooking Lesson" the narrator's observations again raise the issue of women's education and how it affects the spaces and places to which women are relegated. That these matters have not yet been resolved is a reality Castellanos emphasizes to her readers as her narrator insists on her lack of suitability for the task at hand: "I wandered astray through classrooms, streets, offices, cafés, wasting my time on skills that now I must forget in order to acquire others" (207). Thus, too much knowledge can be dangerous as it causes the wife to think and question and gets in the way of her purpose here. She would rather "cook up" reasons why she does not belong.

The description of the kitchen as white and spotless evokes the idea of a blank page on which the wife, as a resistant reader, will write her own recipe for living and dealing with her newly acquired role (O'Connell 192). Its sterility causes the protagonist to connect it with hospitals, sickness, and death, thereby reversing the traditional idea of the kitchen as a warm and nourishing place (Oyarzún 105). Rather, it is analogous to an institution in which the wife is confined, where her madness is an act of sanity in a place of entrapment.

The wife's contemplation of the red frozen meat she has chosen to prepare for her husband's dinner leads to a series of reflections on her past and also to the inevitable association between her and the meat as objects. The color of the meat is linked to the narrator's unromantic description of her honeymoon in Acapulco, a honeymoon during which she experiences the loss of her virginal blood, a symbolic loss representing a bad omen. Red with sunburn, she and her husband make love assuming the classic position—a fact she notes with great irony since only she is the one who suffers: "But I, self-sacrificing little Mexican wife, born like a dove to the nest, smile like Cuauhtémoc under torture on the rack when he said, 'My bed is not made of roses,' and fell silent" (208). By invoking an iconic figure of Mexican history, Castellanos cleverly establishes a connection between the suffering of Cuauhtémoc, the last Aztec emperor, who was tortured and burned by the conquering Spaniards, and the pain her narrator endures while her "conquering" husband selfishly seeks his own satisfaction. Thus the myth of the honeymoon as the first step toward the wife's happiness and fulfillment begins to unravel and suggests that the wife's future will be characterized by her husband's domination of her (Oyarzún 105).

The transformation of the meat during the cooking process closely mirrors the wife's own transformations. Her inability to react to her new name when she is paged in the hotel lobby highlights the difficulty of suddenly losing her former, virginal self and accepting this new married one. Yet what exactly has she gained with her new standing? It is certainly not freedom, since she has gone from one type of prison—that of the older unmarried woman or spinster—to another kind, marriage. As she perceptively observes, her new position is worse than that of a slave: "All the responsibilities and duties of a servant are assigned to me for everything. I'm supposed to keep the house impeccable, the clothes ready, mealtimes exact. But I'm not paid any salary; I don't get one day a week off; I can't change masters" (211).

The protagonist's reflections on her future encompass her husband's inevitable unfaithfulness, an acceptable practice within Mexico's macho culture. Despite her other status, she will be subjected to his distrust of her: "I bear an owner's brand, a property tag and yet you watch suspiciously" (211).

The story closes with the meat burning and the wife pondering what to tell her husband about his dinner. She also indicates that she has discovered something during this cooking process, but does not elaborate further. The final sentence ends with an ellipsis, leaving the text open-ended and inviting the reader to fill in the blanks. What is not in doubt is the wife's personal journey to an altered place/space based on her reflections on her marriage.

"Cooking Lesson" is a work that collides with the values of the dominant culture that objectify, entrap, and annihilate women's sense of self. In this and many other works in which she focuses on ordinary women entrenched in domesticity, Castellanos's feminine discourse breaks through and destroys old myths, replacing them with what *is* possible, another way to be that is better than what was. Her pioneering efforts have slowly reached an audience that has caught up to her farsighted vision. As her friend and colleague the writer Elena Poniatowska has observed, Castellanos's life and works represent the strongest and most effective example of how women everywhere, by immersing themselves in their passions and convictions, can overcome victimization (131–32).

Works Cited

Ahern, Maureen, ed. *A Rosario Castellanos Reader*. Austin: U of Texas P, 1988.

———. "Reading Rosario Castellanos: Contexts, Voices and Signs." *A Rosario Castellanos Reader*. Ed. Maureen Ahern. Austin: U of Texas P, 1988. 1–77.

———. "Rosario Castellanos." *Spanish America Women Writers*. Ed. Diane E. Marting. New York: Greenwood, 1990. 140–55.

Castellanos, Rosario. "Cooking Lesson." Trans. Maureen Ahern. *A Rosario Castellanos Reader*. Ed. Maureen Ahern. Austin: U of Texas P, 1988. 207–15.

———. "Malinche." Trans. Maureen Ahern. Ahern 96–97.

———. "Meditation on the Brink." Trans. Maureen Ahern. Ahern. 111.

———. "Once Again Sor Juana." Trans. Maureen Ahern. Ahern. 222–25.

———. "Self-Sacrifice Is a Mad Virtue." Trans. Laura Carp Solomon. Ahern. 259–63.

WHEN LANGUAGES COLLIDE

Cruz, Sor Juana Inés de. *A Woman of Genius: The Intellectual Autobiography of Sor Juana Inés de la Cruz*. Trans. Margaret Sayers Peden. Salisbury, CT: Lime Rock, 1962.

O'Connell, Joanna. "'Buceando cada vez más hondo . . .' : The Dangerous Memory of Women's Lives." *Prospero's Daughter: The Prose of Rosario Castellanos*. Austin: U of Texas P, 1995. 172–206.

Oyarzún, Kemy. "Beyond Hysteria: 'Haute Cuisine' and 'Cooking Lesson': Writing as Production." *Splintering Darkness: Latin American Women Writers in Search of Themselves*. Ed. Lucía Guerra Cunningham. Pittsburgh: U of Pittsburgh P, 1990. 87–110.

Poniatowska, Elena. "Rosario Castellanos: Vida Nada Te Debo." *¡Ay Vida, No Me Mereces!* Mexico City: Joaquín Mortíz, 1985. 45–132.

ERICA FROUMAN-SMITH, REFLECTIVE PIECE

Rosario Castellanos's career as a writer grew out of a particular cultural context in which women struggled greatly to overcome the barriers of sexism. Any discussion of her writing must inevitably focus on the circumstances she faced. Yet, at the same time, the fact that her achievements came as a result of confronting obstacles contributed greatly to how and what she wrote. Ultimately, what one comes away with after reading Castellanos's work and understanding its context is an appreciation for the powerful role good literature can play in illuminating our own lives.

In structuring this essay, I wanted to highlight relevant texts that reflect her legacy as an innovative writer and thinker on feminist issues. But first, I must establish the important influences on her work. The introduction of the thesis statement at the end of the first paragraph establishes the direction of the essay—that her importance as a writer is intimately tied to the challenges she encountered along the way. The quotation from her colleague in response to Castellanos's death underscores the innovative quality of her work.

Since Castellanos's writing reflects her life, I wanted to provide the reader with some important biographical information about her. What also must be explained are the influences that shaped her vision: her reading of prominent women writers was fundamental to the development of her ideas regarding the status of women. I include quotations from Castellanos's essay on Mexican women to demonstrate the author's perceptiveness on the issue. The other point, that she is a product of her culture, is revealed through an examination of Castellanos's reading of her two most iconic female predecessors, Sor Juana Inés de la Cruz and Malinche. The inclusion of the poem "Meditation on the Brink" is linked to the title of my essay and illustrates Rosario Castellanos's willingness to confront the status quo.

The center of my piece is a close reading of the short story "Cooking Lesson," a work that is representative of Castellanos's writing at its feminist best. Here I wanted to focus on key aspects of her style—her use of irony, humor and candor—through the inclusion of quotations that illustrate that style. An important device to highlight the fact that the author uses to great effect is the incongruousness of situating an educated, middle-class woman in a traditional space. That the narrator speaks directly to the reader is another technique essential to the story's success, the result of which is quite powerful. Nothing gets in the way of the communication between the protagonist and her audience.

Castellanos's innovative use of a feminine discourse—a style in which her gender and her body are inserted in the text—is linked to the central metaphor of the work: her status as an object whose transformations run parallel to that of the meat.

In the closing, I wanted to sum up as well as connect the theme not only to the textual analysis but also to the larger picture of Rosario Castellanos's accomplishments.

"THINK. WRITE. ASK."

1. Erica Frouman-Smith points out for us that one of Rosario Castellanos' rhetorical techniques is to speak directly to the reader. How and where does Frouman-Smith adapt this technique into her own essay? Find a few passages where Frouman-Smith directly addresses her audience; find a few in which her address is more indirect, or technically distant. Which voice you prefer, and why? Are you more persuaded by one voice than the other?

2. What are some of the organizational patterns in "Rosario Castellanos: Charting a Course . . ."? As a reminder, some typical organizational patterns are: definition, narration, classification, comparison and contrast, and analysis.

3. Discuss "analysis," as used above: What is it, exactly? Does it mean different things in different academic settings? How do you decide what it means in any particular setting?

4. There are no headings in this essay. What are some benefits and drawbacks, generally, to using headings to separate and organize a text? How does the flow of this particular text benefit from not using headings?

5. Read again the essay's first two paragraphs, and decide on a few adjectives that best characterize Frouman-Smith's tone: serious? formal? humorous? dry? warm? Do the same with the first two paragraphs of Amy Wysoker's "Profession and Policy in Collision: Nursing, Risk, and Responsibility." Describe the relationships between the tones and the subjects being discussed.

ALL BEGIN

GUY WALKS INTO A BAR

POEMS
BELINDA KREMER
ART
ANGELA PISANO

all begin
guy walks into a bar

permafrost
cosmos
gesture
nothing
3 guys
string theory
horse
renter
translation
nylons
my line
sleepy
queer eye
nebula
hedgehog
sensor
notice
time

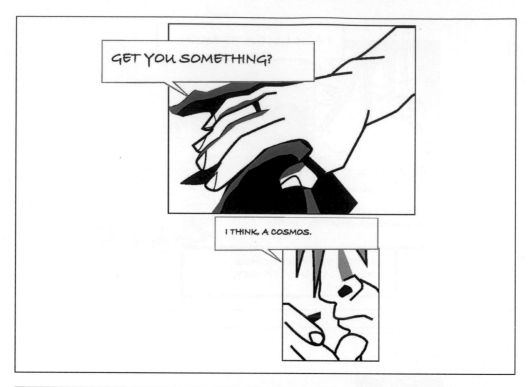

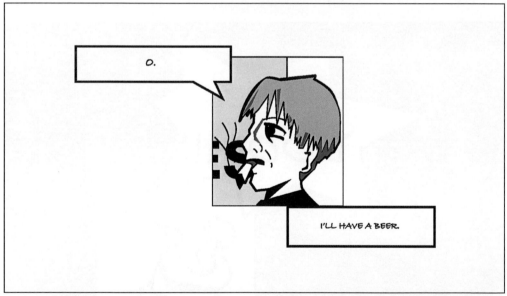

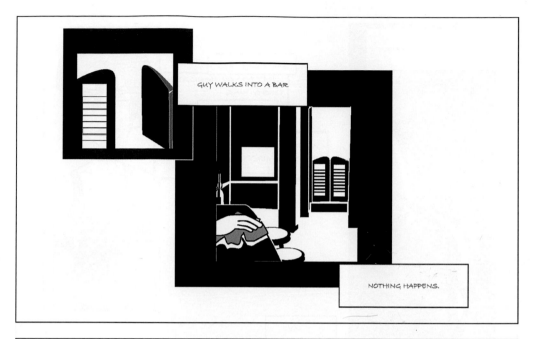

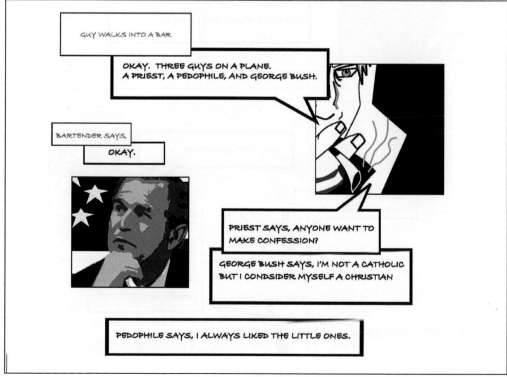

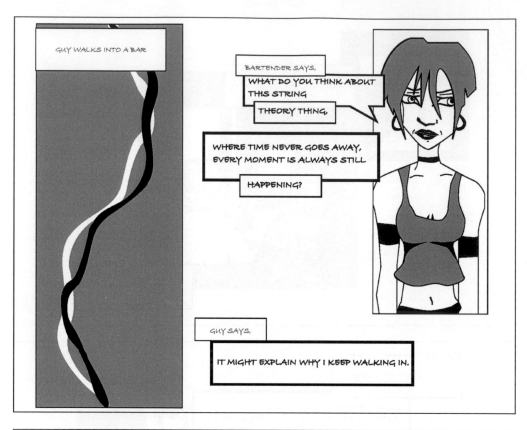

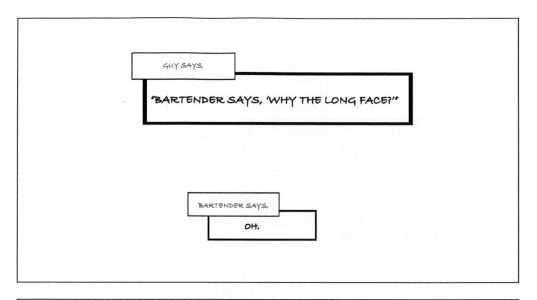

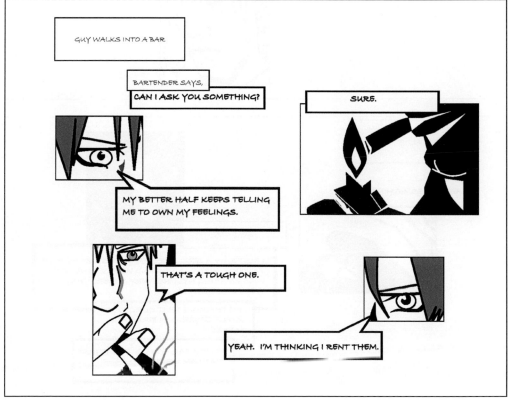

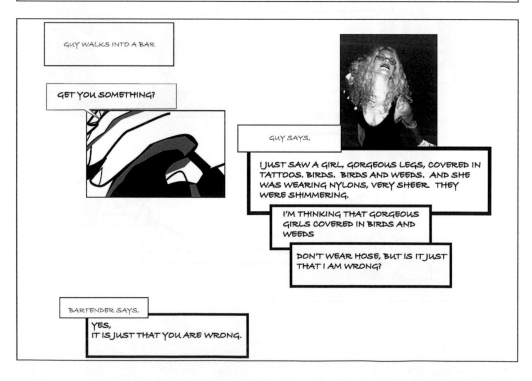

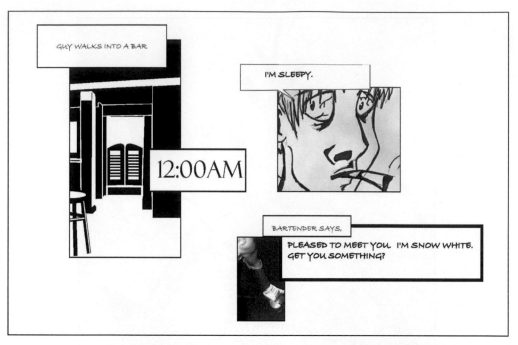

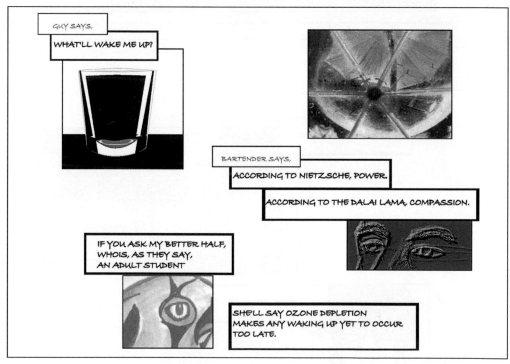

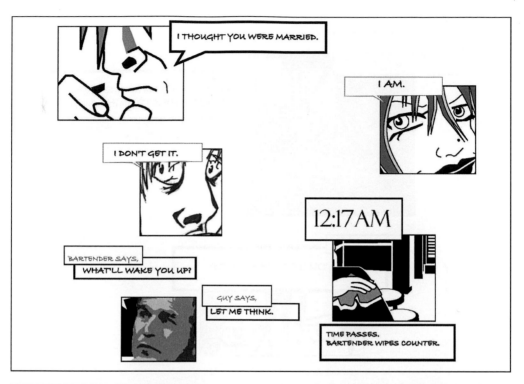

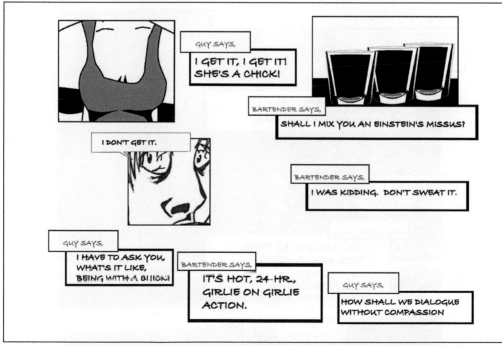

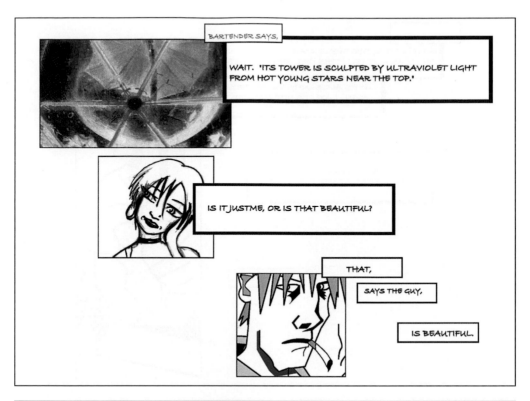

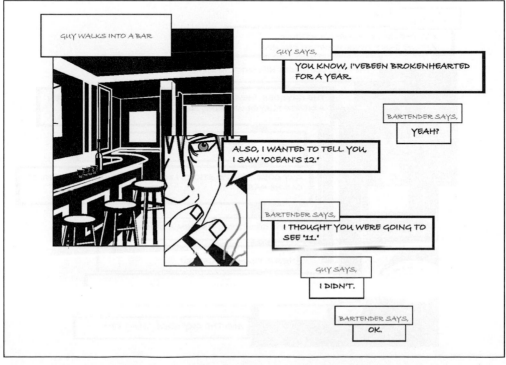

WHEN LANGUAGES COLLIDE

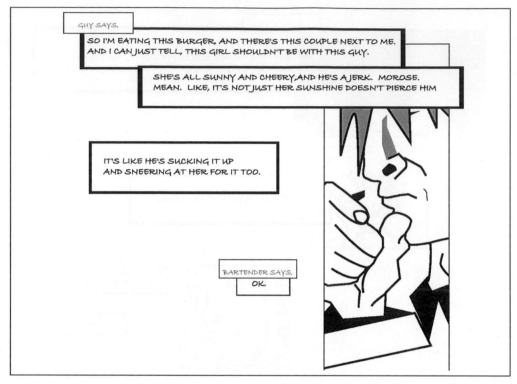

GUY SAYS,

SO I'M EATING THIS BURGER, AND THERE'S THIS COUPLE NEXT TO ME. AND I CAN JUST TELL, THIS GIRL SHOULDN'T BE WITH THIS GUY.

SHE'S ALL SUNNY AND CHEERY, AND HE'S A JERK. MOROSE. MEAN. LIKE, IT'S NOT JUST HER SUNSHINE DOESN'T PIERCE HIM

IT'S LIKE HE'S SUCKING IT UP AND SNEERING AT HER FOR IT TOO.

BARTENDER SAYS,
OK.

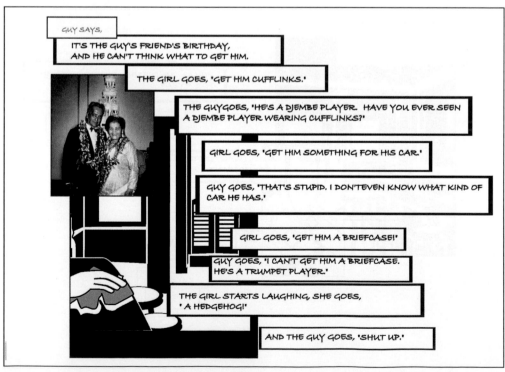

GUY SAYS,

IT'S THE GUY'S FRIEND'S BIRTHDAY, AND HE CAN'T THINK WHAT TO GET HIM.

THE GIRL GOES, 'GET HIM CUFFLINKS.'

THE GUY GOES, 'HE'S A DJEMBE PLAYER. HAVE YOU EVER SEEN A DJEMBE PLAYER WEARING CUFFLINKS?'

GIRL GOES, 'GET HIM SOMETHING FOR HIS CAR.'

GUY GOES, 'THAT'S STUPID. I DON'T EVEN KNOW WHAT KIND OF CAR HE HAS.'

GIRL GOES, 'GET HIM A BRIEFCASE!'

GUY GOES, 'I CAN'T GET HIM A BRIEFCASE. HE'S A TRUMPET PLAYER.'

THE GIRL STARTS LAUGHING, SHE GOES, ' A HEDGEHOG!'

AND THE GUY GOES, 'SHUT UP.'

AND I WANT TO TELL HER, I ALMOST TELL HER AS I LEAVE, 'HE'S NO GOOD FOR YOU.'

BUT I CAN'T DO THAT, RIGHT?

NO,

SAYS THE BARTENDER.

YOU CAN NOT DO THAT.

TIME PASSES.
BARTENDER WIPES COUNTER.

THE THING IS, JUST AS I'M LEAVING,
YOU KNOW THE LAST THING THAT HAPPENED?

BARTENDER SAYS,
NO,

GUY SAYS,
THE GIRL GOES, 'YOU SHOULD GET HIM AN I-POD.'

AND THE GUY GOES, 'WHO.'

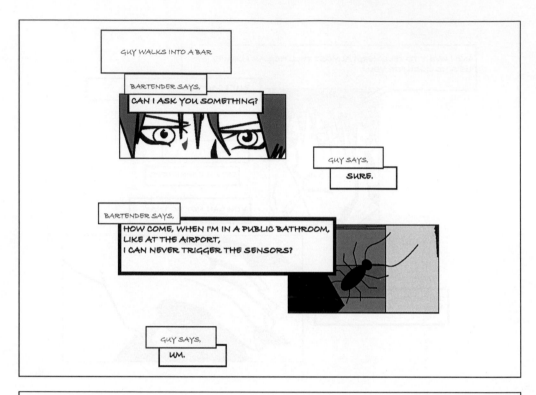

AM I NOT THERE? I MEAN,
WATER'S RUNNING TO MY LEFT, TO MY RIGHT.

I'M WAVING MY HANDS; I'M HOLDING THEM STILL.
WOMEN LOOK AT ME, THEY MOTION AT THEIR SINKS

THEY PANTOMIME HOW TO DO IT, LIKE I'M THICK.
THEY STEP OVER TO SHOW ME;

THEY TRIGGER MY SENSOR. I MOVE MY HANDS
OVER THE PORCELAIN; IT'S ALL JUST AIR.

I'M SERIOUS, MAN. AM I NOT HERE?

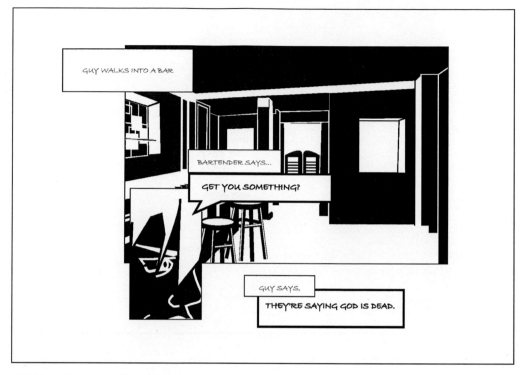

GUY WALKS INTO A BAR

BARTENDER SAYS,
HEY GUY.

GUY SAYS,
HEY.

BARTENDER SAYS,
LAST CALL

BELINDA KREMER, REFLECTIVE PIECE

All Begin Guy Walks into a Bar began for me in an atypical but beautifully
Romanic moment: I was actually that person who sprang awake at 3a.m. and
reached, groggy, for pen and paper, to capture something I just had to get down.
My tools of choice, in this case, were my usual tools for writing: one, a Rhodia
pad (BLOC RHODIA NO. 13), which I have around as much as I can, but occasionally just can't get, which is always very sad; and two, a pen of some kind, the
only aesthetic demands of the pen being that it doesn't offend my eyes, and that
it writes. "Writes" includes that it might stick, clog, blot, resist putting ink to
page; in fact, when I've had a pen for a while, and I get attached to it just as it's
failing, I am willing to put up with a lot as long as it gets something down some
of the time. I think you can be picky about one thing, or a couple of things, but
not everything.

So there I was, at 3a.m., and what was so pressing was this: "Permafrost is sinking Alaska in diamond-shaped lines / clouds without homes are squatting the
sky." We can say, as I just did, that I sprang awake at 3a.m., jolted by a moment
of Romantic inspiration, and wrote down those lines, and that's true; we can
also interrogate the groundwork of that moment, the set of associations and cir-
cumstance and practice that create the 3a.m. moment. What led to it? What led
to it was that 5 hours before, I'd read an essay in *The New Yorker,* or perhaps it
was a piece in *The New York Times'* Tuesday "Science Times," or maybe something in some collected works of John McPhee—in other words, I'd been paying attention to the world through some of my usual and favorite sources (and
if I were writing an academic essay or a conference talk I'd have to go verify
which right now, but I'm not writing an academic essay, I'm reflecting on my
process, which is the fun of this essay, and also of my chosen genre, poetry [that
is: Truth is required, absolute, and essential; but not, necessarily, factual])—and
because, the moment I'd graduated college, I'd ferried up to Alaska to work a sea-
son at Denali, and I had vivid, lived experience of the "drunken pines" described
alongside the sunken "diamonds" in whatever I'd read, and because, for some reason, I'd been thinking about *transpire*, to "give off" and also, "to happen" (though
a dictionary as recent as my ©1983 *American Heritage* notes that "[a]lthough
transpire in the sense of 'to happen' is in widespread use, this recent extension of
its meaning is unacceptable to a majority of the Usage Panel" [—who cares?!!]),
and because, after talking with my sister about a new ordinance in Santa Barbara,
to ban "overnight sleeping," i.e., to make homelessness a crime, I must've, falling
asleep, been thinking about action and place and outcome: their intersection.

WHEN LANGUAGES COLLIDE

(Reflective piece on reflection: I just spent 20 minutes reviewing the previous paragraph, whose final sentence is 250 words long, tracing my dashes [—] and open parens [( ] and parens within parens [[ ]] and close parens [ )], to make sure that while I was having a ball with the infinite, elastic possibilities and structures of the sentence, I was making syntactic sense. Which is for me the whole point of this reflective piece—& of thinking about language? of writing about what I was *doing* when I began *Guy* (though I didn't even know I was beginning it, then)—that we have so many ways to *make sense* and that how we *make sense* and *make sense of* the world through language itself is so varied in structure and investigation and innovation, depending on what we're trying to *do*—that tackling questions of ideas and style and structure can only ever come back the individual, to you: What do you want to do? What are you trying to say? And from there we begin our choices, and whether we choose existing, prescribed structures, or we start from scratch, or we do something in-between, we are simply making choices about what we are trying to do, and we are ultimately mindful of audience.)

So. How much can I say? I could write pages about what went into that first moment, of waking up and jotting down 2 lines that appear early in *All Begin Guy Walks into a Bar.* That's a possibility, but I can sense in me, and I guess in you, that we're about done with that. I could also—and I am going to—change gears entirely, and shift from the *macro* to the *micro*, directly into the aesthetic choices in *Guy*.

Here's what happened as I wrote *All Begin Guy Walks into a Bar:* There was the Romantic jotting. Then there was the waking up the next morning. Then there was, for reasons entirely inexplicable to me, the pressure, after deciphering what I'd written (believe me, this took a while), the pressure of the need to create a *person* who could *say*, "Permafrost is sinking Alaska in diamond-shaped lines / clouds without homes are squatting the sky." I think we can all admit that's not the way people usually talk. But someone had to say it. Meanwhile (apparently in alternate-universe collusion with my subconscious, unbeknownst to me), I spent a couple of really fun days being seized by the need to jot down bits of "guy walks into a bar" jokes, on napkins, fliers, receipts, and so on. Fine; that could be fun. Only: They were *weird* "guy walks into a bar" jokes. I was pretty distracted. I'd be teaching class, and I'd have to keep teaching while I wrote down, on a desk: "Guy walks into a bar. Nothing happens." What was I going to do with that? I didn't know. Or I'd be eating dinner while finishing a grant and be distracted by the awful couple who end up recorded as the story-within-a-story "guy walks into a bar" that ends with the absent boyfriend asking, "Who?"

Late in Day 2 of the Insistent Jotting-Down, I had an epiphany: One of the people in one of the "guy walks into a bar" jokes/poems was the person who would say, "Permafrost is sinking Alaska in diamond-shaped lines / clouds without homes are squatting the sky." I kept recording.

Something was going to happen here.

OK.

How?

You remember, don't you, that I promised the *micro* version here? So I'm going to keep it *micro*, though that's hard, because there's so much to say, even about a text that has as its beginning a dreamy out-of-nowhere inspiration.

Still. Here I try:

As I developed *Guy*, these are the structures I put in place: 1) I would adhere to the "guy walks into a bar"/joke structure, meaning: No back-story, no exposition; in other words, every episode had to function as a dramatic poem, all the lines being pieces of conversation between speakers. 2) I would strive, as much as possible within the oddity of importing joke structure into poetry, for a transparent language and natural diction for the speakers, even if the content (ideation) of their speech was odd and/or complex. 3) I would want to be funny, since "guy walks into a bar" promises a joke. 4) I would be serious, as counterpoint, and because that would be the interesting tension: To say something serious while being funny. 5) I would think about "guy" and "bar," and about our imaginations relative to those terms. 6) I would try to complicate those terms with alternate notions. 7) When I realized that I assumed the bartender was a man, I would investigate the possibilities of the bartender being a woman, thus commenting on my own stereotypical assumptions. 8) I would think of "bar" as a social, and thus potentially transformative, space (as is a poem), and would remain open to whatever developed in the series, even if it seemed strange to me. I would reflect hope about socially transformative conversations and spaces. 9) As the guy and the bartender were *emerging* as characters, I would stay away from *shaping* them as characters. I would try to remain as surprised by, and honest about, each of them as possible.

After about 10 days, even though I felt absorbed in "guy walks into a bar" jokes, and I didn't want to stop, I closed down the process of generating material, feeling that if I went farther, I would lose spontaneity: I could feel processes of *shaping* and *making* affecting even the "original" material. For poetry, that's death. If there's no process of discovery in the writing, how can there be a process of discovery in the hearing or the reading?

With 10 days of *Guy* stuff on napkins, fliers, and so on, I began. I first collated all the material physically, into a pile on my desk. I transcribed these jokes and images and bits onto the computer, remaining faithful to the date order in which they'd been generated.

It seemed like I had quite a bit of order going for me: a genre (*guy walks into a bar* jokes), a time limit, an idea about the speakers, a set of aesthetics.

But what a mess!

It took me about 20 hours to achieve a layout on the page that I felt confident communicated the back and forth between the "guy" and the "bartender."

Then, for each poem within the series, I wrote and revised and rewrote, for clarity, for rhythm, for pace; for narrative, for conflict; for adhesion to the genre. All "guy walks into a bar" jokes are jokes; they're also stories, and they have the demand of narrative (conflict, resolution; conflict; resolution; and so on). Poetry added the necessity of getting the most out of the fewest words; and the demands of surprise, discovery, and invention.

The preceding paragraphs discuss getting *Guy* down as language only, which is where it began, and which is how it still mostly lives in the world; at readings, for example, it is purely spoken-word. A few weeks after finishing *Guy*, though, I was reading a graphic novel, and I thought, "Why not a graphic poem?" The graphic poem excerpt you see here, designed in collaboration with Angela Pisano, has a whole, separate, compositional arc of its own. Angela rose beautifully to the challenge of creating art and a layout that would complement, rather than "illustrate," the text, since "illustration" would be simplistic and limiting. She and I—a visual artist and a poet—had to work out a language with each other, which we did by first creating a broadside of a different, existing poem, and hashing out there our different thoughts on why certain things worked or didn't. We had to decide on aesthetics that pleased both of us, gave Angela room to work as an artist, and enriched the language and ideas in *Guy*. In working out these questions, I came to understand more about my own text, and about the working style of a composer in another discipline. If you have a chance to collaborate cross-genre, I recommend that you take it. Or make your own chance.

"THINK. WRITE. ASK."

1. How might "language" be used to mean other than, for example, "Oaxacans speak a distinct version of the language"? Identify as many "languages" as you can in *All Begin Guy Walks into a Bar*. Describe the collisions or contacts among these languages.

2. Belinda Kremer describes the text she and Angela Pisano created together as a "graphic poem." How would you define a graphic poem? How is a graphic poem different from a comic? For a poet, what are some potential risks and benefits in mixing two "pop-cultural" forms, comics and jokes, with a "literary" form, poetry? What does mixing these forms imply about the boundaries and stability of these genres?

3. If you had to identify another text as "most similar" to Kremer & Pisano's, whose would it be, and why? By quoting from the texts, articulate concretely the similarities you see between *All Begin Guy Walks into a Bar* and the text you chose.

4. Anke Grosskopf, in her reflective piece, mentions *back story*; so does Kremer. What is *back story*? Try and list a few other genres and media in which back story is a way of thinking about narrative. Is it accurate to describe all of the reflective pieces in *Collide* as back story to the accompanying essays? Is there a back story present in the *Collide* text as a whole?

5. Barbara Shorter, in her reflective piece, describes what *motivated* her to do the research that underpins her essay. Kremer describes the process that generated *All Begin Guy Walks into a Bar*. Is Kremer's *motivation* also available in her reflective piece? What motivates *you* to write things you write voluntarily?

WHEN LANGUAGES COLLIDE

WHAT'S SHE TALKING ABOUT?:
POST-FEMINIST NOTES ON SEXIST GRAMMAR

Edmund Miller, Linguistics

ABSTRACT

Though there has been some insufficient sensitivity to the existence of women in the semantic choices of some writers, some feminists writing on grammar confuse language with sexual politics. Gender is not sex, as feminist theory importantly articulates, yet the false assumption that it is has created much of the barbarism and jargon of some feminist grammar. Issues discussed include the masculine as a common gender (jargonic *he or she* with ambiguous antecedents is distinguished from clarifying *he or she* with unknown antecedents), the generic masculine occupation words, the prefix titling system (covering *Ms., Miss* with movie stars,), the *girl/man* pair, and the feminine as a gender of animation. Since most of the new forms and usages are overcorrections and one new usage is sometimes working at cross-purposes to another, style sheets like the N.C.T.E. "Guidelines for Gender-Free Use of Language" arbitrarily and often awkwardly circumscribe a writer's resources without addressing any real issues in sexual politics.

There have certainly been many occasions when the careless writers of the ages and of the current age have produced English insufficiently sensitive to the very existence of women. But discussions of sexist language often collide with common sense.

The kind of material that requires the attention of monitors of sexist language and perhaps their outrage is cited by Julia Stanley in illustration of male semantic space in English in the N.C.T.E. book *On Sexism and Language*. Sometimes a writer begins by using generically words marked for masculine gender but then as he proceeds forgets that he was doing so and shifts to language which cannot be interpreted to include women. In this example from *Feiffer's Album*, *he* and *people* seem generic at first, then are interpreted to apply only to men:

First Satirist: A satirist can't teach people anything if he offends them.

Second Satirist: I offend them. They love it. I make fun of their wives. (Stanley 69)

Of course, this is humor, humor that depends on the reader's ability to understand traditional common gender usage. Jules Feiffer is perfectly aware of this fact, for if as feminists have argued, everyone interprets generic usages as applying exclusively to men, there would be no humor.

But in speech the chief result of the raising of society's consciousness about sexist language has been a self-conscious disruption of the flow of thought, with some people stopping to recast sentences with the fashionable jargon but no changes in subject matter or attitude. I have recently heard the president of my university quoting Henry David Thoreau before an academic audience to the effect that "Philanthropy is almost the only virtue which is sufficiently appreciated by mankind." The President felt it necessary to stop to point out that by *mankind* Thoreau meant *womankind* as well, effectively derailing his discussion of philanthropy to make a point about semantics that everyone in the audience was already aware of.

And even writers on the very subject of sexist language sometimes seem to lose sight of the main issue and take a perverse delight in writing women out of history. The comments of Ann Bodine on the 1850 Act of Parliament which adopted generic *he* are a case in point. A legal protection for women was being made explicit: all laws were made applicable to women even if all people were called *he*. All that Bodine can notice, however, is that the pronoun *she* was not granted generic status (Bodine 136). Nor is it absurd, as Mary Richie Key claims, that a state law reads,

> No person may require another person to perform, participate in, or undergo
> an abortion of pregnancy against his will. (Key, *Male/Female Language*, 42, 89)

While the principal is always a woman in an abortion case, a law like this one that said "against her will" would have a much narrower scope and could not be used against someone forcing a male doctor to perform a (voluntary) abortion at gunpoint—though such wording would still make culpable someone forcing a female doctor to do the same thing.

The use of the masculine pronoun in a variety of different situations has been misconstrued as a single political statement, and consequently several different types of confusion of grammar and politics are at issue. There are sentences that include indefinite pronouns to refer to a mixed group, for example:

When everyone had taken his place, the ceremony began.

The antecedent here is grammatically ambiguous, though the sex of the various persons referred to is presumably known to the writer. Despite feminist assertions to the contrary, the masculine pronoun here refers in turn to several persons, leaving the actual division of the sexes unstated. A similar grammatical situation arises with disjunctive conjunctions, for example:

Either John or Mary has forgotten to pick up his supplies for next week,

meaning that the supplies belong either to Mary or John—the writer does not know which. Anticipating feminist wrath, the most careful writers nowadays, however, would undoubtedly not use *he or she* but recast sentences of this second sort to avoid pronoun use entirely:

Either John or Mary has forgotten to pick up supplies for next week.

In speech, plural reference words are quite regularly used for both of these common gender situations. But *his or her*, *her or his*, and *her* alone (for mixed groups) do not occur in speech except in situations of strained self-consciousness about sexual politics, when the various members of a common class are spoken of in the singular.
But sentences like

The person who committed this crime, whoever he is, must be out of his mind.

are of a different order. The antecedent is not ambiguous since some specific person is referred to. The gender of the antecedent is merely unknown. In speech, plural pronouns ("they") are common for this sort of situation, but *he or she* occurs as well. Surprisingly, however, the common use of the masculine is also frequently heard, perhaps more regularly than with ambiguous antecedents. This is probably because sentences about antecedents of unknown gender are very rare and have an air of formal mystery about them that encourages speakers to search consciously for the best form.
A sentence characterizing a machine

She's on the blink again.

is of yet another type. Such usage ascribes animate gender metaphorically to something with neuter grammatical gender. This poetic device is common in the speech of people at all social levels. And except among certain self-conscious writers, the feminine serves as a gender of animation (as a way of bringing inanimate things to life for a moment). It is available for such use only because English does not have mandatory gender concord as many of the other European languages do.

Of the various usages, this last of ascribed gender is the easiest to understand and I will discuss it at length. It should be distinguished from another poetic tradition also involving conscious pretense—personification. This tradition, which probably never had much occurrence in speech and certainly now has almost none, makes recourse to the gender identifications of Greek mythology. About the only vestige of native Saxon mythology in Modern English is the idea of the man in the moon. Even so, the moon is usually feminine in the Greek way in romantic contexts. Among more common conventions that still occur in poetry, Death is masculine; the Soul is feminine. By a more general agreement, countries and geographical regions are feminine, so a sentence like the following might occur in a news magazine:

The South came into her own in the eighties.

And the use of the masculine pronoun for references to God should be accounted part of this tradition—a convention firmly rooted in popular consciousness. But most of the metaphoric conventions of tradition are not part of popular culture, and the full range of the tradition is a development of English literature after the grammatical gender of nouns and the article and adjective concord of Old English had been lost and after the native mythology of the Angles and Saxons had been forgotten (cf. Musacchio 23–28 and Gershuny, "Sexism in the Language of Literature," 107–29).

But in parallel with this development, popular culture also created a way of making poetic use of the disappearance of mandatory gender concord. Spontaneous animations are still indulged in by people in all walks of life every day. The gender ascribed to inanimate things for the nonce in this way is almost always feminine (Svertengren 261–92, Curme 112–13). The reason for this is that feminine gender (in distinction for female sexuality) is the gender of animation in English. The feminine gender is perhaps available as a gender of animation precisely because the masculine gender was already doing double duty as a common gender.

The National Weather Service's system of giving hurricanes men's as well as women's names (as had been the case), obviously a response to political feminism, runs counter to the natural tendencies of usage. The new policy will probably mean that eventually all people will return to using feminine pronouns for hurricanes with women's names but that less competent speakers may in the next generation twitter self-consciously over pronoun choice when faced with a hurricane that has been assigned a man's name. And it should be noted that it is the will-power and not the destructiveness that makes the gender of animation so frequently seem right with hurricanes. No reference to female destructiveness was intended in the first place, and the whole thrust of the feminist critique of hurricane names was radically unsound. A glacier is more destructive than a hurricane, but since the pace of its devastation allows man to get out of its way, speakers of English do not feel a pressing need for metaphor. On the whole, the gender of animation probably occurs far more often in contexts of affection than of terror. But with the hurricane it is power and self-direction (surely traditional male attributes in the human sexual arena) that produce the popular rhetorical tradition of ascribing the feminine pronoun, a tradition that antedates by centuries and in fact gave rise to the modern convention of assigning actual women's names to hurricanes. The pronoun *she* merely illustrates the animation felt in this force of nature. This happens whether the storm has a name or not. In the decades since the introduction by the National Weather Service of men's names for hurricanes, there has been a marked decrease in the use of the gender of animation for hurricanes, and I see no evidence of any use of masculine pronouns for the hurricanes with men's names, although as recently as 2006 I have heard a television newscaster use *she* in such a case. This impoverishment of the metaphorical richness of the language is undoubtedly temporary. Battleships are often named after men, and yet the feminine gender is retained as a gender of animation for ships so named.

Dorothy Sayers nicely sums up the folk understanding of the gender of animation in this passage from *The Nine Tailors*:

> "Jack has the honour of ringing the oldest bell we have," added the Rector.
> "Batty Thomas was cast in 1338 by Thomas Belleytere of Lynn; but she gets her name from Abbot Thomas who re-cast her in 1380—doesn't she, Jack?"
> "So she do, sir," agreed Mr. Godfrey. Bells, it may be noted, like ships and kittens, have a way of being female, whatever names they are given. (16)

WHEN LANGUAGES COLLIDE

To return to the genuine pronoun problem area: It is important to distinguish between antecedents of ambiguous (mixed) gender and those of unknown gender. Though such pronouns can certainly be cumbersome on occasion, they can be quite meaningful. A passage from the novel *The Last of Philip Banter* by John Franklin Bardin is illustrative: "Philip was as shocked to see Brent [which is a woman's name in this case] as Brent was to see Philip. They stood for a moment, each on his side of the threshold, frozen with consternation" (ch. 5, 396). Some would argue that this is ludicrous, a violation of natural gender. In fact, it is simply an illustration of the way Bardin does in fact invoke the masculine as common gender. To write "Each on his or her side of the threshold" would be to make the sentence about sexual confrontation when it is merely about surprise. And nothing would be gained in clarity—a great deal, indeed, would be lost—by saying "each on his/her side of the threshold." If anyone is troubled by this sort of sentence in the form that Bardin originally wrote it, he is free to recast—in his own writing–and say something like "They faced each other on opposite sides of the threshold, frozen with consternation." It is not reasonable, however, to demand that others recast their sentences in lock-step unison (as does, for example, Lakoff, "Language and Woman's Place," 45–80).

I have heard it argued as a serious complaint against the traditional, conventional use of the masculine as a common gender in English that children do not understand it. Statistics have even been gathered to support the likely enough irrelevance (Nilsen, "Sexism in Children's Books," 165). But were the resources of language limited to what children understand, a great deal would have to be done away with. If children do not understand the traditional system, they will grow up in language usage. If college freshmen do not understand the usage, teachers must explain it to them. Of course it is irresponsible to tell a freshman class that no one ever says *everyone/they*. But it is just as irresponsible not to inform students that many careful writers have traditionally preferred *everyone/he*. And what would be the status of the dangling modifier or the apostrophe if society were to adopt the usage of college freshmen, to say nothing of children, as a standard of excellence? Do writers and speakers of English want to throw over every literary nicety that is not the natural idiom of the untutored?

In fact, teachers have a responsibility to resist proselytizing for their own theories about sexist language to students, even while describing to them the current profusion of experiment in this area. To insist that students, especially those with pressing substantive writing problems, adopt rhetorically clumsy usage to avoid sexism that they do not even feel, is absurd. For indeed their writing indicates that they do not feel the traditional usages to be sexist. On the one hand, their writing indicates that they are not so oblivious to the traditional usage of masculine as a common gender as many feminist polemicists assert. Inexperienced writers are not always consistent with this usage, but it is not foreign to them. And on the other hand, except for an occasional (and typically awkward) *he or she* (masculine always first), the only approved non-sexist usage that ever occurs in freshman writing is plural personal pronouns to refer to indefinite pronouns and to pseudo-example singular nouns in generalizations ("The careful writer proofreads their copy"). Acceptance of this usage in formal writing has been eloquently championed by John McWhorter, but its occurrence in student papers is the result of ignorance of how formal written English differs from spoken English. In the long run, students who become good writers adopt the traditional patterns except when the style sheets of journals they publish in demand other usages.

Grammatical gender is not biological sex despite the fact that the word *gender* has recently emerged in real-world situations where sex is meant (Somers 19–25). Rules of grammar, in fact, reveal nothing about the relations of the sexes. Turkish, for example, has the much-wished-for common-gender third-person pronoun (Farb 163). But rash indeed would be the commentator who supposed on the basis of this fact that the harem girls of the Ottoman Empire led lives of greater dignity than the women who are professors at modern American universities, women who must suffer the lack of such a pronoun.

Current attention to sexist language is often at cross-purposes. Some commentators decry the apparent absence of women from discussions that use generic *man* and compound words with the suffix *-man* or generic *he*, reasoning that, if a writer talks about policemen or chairmen or fishermen, he is not allowing for the fact that these roles are now open to women (Nilsen, "Sexism as Shown," 34–41). Similarly, some commentators deplore forms like *poetess* and lady *lawyer* as calling irrelevant attention to sex (Bolinger 112; see also Lakoff, "You Are What You Say," 63–67; and Meredith 476–81). This second complaint is closer to the mark. It is undoubtedly true that at some time in history *policeman* and *chairman* and most of the other *-man* titles (though not of course the word *woman*) could, it was thought, apply only to men because they did apply only to men. But women had been serving as *chair* and *chairperson* for a long time before it entered common usage. No women's rights issue is moved forward by insulting the memory of such women now.

Similarly at cross-purposes is the prefix title *Ms.* The editors of *Ms.* magazine succeeded only too well in giving wide currency a title with a new-fangled look to address this non-problem. The problem was stated to be that women were denigrated by being forced to reveal their marital status in situations where men did not reveal theirs.

Of course, the introduction of the new title *Ms.* has not eliminated the old titles. As recently as 2006, the *New York Times* used *Mrs.* throughout its front-page obituary of Coretta Scott King (Applebome). So there are now three common titles for women, marking women as, if anything, more inferior to men than they were before, since a new subtlety has been introduced into the process of choosing the correct title for a woman but not for a man. In fact, feminist researchers have shown that the new variety of prefix titles for women has been reinterpreted by society to support sexist ideology (Ehrlich and King).

If separate were always unequal, then of course the thing to do would be to grant the prestige title *Mr.* to everyone. No one advocates this, although the lawyers' suffix title of *esquire* is now accorded women as well as men, and the air of strangeness has disappeared. But, in contradiction, *Ms.* is a title that more than one writer cautions against indiscriminate use of to refer to such people as, for example, a friend's grandmother (Miller and Swift 157). And Maureen Dowd notes the decline of the usage among twenty-first century professional women (54; 64–65 in rpt.).

It is also simply not true that women were forced by the traditional titling system to reveal their full marital status. In the twentieth century, not every *Miss* was unmarried. Before the introduction of the title *Ms.*, many career women—many academic women—used a surname and the title *Miss* though happily (or unhappily) married in private life. 'Miss' had, in fact, established usage as a career title on a fairly wide scale.

Miss was demonstrably part of the public consciousness in this sense before *Ms.* was invented. No matter how many times Ginger Rogers or Elizabeth Taylor married, the only title ever used for her was *Miss.* Even more indicative of fixed popular understanding of *Miss* as the proper title for a woman acting on her own in the world regardless of marital status during the bulk of the twentieth century is the fact that actresses and other performers who acquired their professional surnames through marriage were still always called 'Miss' during this period, never 'Mrs.'. This is the situation with silent film star Alieen Pringle, Roaring Twenties Paris nightclub performer Josephine Baker, 1950s sex symbol Jayne Mansfield, 1960s sex symbol Raquel Welch, 1980s sex symbol Bo Derek, nighttime soap star Priscilla Presley, and feminist icon Susan Sarandon, for example. This well-established usage of *Miss* represents a natural change that had occurred in language, since until the early part of the last century even actresses did not have names of their own–Mrs. Siddons, Mrs. Patrick Campbell.

The problem for English is that the modern world gives married women frequent opportunities to act on their own apart from their husbands, and they need a prefix title for when they are acting in this way. *Ms.* could fill this gap although married women are not using the title in this way. Women are clinging to the title *Mrs.*, though many are defying the etiquette books by following *Mrs.* with their own given names ("Mrs. Mary Smith", not "Mrs. John Smith").

Sometimes complaints about sexist language collide with the position of women in history. Mary Ritchie Key, for example, deplores a reference to Queen Elizabeth I of England as a "true prince" (Key, *Male/Female Language* 42). Clearly such usage should be applauded as non-sexist: *prince* is being used here to mean a ruler of authority, justice, and nobility of character. To say that since Elizabeth was a woman everyone must call her a ruler and not a prince is to circumscribe irrationally the resources of language. Key also cites as ludicrous the fact that Pearl Bailey received a Man of the Year award. There would be far greater cause for complaint if she had been ruled ineligible by reason of her sex.

It would be folly for English speakers to redefine occupation words to exclude women just now when women have expanded their occupational horizons. Yet this is exactly the implication of a form like *chairperson*. It says the user thinks women cannot make satisfactory chairmen. To insist on a term like *chair* or *head* for the person presiding in the chair carries the same implication and merely cloaks it in jargon.

Another collision of feminism and common usage concerns the term *girl* as a reference to a woman of mature years. While the usage is certainly sometimes a way of dismissing the contributions of women, much of the verbiage on the subject assumes that men of mature years are called *men* in contexts similar to those in which women of mature years are called *girls* (e.g. Key, *Male/Female Language*, 41; Gershuny, "Sexism in Dictionaries and Texts," 155). In fact, in at least one of these contexts men are called *boys*: *boys' night out*. Perhaps it is unfortunate that *girl* is used for female children, but it is unambiguous in context since no one ever thinks that female children are being referred to.

The slang form *guy/gal* is a possible pair, but to most speakers of English *gal* is worse than *girl*, more dismissive. And *guy* is achieving some real currency as a sex-neutral term among high school students and other ordinary speakers (not just feminist theorists). But this is the old masculine-as-common gender reality that upsets some people so about common-gender pronouns and the *-man* words. In addition, Daryl McGrath has described and validated the return of *girl* to general usage while still warning men off.

The 1975 National Council of Teachers of English "Guidelines for Non-Sexist Language" are a bellwether for what is wrongheaded with the original feminist critique of traditional usage and what continues to be wrong. Revised in 2002 as "Guidelines for Gender-Free Language," these guidelines, while claiming to offer no new dogmatism, in fact require a radical overthrow of living language patterns.[1] The assertion that -*man* words are now closely associated with male sexuality, for example, is contradicted on almost every page of any daily newspaper or popular magazine taken at random. That radicals advocating the new usages do not wish to clarify language but wish to reorder society at the expense of language is evident from the fact that, despite the wide disagreements even among feminists, editors of N.C.T.E. publications were originally empowered to decide for authors what is and what is not sexist language (National Council of Teachers of English 181–91). The N.C.T.E. concedes the student's right to his own dialect but, even in the revised guidelines of 2002, does not concede a similar right to the scholar: "In the case of language inconsistent with these guidelines, the editor's duty is to question the author's vocabulary or usage. The author has the right to insist on its use, but a footnote will be included to reflect such insistence." The *Guidelines* have inundated the pages of *College English* and many other journals with barbarisms, including in the first flush of enthusiasm the unpronounceable and therefore peculiarly offensive *s/he*, but they have ushered in no compensating millennium of sexual equity. Rational arguments in lucid prose are more likely to improve the relations of the sexes than word counts of *she or he* in learned journals. And editorial practices that change style for the worse are only unprofessional bullying.

Until non-feminist voices are heard on issues of grammar and gender, society will not arrive at a real understanding of the nexus of these topics.

---

[1] This is the unacknowledged truth of much of feminist grammatical theory. Rosalie Maggio, for example, has reprinted and expanded her 1987 list of sexist usage without noticing that she is redefining words actually used in ungendered ways or that it can sometimes falsify the past to impose revised gender language in historical contexts. A useful corrective to the narrow-mindedness of much feminist writing about grammar is provided by Eugene August's clear catalogue of the ways that traditional English usage shows substantial bias against men and not exclusively bias against women. See also Kakutani.

Works Cited

Applebome, Peter. "Coretta Scott King, 78, Widow of Civil Rights Giant." *New York Times*, 1 Feb. 2006, 1+.

August, Eugene R. "Real Men Don't: Anti-Male Bias in English." *University of Dayton Review* 18 (1986–87). Rpt. Paul Escholtz, Alfred Rosa, and Virginia Clark, eds. *Language Awareness: Readings for College Writers*. New York: Bedford, 1990 (rpt. revised in later editions through 2005). 289–300.

Bardin, John Franklin. *The Last of Philip Banter* (1947). *The John Franklin Bardin Omnibus*. Clinton: Penguin, 1976.

Bodine, Ann. "Androcentrism in Prescriptive Grammar: Singular 'They', Sex-Definite 'He', and 'He or She'." *Language in Society* 4 (1975): 129–46.

Bolinger, Dwight. *Aspects of Language*. New York: Harcourt, Brace, and World, 1968.

Curme, George O. *English Grammar*. New York: Barnes and Noble, 1947.

Dowd, Maureen. "What's a Modern Girl to Do?" *The New York Times Magazine*. 30 October 2005: 50–55. Rpt. as part of the chapter "How to Set Your Bear Trap in the Mink Department of Bergdorf's" in Doud's book *Are Men Necessary: When Sexes Collide*. New York: Putnam's, 2005. 15–76.

Ehrlich, Susan, and Ruth King. "Feminist Meanings and the (De)politicization of the Lexicon," *Language and Society* 23 (1994): 59–76.

Farb, Peter. *Word Play: What Happens When People Talk*. Toronto and New York: Knopf Bantam, 1973.

Gershuny, H. Lee. "Sexism in Dictionaries and Texts: Omissions and Commissions." Nilsen et al. *Sexism and Language*. 161–79.

———. "Sexism in the Language of Literature." Nilsen et al. Sexism and Language. 107–29.

Kakutani, Michiko. "The Word Police." *New York Times* (31 Jan. 1993): 9 (Style).1.

Key, Mary Ritchie. *Male/Female Language: With a Comprehensive Bibliography*. Metuchen: Scarecrow Press, 1975.

———. "The Role of Male and Female in Children's Books." *Wilson Library Bulletin* 46.6 (October 1971): 167–76.

Lakoff, Robin. "Language and Woman's Place." *Language in Society* 21.1 (April 1973): 45–80.

———. "You Are What You Say." *Ms.* (July 1974): 63–67.

Maggio, Rosalie. *The Non-Sexist Word Finder*. 1987. Recycled as *The Dictionary of Bias-Free Usage: A Guide to Nondiscriminatory Language*. Emeryville CA: Oryx, 1991.

McGrath, Darryl. "The Return of Girl." *Women's News* 2000 website. Rpt. in *What's Language Got to Do with It?* Ed. Keith Walters and Michael Brody, eds. New York: Norton, 2005. 371–74.

McWhorter, John H. "Missing the Nose on Our Face: Pronouns and the Feminist Revolution." *The Word on the Street: Fact and Fable about American English*. 1998; rpt. *Word on the Street: Debunking the Myth of a "Pure" Standard English*. New York: Perseus, 2001. Rpt. in *What's Language Got to Do with It?* Ed. Keith Walters and Michael Brody, eds. New York: Norton, 2005. 376–82.

Meredith, Mamie. "'Doctresses', 'Authoresses', and Others," *American Speech* 5 (1930): 476–81.

Miller, Casey, and Kate Swift (AKA Kate Miller and Casey Swift). *Words and Women.* Garden City: Anchor, 1976.

Miller, Edmund. "Name Reference." *The Missouri English Bulletin* 28.4 (October 1971): 20–24.

Musacchio, George L. "Milton's Feminine Pronouns with Neuter Antecedents." *Journal of English Linguistics* 2 (1968): 23–28.

National Council of Teachers of English. "Guidelines for Nonsexist Use of Language in NCTE Publications." 1975; Nilsen et al. *Sexism and Language.* 181–91. Subsequently revised 1985 and revised and renamed "Guidelines for Gender-Free Use of Language" in 2002.

Nilsen, Alleen Pace. "Sexism as Shown through the English Vocabulary." Nilsen et al. *Sexism and Language.* 34–41.

———. "Sexism in Children's Books and Elementary Classroom Materials." Nilsen et al. *Sexism and Language.* 131–40.

———. "Sexism in English: A 1990s Update." Paul Escholtz, Alfred Rosa, and Virginia Clark, eds. *Language Awareness: Readings for College Writers.* New York: Bedford, 1990 (rpt. unrevised in later editions through 2005). 277–87.

Nilsen, Alleen Pace, et al. *Sexism and Language.* Urbana: National Council of Teachers of English, 1977.

Romaine, Suzanne. *Communicating Gender.* Nahwah: Erlbaum, 1999.

———. *Language in Society: An Introduction to Sociolinguistics.* 1994; London: Oxford U. P., 2000.

Sayers, Dorothy L. *The Nine Tailors.* 1934; New York: Harcourt, Brace, and World, 1962.

Smith, Joan. *A Masculine Ending.* New York: Fawcett, 1987.

Sommers, Christina Hoff. *Who Stole Feminism? How Women Have Betrayed Women.* New York: Simon, 1994.

Stanley, Julia P. (AKA Julia Penelope). "Gender Marking in American English: Usage and Reference." Nilsen et al. *Sexism and Language.* 43–76.

Svertengren, T. Hilding. "The Use of Feminine Gender for Inanimate Things in American Colloquial Speech." *Moderna Språk* 48 (1954): 261–92.

This essay was inspired by an on-going concern for the little niceties of English grammar as feminist theory collided with grammar in the late 1970s. It seemed to me early on that feminists of this period had adopted a theory that rules of grammatical gender in English make a political statement of a sort that it is not even possible for grammatical rules to make. In addition, they had convinced an influential portion of the scholarly community that it was necessary to legislate changes in the appearance of scholarly writing that did not make it clearer, that often did make the writing less elegant, and that had no effect on the real-world issues legitimately brought to the attention of the scholarly community and the general public by feminism. The thesis that some feminists confuse language with sexual politics was in my mind from the beginning. I planned to point out that gender is not sex and to show that this false assumption has introduced a particular kind of awkwardness into contemporary writing.

The mode of discourse throughout is primarily forensic; that is, an analysis of evidence, explaining how a situation arose and holding responsible those who brought the situation into being. In addition, there is clearly a framing structure of polemic since feminists are blamed for grammatical innovations that fail to address the social issue claimed and that may have encouraged awkward prose style. While this polemic tone is perhaps alienating, it is mild compared to the polemic tone of much feminist discourse on the topic. Reasoned analysis seems not to get much attention in this arena. Accordingly, the conclusion is explicitly polemic.

A portion of this paper under the title "Sex and Grammar" was read at the 1979 Convention of the Council on College Composition and Communication, Minneapolis, 7 April 1979. This early version of the paper is included in E.R.I.C. reports, ED 177,603, 29 February 1980, abstract in *Resources in Education*, March 1980. At the convention session itself, the session on Feminism and Grammar had four male panelists and an audience of over a hundred women and one man. I was surprised by the emotional reaction of the audience. Several speakers seemed to damn the panel as a whole for my views although two of the men were actually advocating feminist positions that I was rejecting and the third was making a very narrow point (about the etymology of *-man*, I believe). I was not able to get the paper published at the time either because editors tended to give it to feminists, rather than grammarians, to referee or, even more tellingly,

as one editor remarked, because "Women might not like it." A curious standard
of scholarly exchange.

The points raised in that early version of this paper have not been answered.
Feminist grammarians have been unwilling to confront the implications of their
own theories, perhaps because feminist theory privileges personal feelings. If so,
this is a devastating critique of feminism as a theory that allows feeling to trump
thought. I have been adding bits and pieces of evidence to the argument over the
years.

The paper is organized by addressing in turn a number of issues raised by the
feminist grammarians: the masculine as a common gender, the generic masculine occupation words, the prefix titling system, the supposed "girl"/"man" pair,
the feminine as a gender of animation. The tone is perhaps provocative but no
more so than the tone some of the feminist grammarians cited in the piece. In
the process of revision I removed some of the more provocative language as perhaps better suited to oral presentation. I also cut a section on grammatical gender in other languages to focus more on English and to shorten the piece.

Both at the time of original writing and at many stages of revision, I had difficulty with deciding on the right documentation format since linguistics is a
discipline variously regarded as a humanity, a social science, and a science. For
the most part, I stay with M.L.A. style. I do so primarily because I wish to reach
an audience in the humanities, perhaps prepared to believe scholars in the other
fields are beyond reach.

The abstract serves as a map of the topics covered in the essay. The research
materials are very mixed, including both popular and scholarly feminist discussions of the grammatical issues as well as more traditional approaches. There are
also illustrations of particular points of usage drawn from popular literature,
including detective stories and newspaper articles. The feminist articles are
included to raise the substantive issues in dispute. The traditional grammarians
are included to describe the way the issues were understood before the Women's
Movement. The popular materials are included for yet another reason. It seemed
to me important to look at popular traditions because they are closer to unself-
conscious usage. Despite its innovative agenda, feminism seem to be returning
to the abandoned model of prescriptive grammar, the theory that scholars may
legislate grammatical correctness without the authority of usage.

"THINK. WRITE. ASK."

1. Edmund Miller describes his tone as "provocative" and "polemic." In the context of argumentative writing, what might provocation achieve? Locate a few passages where Miller's tone is provocative, aggressive, or polemic. What is the effect of this approach? Do you like this style in an argumentative essay?

2. Miller puts into practice his theory about the use of generic masculines as common gender forms. Find two places where he uses *he* as a common gender pronoun or uses a *-man* word generically. Did you notice these usages as you were reading? Did they strengthen, weaken, or have no effect on the persuasiveness of Miller's argument?

3. Choose a couple of other essays in *Collide*, and note how the authors deal with the grammatical issues discussed by Miller. Which choices do you like best? When writing a sentence containing "a student," would you refer to the student as "he," "she," "s/he," "he or she," or some other way? Alternatively, would you rephrase the sentence to avoid the choice necessitated by the use of the singular "student"? In making your choice, what factors would you consider?

4. Many writers and professional organizations advocate strongly for the use of bias-free language; such advocacy constitutes the counter-arguments to Miller's argument. Are these counter-arguments stated clearly in Miller's essay? If so, are they refuted convincingly? If not, what does Miller risk in not detailing the counter-arguments?

5. Miller's and Estelle Kamler's essays could be said to argue with each other. How so, since their subjects are quite distinct? How so, since Miller's essay originated in the late 1970s and Kamler's in 2004? What are some of the benefits of texts being able to argue with other across subject and over time?

WHEN DATA AND PERCEPTION COLLIDE: WRITING EDUCATIONAL AND DIAGNOSTIC REPORTS

Steven Nathanson, Special Education and Literacy

"Things should be described as simply as possible . . . but no simpler."

Albert Einstein

"Men are tormented by the opinions they have of things, rather than by the things themselves."

Old Stoic proverb

It was a familiar episode of a highly popular "crime scene investigators" television show. A team of forensic scientists intrepidly scour a dangerous, bloody crime scene, calmly gathering evidence. As they dust for fingerprints, gather blood samples and take photographs, they make broad but infallible leaps and propose hypotheses to explain events. The well-coordinated efforts of this team of individuals eventually get to the root of the crime and identify the suspect, between the final commercial block and the end-of-show credits. Another victory for science; another piece of justice done!

As a professor who has supervised graduate education students in literacy clinic internships, it is my responsibility to train clinicians to administer a variety of diagnostic tests, conduct interviews and apply screening instruments to develop a working case study plan for remediating a client. Such activities are roughly akin to educational "forensics"; clinicians apply a series of measures to build a working hypothesis to remediate successfully a literacy client. Yet, while forensics always solve the case, clinical work is more complex, and its instruments are by their nature limited in terms of reliability and validity. Sometimes, though, I have noticed what I think of as "the CSI phenomenon" creeping in. Each piece of test data is regarded as a vital "clue" to a working hypothesis and interpreted as such. In their well-intentioned and earnest haste to solve the puzzle, the clinical students may make erroneous causal leaps and assumptions about their clients. Yet premature conclusions or false assumptions based on improperly or incompletely applied knowledge of literacy processes "taint" the evidence and perhaps obscure rather than clarify the treatment. As Ekwall (1976) pointed out, "a remedial program that is not based on the results of a thorough

diagnosis is likely to fail." We know that literacy failure can be caused by a complex, interacting set of problems and causes—indeed, as Lipson and Wixson
pointed out: "reading and writing disability, like ability . . . no longer [should]
be viewed as the absolute property of the learner, but rather as the relative property of the interaction between specific learner and contextual factors" (*Assessment and Instruction of Reading and Writing Difficulty*, 2003, p. 52). Clinical
supervisors, professors, teachers and all others involved in the educational assessment and remediation process need to guard against the improper collision of
signs and symptoms revealed by test data, and make every attempt to produce
rigorous, objectively transparent, and clinically appropriate reports to their various constituencies. That goal, the execution of a clear and accurate written
communication about an educational performance, is the purpose of this essay.

I. EDUCATIONAL "FORENSICS": TESTING DATA
FOR EDUCATIONAL DIAGNOSIS AND PRESCRIPTION

Unlike television-based forensic shows, educational investigation is not a
60-minute exercise in serendipity, but rather, a slow and gradual process in which
the assessor must gather clues while avoiding premature and possibly erroneous
diagnosis. Thus, in "Assessment Literacy for the 21st Century," Stiggins (1995)
wrote that competent assessors must be skillful in applying five key principles of
assessment, which can be summarized as follows:

1. starting with clear purposes such as the need to identify individual needs
   of a student.
2. focusing on achievement targets such as understanding the content or
   proficiency level necessary for success in the classroom.
3. selecting proper assessment methods including a diversity of measurement instruments.
4. sampling students' achievement by looking at performance in a variety
   of the instruments and school contexts.
5. avoiding bias and distortion by reporting out the data in a clear, concise,
   sympathetic, yet objective manner.

The clinical interaction between client and evaluator and his or her client
can be seen as a form of action research for individual pupil improvement, leading to the development of an educational plan. Thus, Upcraft and Schuh (2002)
and Asselin (2003) distinguished between testing and research, with Asselin

defining the latter process as an attempt to gather evidence to create and then test hypotheses.

Katz, Earl and Olson (2001) noted that "assessors are caught in a paradox. . . . [Testing] attempts to serve competing purposes that are intimately bound to alternate conceptions of competence," since the very same tests used to label, partition and make judgments about pupils, classes, programs, or districts are supposed to provide information about how to help students and differentiate their learning needs. Katz, Earl and Olson believe that these competing purposes and conflicting paradigms of learning complicate how assessors use and interpret test data. One paradigm is the "top-down" theory of learning in which students are evaluated in terms of how well they've learned the facts and concepts of the culture. In this view, tests are seen as providing clear delineation about how well a pupil can give back these facts, and testing is aligned with curricula. Katz, Earl and Olson described a different paradigm which was developed from the child-centered educational philosophy of Dewey and strengthened by constructivist models of human learning. In this paradigm, new forms of data collection and interpretation are accomplished through performance assessment, portfolio assessment, and the application of benchmarks or rubrics. Thus, assessors hope to obtain data not on what is "known" or "taught" but on the "knower."

This paradigm shift, however, does not solve the basic problem of testing. As Crittenden (1992) puts it: "a test is anything in which a student is asked a question to which the examiner or questioner knows the answer." Thus, even if you apply Stiggins' assessment principles such as understanding the purposes for the testing, keeping an open mind, or sampling performance with a variety of performance data, the information obtained from formal testing inherently reflects what is taught, not what the pupil actually knows or how he or she thinks. The limitations of testing for certain populations of special need learners is central to Fletcher and Coulter's (2004) criticism of the "test and label" model for labeling special education children. These researchers instead proposed a "treat and then test" approach in case studies. Clarke, Madau, Horn and Ramos (2000) reviewed twentieth-century assessment policies and tests, and concluded that the new forms of tests based on new models of teaching and learning are not necessarily better than the old tests in charting pupil progress. Their findings cast doubts on the high-stakes testing programs used to measure pupil progress and assign certain pupils to remedial tracks.

Hargreaves, Earl and Olson's (2002) review of assessment reform (2002) also suggested that this paradigm shift complicates the use and interpretation of assessment data. Bourdett, Murname, City and Moody (2005) pointed out that little has been done to help teachers use assessment data to guide instructional improvement and outlined a professional development approach in which teams of educators evaluated individual pupils using multiple forms of data.

Assessment experts would not eliminate tests altogether; instead, they would have educators, clinicians, and evaluators make more informed use of tests and change the way we report and use test data. The recommendations of experts in the field of assessment and data reporting would have us avoid what Greenspan (2005) considered the overarching problem with testing: allowing tests to determine what it is that we value instead of applying observation and common sense. In the process of learning how to conduct tests, interact with clients, and develop a case study, clinicians-in-training and well-intentioned yet misinformed educational personnel often lose sight of these points, getting lost in the trees, instead of seeing the forest. However, this muddled vision is not always the fault of the clinician; during a case study, many factors contribute to potential distortions and misinterpretations during assessment/diagnosis, and these factors—limitations of tests and potential for examiner bias—are discussed below.

II. PITFALLS IN THE CASE STUDY DIAGNOSTIC AND REPORTING PROCESS

If the literacy clinician or educational evaluator, like the forensic examiner, had only the task of obtaining *physical* evidence and evaluating the evidence with an ever-growing host of chemical and technological tools, again like the forensic examiner, the task of pinpointing the problems and cures of the struggling student would be easy. Unfortunately, educators do not have discrete physical evidence, and the case study process is complicated by both the limitations of tests themselves and the competence, experience and skill of the evaluator. Before discussing what evaluators and clinicians can do to prepare and report case study data, I would like to discuss how the role of tests and the perceptions of the examiner complicate the assessment reporting process.

A picture or a snapshot is an attempt to capture a reality on film, yet it is a selective view. Similarly, tests can be seen as snapshots of learning, not learning itself, and thus, must be viewed with careful, informed detachment. How helpful is the data obtained from tests in providing insight into a struggling learner? If the picture is distorted, incomplete, or blurry, how valid a depiction is the picture? The "photograph" metaphor summarizes the concerns about testing and reporting raised by researchers.

A. Limitations in the test instruments used for case studies

In outlining an interactive model for case study work which stresses intervention, use of multiple forms of data, and continuous and on-going diagnosis, Lipson and Wixson (2001) pointed out that standardized tests are problematic because they focus on static and isolated skills rather than on complex performances, Lipson and Wixson base their argument on Resnick and Resnick's (1992) "decontextualization assumption": standardized test-makers develop questions by sampling curricular materials and devising questions that reflect content-based skills such as reading a map, identifying word meaning, or solving a math problem. Test construction is based on a fallacious assumption on the part of the test makers that a skill in a test accurately reflects instruction in the classroom or real-life situation. According to Resnick and Resnick this assumption can never be true. Diagnostic and achievement tests—instruments typically used in case studies by educational evaluators—are particularly prone to this decontextualization fallacy. Decontextualization is not merely limited to formal written diagnostic tests; it also applies to instruments used in case studies including informal performance assessments and informal screenings.

Because of the decontextualization fallacy, many researchers have questioned the validity and reliability of test information used for pupil diagnosis and placement. For example, Gunderson and Siegel (2001) studied the use of IQ tests for defining learning disabilities for first and second language learners and concluded that IQ tests may not be effective due to question content difficulties, which include culturally biased items and reliance on verbal interaction that penalizes certain pupils, especially ESL pupils. Also, in a meta-analysis of IQ testing conducted by Stuebing, Fletcher, LeDoux and Lyon (2002), they found that IQ tests could not be used to predict or label disabled readers. Similarly, Shaul and Breznitz (2004) found no difference between adult and juvenile readers and adult and juvenile dyslexics, *except* in speed of reading lists of words and pseudo-words. These researchers acknowledged that their experimental data did not simulate actual conditions and situations of reading. For some time literacy researchers such as Smith (2003) and Allington (2005) have consistently argued that the use of tests made up of isolated skills, such as decoding pseudo-words, makes it impossible to demonstrate that one type of reading method or material is more effective than any other for the teaching of reading, echoing cogent criticism against the National Reading Panel's Report on Teaching Children to Read (2000) by Yatvin, Weaver and Garan (2000) and Garan, Shanahan and

Henkin (2000), among others. Using the photograph analogy, researchers have suggested that test data is a snapshot, a "two-dimensional" representation of an instance in time, and not a complex three-dimensional entity such as the act of reading, writing, or problem-solving. Crime scene experts do not limit their forensic evidence to photographs; by extension, educators cannot rely on decontextualized test data for making valid prescriptive generalizations.

More sweeping criticism of using testing has come from psychologists and cognitive neuroscientists through studies of how the human brain learns. In the view of cognitive psychology, high-stakes testing and assessment programs have limited value for tapping into the immense potential and complexity of the brain. Brain research and advocates for differentiating instruction focus on the learner, not the teacher or assessor. As Caine and Caine put it, we must re-think who "'owns' information and how it reaches children" (*Education on the Edge of Possibility*, 1995, p. 4). Thus, a brain-friendly approach minimalizes testing and relies on differentiating instruction according to the strengths of the learner. For example, Caine, Caine, McKlintic and Climek (2004) pointed out that the brain can memorize facts and perform activities to demonstrate understanding, yet it is also capable of making intellectual and practical use of experience, entities that are not normally measured in any tests. Thus, Wolfe (2001) reviewed the different verbal and non-verbal memory processes associated with learning and indicated that tests measure constructs stored in our semantic (verbal) memory. She pointed out that "reasons for remembering and forgetting are more complex than repetitions of experience." Similarly, Spenger (2001) described five distinct types of memory systems in the brain which are combined and used differently in each individual. In her view, memory is an on-going process, and memories are made and retrieved differently in each learner.

Schenk (2002) suggested that because of the complex memory system of the brain, pencil and paper tests can only be used for items taught as pencil and paper constructs. Caine and Caine (1991) and Kovalik and Olson (2002) developed learning/teaching models reflecting the premises that: (a) each brain is a unique entity; and (b) each person learns and demonstrates learning in a unique way. Jensen (2005) presented a list of complex variables in the learner which may affect the test results, including: (a) quality and timing of the original learning; (b) degree of rehearsal of material prior to testing; (c) format of the test [essay or short answer]; (d) the test taker's level of motivation for testing; (e) the test-taker's ability to manage stress; and (f) the physical and emotional health of the test-taker. Although Jensen believes that educators and assessors can understand these factors and use them to advantage in testing, in reality, the case study clinician or teacher who administers tests does not always have the opportunity, the skill or the knowledge to consider these factors when conducting mandated pupil or case study evaluations.

In conclusion, relying on test data in case studies provides a "two-dimensional" snapshot view of the learner that can result in over-interpretation and faulty educational prescriptions based on limited data. Unfortunately, the limitations of testing instruments are not the only difficulties facing clinical assessors. The next section deals with another difficulty—examiner bias—which can, and often does, occur during and after the diagnostic process.

B. Examiner bias in scoring and interpreting test data

In discussing how case workers need to examine their prejudices and preconceptions when counseling at-risk youth, Manning and Baruth (1996) reminded clinicians, therapists and educators to look to themselves when they begin to label and make assumptions about clients. "Look to thyself" is certainly an important principle for literacy clinicians and educational evaluators when they base prescriptions on diagnostic data. Therefore, assessors and educational specialists have to recognize and identify instances of rater bias, during and after testing, and in the preparation of reports. Before discussing what assessors can do about rater bias, I would like to discuss the problem of rater bias in some detail.

One aspect of rater bias that I have found in my experience with literacy clinicians is the proficiency of the test administrator. Certain non-standardized tests and standardized tests are complicated to administer and score. In our program at C.W. Post, students are taught the rudiments of test administration and then do "action research" in the form of a case study. Supervisors evaluate clinicians on their testing practices, verbal interactions with clients, and expertise in scoring and interpreting test data. Clinicians' training in the use of test protocols and rubrics is extensive. However, these interventions do not solve the problem of inter-rater reliability. Dennis, Newstead and Wright (1996) identified three potential sources of bias that typically contaminate assessments: (1) when the student whose work is being assessed is personally known to the marker; (2) when raters tend to generalize about the performance of the student from previous performance; and (3) when the individual's performance on an exam is interpreted in the light of performance on other exams, the so-called "halo effect." Also, Shay (2004) noted that "assessors' interpretations are powerfully shaped in predictable and unpredictable ways by their disciplinary orientations, experience levels, and levels of involvement with students" (p. 307). Paris and Carpenter (2003) pointed out that Informal Reading Inventories (IRIs), commercially published series of reading passages used for oral and silent reading assessment, are among the most frequently used instruments in literacy case studies. However, Spector (2005) surveyed statistical data used to establish validity for IRI's and found that the test producers failed to demonstrate satisfactory statistical reliability between different IRI tests or different raters. I also recalled the words of an experienced reading teacher who has conducted hundreds of evaluations using an IRI: "The IRI information is only as good as the person administering the test." Spector is correct in urging school psychologists and clinicians to become "well informed about the limitations of these tests . . . and educate teachers about these issues" (p. 601).

Most educational theorists differentiate between sex, biological status, and gender, a social-derived role construct. Reeder (2005) pointed out that gender is developed through interaction (including classroom interaction) in which language plays a major role. Hunter and Chick (2005) stated that "gender roles are learned from birth, and shared assumptions about human ability, behavior and thought are said to affect the development of boys and girls profoundly" (p. 65). In acknowledging the role of gender and gender-related perceptions, other researchers have suggested that gender creeps into the assessment process. Dennis, Newstead and Wright's experimental study (1996) tended to affirm previous studies by Bradley (1984) suggesting that gender stereotypes are one of several forms of assessor bias that may affect educational assessments (p. 517). Also, Okpala (1996) observed student-teacher interactions in elementary classrooms and found evidence of gender-related differences. Teachers seemed to praise girls more than boys; however, teachers were also far more punitive in response to girls' disciplinary infractions and responded to girls' questions less energetically. Peterson (1998) studied teachers' perceptions of sixth-grade student writing, and found that teachers tended to view girls' classroom writing as being more literate and sophisticated than boys' writing. Tiedemann (2000) investigated gender-related beliefs about the mathematical competence of boys and girls, and found that teachers' perceptions of male and female ability are influenced by gender. For example, "teachers believe that girls are less logical than boys; boys more adept at problem-solving than girls" (p. 206). In *"Reading Don't Fix No Chevys,"* Smith and Wilhelm (2002) argued that educators often fail to recognize and thus differentiate the reading preferences of female and male readers. Thus, males often dislike and resist the fictional materials provided for female students, leading to the erroneous conclusion that boys are poor readers. Similarly, Riordan (2003) compared achievement of males and females in twentieth-century American schools, concluding that "males, not females" are increasingly on the unfavorable side of the gender gap in education [achievement] and developmental matters" (p. 369), performing less well than girls in terms of dropout rates, U.S. Department of Education reading achievement tests scores, and studies of writing skills. Riordan argued that negative perceptions about the skills of male students appear to accompany declining male achievement in critical areas. Whether or not the "gender gap" has been caused by a mismatch of student to materials or a complex set of interactions between teachers and their students, in my experience with clinical case studies, clinicians often fail to recognize gender or the mismatch phenomenon in interpreting case study data and making recommendations.

In conclusion, research has certainly implied, if not emphatically proven, that the assessment and reporting process seems rife with possibilities for distortion or misinterpretation, because imperfect data collides with a human observer. However, despite inherent pitfalls in both the instruments and the raters, most educators and researchers would agree with Popham (1995) that: (1) testing drives instruction; and (2) educators must be literate in the use and interpretation of test data. Because testing is not going away, the question becomes how to best make use of its data as part of an on-going process of educational improvement, as Lipson and Wixson describe it. Morrow (2005) pointed out that effective report writing is linked to this rigorous diagnostic process:

> In addition to adequacy of data, the adequacy of interpretation during the process of data analysis, interpretation and presentation is essential to round out the criteria for trustworthiness. Data analysis, interpretation, and writing are a continuous and interactive process, often leading the investigator back into the field for additional data. . . .
>
> The writing should also be characterized by thick [observable] description, and by clarity of presentation, and subheadings, tables, and figures used as needed to assist the reader in following the interpretation. (p. 256)

What can educators and consumers of testing data do to gather, organize, and report this information in forms that can be useful for instructional improvement? The next section of this essay consists of suggestions based on my experiences as teacher, clinician and clinician-supervisor.

WHEN LANGUAGES COLLIDE

IV. AVOIDING THE COLLISION OF TEST DATA
AND INTERPRETATION—WHAT EDUCATORS *CAN* DO

Rather than deny or ignore the potential subjectivity and built-in distortion in the testing process, clinicians and evaluators need to observe important conventions of written reports that help to minimize subjectivity, inaccuracy of interpretation, and bias. Therefore, in my clinic seminars, before providing training in how to administer various types of tests, I provide my clinicians with the following guidelines for reporting and writing about what the test data means. These guidelines are listed below.

A. Applying Ockham's Razor—the simplest explanation is the best

As Einstein said in the epigram that opens this essay, things should be described simply; however, "simply" does not mean "simplistically" or "inaccurately." Einstein was applying the centuries-old principle known as Ockham's Razor, developed by the thirteenth century philosopher and theologian, Sir William of Ockham: "entities are not to be multiplied beyond necessity" (Reese, in DeCicco and Allison, 1999). In the clinical testing/diagnostic reporting process, "what can be done with fewer assumptions is done in vain with more" (Cambourne, 2001, p. 784). Clinicians must therefore take pains to describe observations as simply and transparently as possible. Consider, for example, the following report remarks about results from an Informal Reading Inventory:

> *Clinician A*: "According to the results on the reading passages, James' cognitive processes for solving words include recognizing them, taking them apart, and putting them together at the 2nd grade independent level."

> *Clinician B*: "James' oral accuracy for second grade passages show fewer than 2 errors, at the independent level."

Clinician A suggests that James goes through some form of internal process for "solving words" by recognizing them in his head and putting them together. How can the clinician know the internal processes? Moreover, what indicators are given to prove this assertion? There are no provisions in the Informal Reading Inventory for the student to discuss or verbalize his or her reading strategies; these comments merely represent Clinician A's assumptions and extrapolations. Clinician B, by contrast, reports the data and specifies that it was based on one limited application. The person reading the data from Clinician B's report can grasp the context in which this data was derived and use it for future applications and instructional programs. Clinician A's information may or may not be supported by actual clinical intervention, and may actually confuse, rather than clarify, the subject's performance. As literacy expert Cambourne puts it, "'Keep it simple stupid' would be a loose [but accurate] paraphrase of Ockham's razor applied to educational reporting."

B. Taking Ockham's Razor one step further—using a transparent writing style

Undergraduate students and graduate clinicians alike should avail themselves of an effective, clear and comprehensive writing style guide such as the *Publication Manual of the American Psychological Association* (2001), better known as the APA guide. The APA guide is the 'gold standard' for research writing; however, its actual purpose goes far beyond mere conventions of citing references and preparing manuscripts for scholarly publication. The goal of the APA manual is to help the researcher, evaluator, or clinical report writer develop accurate, easily understood and transparent written style consistent with the principles of Ockham's Razor. "Inexperienced researchers tend to have unbridled faith in the strength of their results" (2001, p. 328); however, judicious editors insist and know that the strength of the research is its clarity and transparency. To that purpose, the APA guide provides explicit advice in elimination of all forms of bias and distortion, as the following abridged topic list from the table of contents suggests:

Expressing Ideas and Reducing Bias in Language
Orderly Presentation of Ideas
Smoothness of Expression
Precision and Clarity
Guidelines to Reduce Bias in Language:
 Specificity
 Labels
 Gender
 Racial and Ethnic Identify
 Disability (p. vi)

All sorts of researchers, from dissertation preparers analyzing massive amounts of statistical data, to the clinician preparing an educational assessment on a single struggling student, can benefit by keeping this point in mind and using a style guide such as APA. Also, in order to avoid the pitfalls of the collision of data and perception, the APA editors remind the research writer about stylistic "deadly sins." These "sins" include: (a) overuse of the passive voice; (b) pedantry; (c) artificiality (overuse of the conditional); (d) redundancy; (e) extraneous language; (f) excessive reporting and repetition; (f) lack of explicit detail; and finally, (g) poor grammar (*APA Manual*, p. 328). The following samples culled from numerous clinical reports provide models of how to—and not to—follow a transparent style consistent with Ockham's Razor, and the principles expressed in the APA manual.

For example, with respect to use of the active voice in report writing, compare the following Clinician 'A' and 'B' statements for nuance and tone:

Clinician A: "James was given the informal reading inventory by Jerry Johns for assessing his oral and silent reading accuracy and comprehension by the clinician."

Clinician B: "The clinician administered Johns' Informal Reading Inventory to James to evaluate his oral and silent reading accuracy."

The difference of these two statements is more than just syntactic subtleties. Clinician A places James, not the diagnostic investigation, at the forefront of her report by using the passive voice. Clinician B makes it clear that she is in charge of the investigation, and yet she effectively links the test to its explicit purposes, setting the stage for clear reporting of results.

Besides problems with nuance and tone associated with the use of the passive voice, clinicians and report writers have to consider the perils of providing "too much information." For example, compare the following pairs of statements about a spelling test.

Clinician A: "The Test of Written Spelling is a norm-referenced diagnostic assessment used to provide evidence whether a person can spell words in written form when dictated to them. The test has three purposes: (a) to identify if a student needs direct spelling instruction; (b) to record improvement in spelling and (c) to accurately record achievement in spelling with children who have learning disabilities."

Clinician B: "The Test of Written Spelling is a wide-range dictation test used to determine an overall level of spelling achievement."

Compared to Clinician B's clear and concise description of a test, Clinician A committed several of the APA's deadly writing sins. He over-applied jargon ("diagnostic," "norm-referenced"), committed several redundancies and made extraneous, if not preposterous assertions. What student, for example, would not benefit from direct instruction in spelling? 'A' provides a broad menu of purposes of the instrument, although the specific purpose for his client is not given. Furthermore, he incorrectly calls the test "diagnostic," which it is not.

Also, clinicians who present data as a neutral window on the performance of a student need to remember that the conditional—'might' or 'should' statements about data or the client—have no place in transparent, neutral report prose. Both Clinician A and Clinician B in the following examples mix data reporting with behavioral analysis and prescriptive comments:

Clinician A: "Lindsay's average reading rate on the silent reading passages was 136 words per minute although she should be reading easier material in order to develop fluency and confidence."

Clinician B: "Chris scored at the frustration level for comprehension at the 7th grade level, although Chris' response to questions might vary because he seemed to prefer stories about war to stories about animals."

Statements such as "Lindsay should be reading easier material" mix data reporting with diagnosis and treatment. An important convention of research writing, which is followed in clinical practice, is to separate descriptions of performance from recommendations. For example, researchers typically have a 'results' or 'findings' section in a scientific study or dissertation which precedes and is separated from the discussion and recommendation sections. The use of discrete sub-sections is another way to achieve clarity and organization in writing when the data covers experiments using massive population samples; it also applies in a clinical case study of a single individual. When the clinician separates findings from her behavioral observations, judgments and recommendations, the reader of the report is in a better position to understand and apply or test this information during clinical intervention. As can be seen from Clinician B's statement above, unless Clinician B has corroborating evidence or has surveyed her client Chris to determine reading preferences or dislikes, her speculations or prescriptions concerning Chris's fluency are over-interpretation, a classic collision between what the data says and her perception about what Chris needs in order to become a successful reader.

C. Avoiding labels—using adjectives and terminology cautiously

In an analysis of why labels and literacy jargon often confuse rather than enlighten the clinical practitioner, Bontrager (2004) points out that the over-use of terminology (a) fosters an erroneous belief that there is one correct way of doing something; (b) puts labels on pupils in a manner that is false to the uniqueness of individuals; and (c) fosters "diagnosogenic," i.e., fragmented descriptions of symptoms. Bontrager would have us eliminate not the report-ing of data but the use of educational labels. As he puts it, labels, adjectives, and "current fads" in diagnostic terminology are flaws that confuse rather than clarify:

> Mothers read articles about 'reversal,' 'word blindness,' 'eye movements,' 'attention span,' etc., and come to the clinic prepared to name the demons with which little Willie is afflicted. I interview mother, teacher and child individually and in their responses to my question, "What do you think is the difficulty?" they parrot the same mysteries. (p. 500)

Bontrager's anecdote would be corroborated by style manuals such as the APA guide. The APA guide devotes a whole chapter to helping writers express ideas clearly, stating that carefully crafted, clear and transparent prose contributes as much to the body of scientific research as the experiment itself. Accordingly, in the clinical seminars, I remind my clinicians that: (a) adjectives, jargon and labels are a trap; (b) scores and descriptive terms must be carefully used and presented; (c) descriptions should focus on behaviors observed; (d) tables and charts must be accompanied by narrative explanations; (e) multiple sets of scores must be described in a descending or ascending order; (f) the sty-listic voice and audience for the clinical report must always be considered. How these guidelines help to avoid the collision of data and perception fol-lows below.

I remember an English teacher in a writing process workshop years ago requir-ing us to write a paragraph without adjectives, "Hemingway-style." No reader would confuse a clinical case study report with *Farewell to Arms;* however, the trainer's point remains valid: adjectives can confuse, label, or limit. In striving for transparency and objectivity, the clinician should strive to use adjectives as spar-ingly as possible. Consider the following pairs of report statements:

Clinician A: "Kristi achieved excellent results on the Test of Written Spelling, scoring at the 98th national percentile rank."

Clinician B: "Kristi is a phenomenal speller. She got the surprising score of 98th percentile on the Test of Written Spelling."

As can be seen in this pair of statements, Clinician A uses the word 'excellent' but quickly identifies the source of the excellence, Kristi's high test score. Clinician B, by contrast, makes the broad, if not unsupportable, statement that Kristi is a phenomenal speller, and then, in the next sentence, suggests that Kristi's score 'surprised' him. What is the basis for this surprise? Has Kristi demonstrated solid performance on spelling quizzes in the classroom? Has she handed in exemplary classroom essays or gotten an 'A' in English? Or has the clinician never encountered a speller with a 98th percentile score? We'll never know, and the reader should not be asked to speculate about the source of the surprise during a clinical case study investigation.

Another descriptive pitfall is an error of omission: failure to describe, in the narrative text, a bit of statistical data presented in a table. Thus, consider the following table (Table 1) from a Slosson Intelligence Test (revised edition) report:

Table 1

Total Standard Score	Classification of Intelligence	Mean Age Equivalent	Percentile Rank	Stanine	Confidence Interval [@ .95]
104	Average	9.8 yrs.	59%	5	96–112

Each one of these statistical constructs given in the score table needs to be described and explained in the text of a report through simple explanations of what each of the different statistics means, as well as the descriptor in the 'classification of intelligence' column. Attention to these details demonstrates clear understanding of stylistic voice as well as the audience for the report. While a school psychologist or test expert would understand these statistics, the parent or child advocate reading the report would need explanation going beyond mere numbers. Therefore, the rule of thumb *"If it's in the table, explain it in the report"* is an important principle for considering the varied constituencies who make up the audience for a diagnostic report: parents, lay advocates, general educators, specialized school support personnel, and psychologists. The report writer who

WHEN LANGUAGES COLLIDE

does not fully and clearly describe the data may cause more harm than if he had given no data at all.

Descriptive language used to label or classify can also have a downside: implying exclusion, discrimination, and bias. With respect to labeling by educational classification, race, group or gender sexual-preference, the APA publication guide cautions: "A common occurrence in scientific writing is that participants in a study tend to lose their individuality by being broadly categorized as objects or in the case of disabilities . . . equated with their conditions—amnesiacs, depressives, learning disabled" (p. 63). When labels are necessary, the APA recommends "balancing sensitivity, clarity and parsimony" of language (p. 64). In the statement below, note how Clinician A subjectively interjects his own prejudices about Kristie's performance, while Clinician B more neutrally applies a descriptive label drawn from the investigation:

Clinician A: "Kristi's IQ score on the Slosson Test of Intelligence was 78, indicating Kristi is mentally handicapped and should be placed in specialized slow learner classes."

Clinician B: "At this time, Kristi's total IQ score on the Slosson Test of Intelligence was 78, at the borderline mentally handicapped range."

Standardized tests such as the Slosson Intelligence Test (2001) provide psychologists and clinicians with tables of empirically determined norms and descriptive terms associated those number values. These are based on a bell curve distribution and their derivation and use is described in the examiner's manual. An IQ score of 78 falls within the 'borderline mentally handicapped' range of the distribution. Both Clinician A and B took the label 'borderline MH" from the manual; however, there are important differences. Clinician B correctly juxtaposed the IQ score and the appropriate label. Clinician A, however, described the subject, not her educational condition, and inserted a placement recommendation as well. In the real world of a CSE meeting, school-based support team conference, or parent-teacher consultation, such prescriptive statements might be incorrect, redundant, inflammatory, or all three.

When sets of data such as item analyses or sub-scores of multi-part diagnostic tests must be provided in a report, descriptors should be used correctly and the narrative re-organize the information for the reader. Note how data in the following table are presented in the diagnostic report:

Table 2   Chris' Slosson Item Analysis Results

Question Type	Percentage Correct	Classification of Results
Vocabulary	33%	Average
General information	54%	Average
Similarities & differences	89%	High
Comprehension of social cues	25%	Below Average
Quantitative reasoning	95%	High
Auditory memory/ recall	25%	Below Average

Clinician C: "An item analysis of questions was conducted and the percentage of questions correct to questions attempted is displayed in Table 2. Percentages indicate Chris scored at the high range in questions of quantitative reasoning and similarity/difference comparison. He scored in the average range in vocabulary-related items and questions of general information. Chris scored at the below average range in questions of recall (auditory memory) and comprehending socially appropriate behavior."

In the above narrative, Clinician C presented the item analysis percentages in descending order. By receiving data in this manner, the reader is able to note the subject's performance strengths and weaknesses. Sets of data organized in ascending or descending order provide another window on the subject's performance, facilitating pattern detection and assisting in the intervention process.

The reporting of client test behaviors also requires careful practice. In my clinic seminars, clinicians are instructed to report client behavior during the testing process as a means of supporting or qualifying a particular performance. Compare the following pair of report statements in which the first statement focuses on observable, obtained behaviors, and the second reveals internal speculation and descriptive vagueness:

Clinician A: "James appeared relaxed and comfortable during testing. He remained smiling and attentive throughout the testing session. When he did not know an answer, he made several attempts to answer or verbally elaborate a response until the examiner told him, 'pass.'"

Clinician B: "Max disliked the test because he didn't do well. Results are due, in part, to a lack of motivation on his part."

WHEN LANGUAGES COLLIDE

Clinician A concentrates on describing, to the best of his ability, James' body language and verbal comments during the testing period. Whether James' scores were high or low, or whether or not James' intelligence is commensurate with his actual school performance or behavior, we have reason, based on the examiner's observations, to accept the accuracy of this testing session. By contrast, Clinician B's statements provide no corroboration about Max's state of mind and opinions; one can neither prove nor refute the evidence that this performance represents Max's sincere best. Test objection sustained: speculative statement by the clinician!

D. Technical precision—going beyond editing skills into the caring zone

Sanacore (2004) wrote about the importance of providing a "caring" attitude for literacy learners: "An important aspect of genuine caring is for educators to persevere in developing an understanding of and a sensitive response to their students' culture." Indeed, the use of appropriate clinical labels, adoption of neutral, bias-free language and avoidance of unsupported assumptions do more than demonstrate respect for scholarly convention or political correctness—they demonstrate the caring of the clinician, teacher or evaluator. As the APA manual points out, grammatically correct, concise writing helps the reader better understand and make use of the data in the report for future research. However, common errors such as misplaced or dangling modifiers, errors of subject and verb agreement, improper verb tense shifts, lack of parallel structure, and improper pronoun referents cloud the window of transparency and comprehensibility in case study reports. A precise and concise report demonstrates a caring, professional attitude and attention to detail consistent with a successful conclusion of the "educational forensics"; however, it transcends the sum of its well-written parts. Therefore, by exerting tight editorial control in the final product, the clinician demonstrates what Morrow (2005) identified as ethical standards for quality clinical reporting: "validity, credibility, rigor or trustworthiness." In clinical seminars, my graduate students discuss the importance of establishing empathy and rapport with the client and client's caregiver early in the assessment and intervention process. When we write in a culture-free, bias-free and technically transparent manner, we extend that clinician-client empathy to a third party: the reader. A diagnostic report that avoids the collision between data and perception is faithful to the ultimate goal of assessment: changing the life of a struggling learner by facilitating educational improvement.

References

Allington, R. (2005, December/ 2006, January). What counts as evidence in evidence-based education? *Reading Today*, 16.

American Psychological Association. (2001). *The Publications Manual of The American Psychological Association* (5th ed.). Washington, D.C.

Asselin, M. (2003). Assessment issues and recommendations. *Teacher Librarian, 30*(5), 52–54.

Bontrager, O. R. (2004). Re-education in reading: A report on applications of general semantics in remedial work in reading. *Et Cetera, 61*(4), 494–503.

Boudett, K. P, Murnane, R. J. City, E. & Moody, L. (2005). Teaching educators how to use student assessment data to improve instruction. *Phi Delta Kappan, 86*(9), 700–706.

Caine, R. N., & Caine, G. (1997). *Education on the edge of possibility*. Alexandria, VA: Association for Supervision & Curriculum Development.

Caine, R. N., Caine, G., McClintik C., & Klimek, K. (2005). *12 brain/mind principles in action: The fieldbook for making connections, teaching, and the human brain*. Thousand Oaks, CA: Corwin Press.

Cambourne, B. (2001). Why do some students fail to learn to read? Ockham's razor and the conditions of learning. *Reading Teacher, 54*(8), 784–786.

Clarke, M. L., Madaus, G. F., Horn, C. L, & Ramos, M. A. (2000). Retrospective on educational testing and assessment in the 20th century. *Journal of Curriculum Studies, 32*(2), 159–181.

Daniel, L. G., & King, D. A. (1998). Knowledge and use of testing and measurement literacy of elementary and secondary teachers. *Journal of Educational Research, 91*(6), 331–345.

DeCicco, E., & Allison, J. (1999). Ockham's razor applied: It's mission clutter. *Childhood Education, 75*(5), 273–275.

Dennis, I., Newstead, S. E., & Wright, D. E. (1996). A new approach to exploring biases in educational assessment. *British Journal of Psychology, 87*(4), 515–535.

Einstein, Albert. Quoted in Are Jews Smarter? Why the controversial new study of Jewish intelligence has everybody plotzing. *New York Magazine*, Oct. 24, 2005, 30–35; 158.

Ekwall, E. E. (1977). *Diagnosis and remediation of the disabled reader*. Boston: Allyn & Bacon.

Fletcher, J. M., Coulter, W. A., Reschly, D. J., & Vaughn, S. (2004). Alternative approaches to the definition and identification of learning disabilities; Some questions and answers. *Annals of Dyslexia, 54*(2), 304–332.

Garan, E., Shanahan, T., & Henkin, R. (2001). What does the report of the national reading panel really tell us about teaching phonics? *Language Arts, 79*(1), 61–73.

Greenspan, S. I. (2005). The problem with diagnostic labels. *Scholastic Early Childhood Today, 19*(6), 18–19.

Gunderson, L., & Siegel, L. S. (2001). The evils of the use of I.Q. tests to define learning disabilities in first- and second-language learners. *The Reading Teacher, 55*(1), 48–55.

Hargreaves, A., Earl, L, & Schmidt, M. (2002). Perspectives on alternative assessment reform. *American Educational Research Journal, 39*(1), 69–95.

Jensen, E., & Dabney, M. (2000). *Learning smarter: The new science of teaching*. San Diego, CA: The Brain Store.

Katz, S., Earl, L., & Olson, D. (2001). The paradox of classroom assessment: A challenge for the 21st century. *McGill Journal of Education*, *36*(1), 13–26.

Kovalik, S. J., and Olsen, K. D. (2002). *Exceeding expectations: A user's guide to implementing brain research in the classroom* (2nd ed). Covington, WA: Books for Educators.

Lipson, M. Y., & Wixson, K. (2003). *Assessment & instruction of reading and writing disability: An interactive approach.* Boston, MA: Pearson Educational Publishing.

Manning, L., & Baruth, L. G. (1996). Learners at risk: Three issues for educators. *The Clearing House*, *69*(4), 239–242.

Miller, R. (2005). Integrative learning and assessment. *Peer Review*, *7*(4), 11–16.

Morrow, S. L. (2005). Quality and trustworthiness in qualitative research in counseling psychology. *Journal of Counseling Psychology*, *52*(2), 250–260.

National Institute of Child Health & Human Development. (2000). *Report of the national reading panel: Teaching children to read.* Washington, D.C.: U.S. Department of Health and Human Services.

Nicholson, C. L, & Hibpshmann, T. L. (Eds.). (2002). *Slosson Intelligence Test-Revised.* East Aurora, NY: Slosson Educational Publications.

Okpala, C. O. (1996). Gender-related differences in classroom interactions. *Journal of Instructional Psychology*, *23*, 275–285.

Paris, S. G. (2005). Reinterpreting the development of reading skills. *Reading Research Quarterly*, *40*(2), 184–202.

Popham, W. J. (1995). *Classroom assessment: What teachers need to know.* Boston: Allyn & Bacon.

Reeder, H. M. (2005). Exploring male-female communications: Three lessons on gender. *Journal of School Health*, *75*(3), 115–117.

Resnick, L. B. & Resnick, D. L. (2003). Assessing the thinking curriculum: New tools for educational reform. In M. Y. Lipson, K. Wixson (Eds.). *Assessment & instruction of reading and writing disability: An interactive approach.* Boston: Pearson Educational Publishing.

Riordan, C. (2003). Failing in school? Yes; victims of war? No. *Sociology of Education*, *76*(4), 369–372.

Ross, S. (2002). Becoming a good consumer of evidence. *Principal Leadership*, *3*(2), 10–12.

Sanacore, J. (2004). Genuine caring and literacy learning for African American children. *The Reading Teacher*, *57*(8), 744–753.

Shaul, S. M., & Breznitz, Z. (2004). Electrocortical measures during a lexical decision task: A comparison between elementary school-aged normal and dyslexic readers and adult normal and dyslexic readers. *The Journal of Genetic Psychology*, *165*(4), 399–424.

Shay, S. B. (2004). The assessment of complex performance: A socially situated interpretive act. *Harvard Educational Review*, *74*(3), 307–329.

Smith, F. (2003). *Unspeakable acts, unnatural practices; Flaws and fallacies in "scientific" reading instruction.* Portsmouth, NH: Heinemann.

Smith, M. W., & Wilhelm, J. D. (2002). *"Reading don't fix no chevys": Literacy in the lives of young men.* Portsmouth, NH: Heinemann.

Spector, J. E. (2005). How reliable are informal reading inventories? *Psychology in the Schools*, *42*(6), 593–603.

Sprenger, M. (1999). *Learning and memory: The brain in action.* Alexandria, VA: Association for Supervision & Curriculum Development.

Stiggins, R. J. (1995). Assessment literacy for the 21st century. *Phi Delta Kappan, 77*(3), 238–246.

Stuebing, K. K., Fletcher, J. M., LeDoux, J. M., & Lyon, G. R. (2002). Validity of IQ-discrepancy classifications of reading disabilities: A meta-analysis. *American Educational Research Journal, 39*(2), 469–518.

Tiedemann, J. (2000). Gender-related beliefs of teachers in elementary school mathematics. *Educational Studies in Mathematics, 41*(2), 191–207.

Upcraft, M. L, & Schuh, J. L. (2002). Assessment vs. research: Why we should care about the difference. *About Campus, 16*, 16–20.

Yatvin, J., Weaver, C., & Garan, E. (2003). Reading first: Cautions & recommendations. *Language Arts, 81*(1), 28–33.

Wolfe, P. (2000). *Brain matters: Translating research into classroom practice.* Alexandria, VA: Association for Supervision & Curriculum Development.

WHEN LANGUAGES COLLIDE

STEVEN NATHANSON, REFLECTIVE PIECE

This essay was a written transformation of notes, conversations, and editorial responses to a long line of graduate clinicians I have had the good fortune of supervising in my years at Long Island University. It was particularly easy to develop a framework and purpose for this article because as I wrote it I always envisioned my graduate students and my class discussions. At the same time, I always harked back—as educators frequently do—to my own professors, scholars and teachers who influenced and inspired my own professional training. Dr. H. Alan Robinson, keen of mind and sharp of editorial pen, always challenged us to write the best and most honest essays, research summaries, and technical reports. As I wrote this article, it was easy to conjure the image of Dr. Robinson's research seminars: tough, exacting, but always focused on professional growth. Dr. Robinson, I am certain, would approve of the image of the collision between raw data and perception. He was a stern but dedicated Socratic teacher who constantly challenged graduate students to "mean what we say, and say what we mean." Isn't that what we want our own writing to do and to be . . . reflections of our best thoughts, and yet also works-in-progress that will enable other scholars, clinicians or researchers to move forward?

As a former staff developer in public education who once made a point of attending workshops and seeking out exemplary presenters, I was once given the advice to begin every article with a story, brief anecdote or narrative. In my writing, I have carried this principle out; indeed, my own research studies on this topic have convinced me that no matter how discursive the topic, a narrative is always the exact way to meet and greet your audience. In the chapter I submitted for the "collisions" project, I used the image of the "crime scene" forensics specialist, drawn from contemporary popular culture, to draw my reader in and crystallize the central problem of the essay: overcoming the inherent flaws in the educational diagnostic/prescriptive process. I even extended this image into a metaphor of sorts: educational testing as a form of "educational forensics." The use of this imagery is recursive in my essay, but it too is based on my classroom experiences: I often talk to my clinicians about the importance of doing a careful case study since every pupil is a unique mystery to unravel. I know that my graduate students or the undergraduates who may become educational majors or minors will grapple with the challenge of performing educational assessment and diagnostic, prescriptive conclusions. One of the special joys of writing this essay was in knowing the purpose and my goals before I started, and still being able to play the role of storyteller.

Several features of the discourse were also conscious and deliberate. For example, research is a tapestry that tells a story not about interactions of literary characters but a story about overlapping findings and recommendations which help to reveal effective practice. Thus, in my research, I was able to find and draw upon many experts in testing and diagnostic/ prescriptive assessment in support of my central thesis about a need for clarity. The challenge here was to provide a delicate balance between focus and the need to accurately reflect the writers' views. I was extremely fortunate in that not only did I have recognized stylistic guidelines from the American Psychological Association and other scholarly writing from which to draw, I also had an effective conceptual framework cogently advanced by the editors (Marjorie Lipson and Karen Wixson) of the textbook I use. Another feature of the research is that it was necessarily eclectic: I drew upon literacy experts, testing and measurement experts, neuroscientists, and semantics experts. I felt that it was necessary to examine the problem of testing and reporting from different, yet mutually supporting frameworks, applying these sources as different lenses to look at testing, labeling and educational placement. The nature of the subject matter—why style matters and what kind of style matters—was not supported by referring to a single experimental study, meta-analytic study, or even a case study. Instead, I concentrated on studies where direct or indirect findings, experiments or retrospectives about educational trends, would provide insight about framing data in the most effective manner possible.

Another key component of this article, the recommendations section, was easy to document and write. From clinical reports submitted over the years and numerous in-class discussions with my students, I was able to obtain and use examples of "good" and "bad" writing. Furthermore, by selecting these, I was able to apply yet another aspect of my own experience: people learn to write when explanatory models of the discourse are provided by the teacher.

Editing this article was another way to apply the central tenets in the recommendations section (part IV) of this chapter. Because my research orientation was breadth rather than depth, studies were listed chronologically and conceptually. This represents a special challenge for editing. Noun and pronoun referents in particular have to be tight and transparent, verb tense consistent, and voice and tone have to be crisp, authoritative, and professional. The writer's challenge is similar to boxer Muhammad Ali's famous style: "float like a butterfly" through the research, but find your point and make it "sting like a bee." Throughout the essay, I varied my sentence structure, complexity and length in order to "bob and feint" in support of interest, clarity and argumentation. Somewhere along the way, I hope the ideas hit home.

WHEN LANGUAGES COLLIDE

In the essay, I make the point that educational reports have discrete sections to separate findings from discussion, which provides another way to achieve transparency and comprehensibility. Thus, I divided the article into sections: there is research about problems of tests and observers which result in collisions. The last section contains models and examples of what to strive for, and what to avoid, and has been further sub-divided into "A," "B," etc. The concluding section ratchets up the discussion by framing clear writing in a new dimension, the moral and ethical standards required in clinical work:

> When we write in a culture-free, bias-free and technically transparent manner, we extend that clinician-client empathy to a third party: the reader. A diagnostic report that avoids the collision between data and perception is faithful to the ultimate goal of assessment: changing the life of a struggling learner by facilitating educational improvement.

To that end, I hope the essay reflects the precise values and style that I promulgate for my readers. By taking the moral high road, my readers—I hope—will end up at a better place than they or I have ever achieved!

"THINK. WRITE. ASK."

1. Steven Nathanson uses a number of sentences like the following: "Before discussing what evaluators and clinicians can do . . . I would like to discuss how the role of tests and the perceptions of the examiner complicate the assessment reporting process." Identify one or two other similar statements. Why do you think Nathanson includes such statements?
2. Nathanson tells us that he varied his sentence structure, complexity, and length to produce clearer, more interesting prose. Pick several paragraphs longer than five sentences, and imitate the paragraphs' sentence structures (use different subject matter, real or invented). Are your imitative paragraphs more or less varied compared to your usual prose? Why might varied and complex sentence structures be valued in many kinds of prose?
3. Nathanson outlines a writing process which has its goal minimizing inaccuracy in the presentation and interpretation of test data. Locate the section in his text where he outlines this process, and re-read it; then find a news story in the *New York Times* or another national, daily newspaper,

and edit the paragraphs according to Nathanson's principles. Be ready to describe the effect of your editing on the news story.

4. Nathanson references "Ockham's Razor." In your own words, explain "Ockham's Razor." In what analytical situations might Ockham's Razor thrive? Can you imagine places it might fail, or where it might not serve a writer or reader well? If you apply Ockham's Razor to Belinda Kremer & Angela Pisano's *All Begin Guy Walks into a Bar*, what happens?

5. Nathanson tells us that *ethical standards* require that we try to use bias-free language. Miller vehemently disagrees. Do you think a commitment to avoiding bias in language is an *ethical* commitment? Do you think the effort is worthwhile? Why or why not?

WRITING PROJECTS RELATED TO LANGUAGES IN COLLISION

A. The final section of *Collide* has to do with collisions of language.

    Compose and record a 5-minute long podcast (or other type of audio file) that examines the types of collisions these authors discuss. What sorts of reasons have authors given for the collisions they chose to write about? What sorts of collisions seem, at this moment, striking or important to you?

B. Each author in *Collide* discusses his or her own writing process.

    On a class blog, post a 600–900 word "Reflective Piece," modeled on the many reflective pieces you've read in *Collide*, about a text you wrote, or are writing, this semester, for any course. Your class can decide together whether to use a free commercial blogging software, or a platform provided by your university. As an accompanying rhetorical exercise, be sure to view the blogging template together, and to determine as a group whether you'll embrace some or all of the suggested conventions of the site. Also as a group, develop a rhetorical strategy that encourages class members' interactions with each other's posts.

C. Pick two essays, from two different sections of this anthology, that you find most interesting.

    Write an essay analyzing the rhetorical strategies the authors chose to use. Determine an appropriate length for the level of detail desired. Use the following guidelines to help frame your essay:

(a) Introduction: How do the authors lay out the topic or problem? How is the topic/problem set within the context of professional conversations that have gone on before? What kind of justification and evidence do they use to identify the topic/problem (e.g., citations of previous research studies, narrative evidence, observational evidence, citation of major texts within the field, citation of experts within the field, direct quotations from authoritative sources, etc.)? Do they provide guides to reveal the organization of the essay?

(b) Body: Within the body of the article, how do the authors construct their arguments and points? What kinds of evidence do they use for these arguments/points? Think, for example, about whether or not in a particular essay the author uses narratives or informal observations. What other types of evidence does she use? Statistical data, case-study data, ethnographic data, direct quotations from literary or traditional sources, analogy and metaphor, citations to previous research, etc.? How would you describe the form of each essay's argument and claims?

(c) Conclusion: What are some of the rhetorical moves characteristic of the authors' conclusions? Do they make references to future research, work, scholarship, and observation? Do they speculate about interesting connections with other areas of study? Do they discuss the implications, evaluations, or professional responsibilities of their topic or problem?

(d) Discourse features: What are some of the discourse features of each essay? Search for trends and patterns of voice or tone; sentence length, variety, and pattern; stylistic features; punctuation usage.

Suggested length: Instructors will want to tailor the length to the level of detail required.

D. Return to Writing Project A, above, and re-consider its final question: What sorts of collisions, seem at this moment, striking or important to you?

In a visual medium of your choice, relate to viewers a collision that matters to you, as well as why it matters.

ABOUT THE WRITERS

SIMONE WEIL DAVIS, formerly of C.W. Post, is a visiting associate professor of English at Mount Holyoke College in South Hadley, Massachusetts, where she teaches courses on American literature, American Studies and Gender Studies. Her research interests include the history and impact of the advertising industry, the effect of the media on contemporary sexualities, and prison literature. Publications include *Living Up to the Ads: Gender Fictions of the 1920s* (Duke 2000) and "Loose Lips Sink Ships" (about labiaplasty) in the Spring 2002 issue of *Feminist Studies*. In an upcoming project, "Voices and Doors: What Workshops Allow," she considers the possibilities and challenges of creative writing workshops for women behind bars.

SUSAN DINAN's research examines the role of women in poor relief efforts in early modern France. While at C.W. Post, she taught Western Civilization to 1789 and Western Civilization since 1789, as well as The Renaissance, The Reformation, Eighteenth-Century European History, Early Modern France, The French Revolution, and The Family in Early Modern Europe. Her publications include *Women and Poor Relief in Seventeenth-Century France* and *Women and Religion in Old and New Worlds*, edited with Debra Meyers. She has published several articles, including "Motivations for Charity in Early Modern France," in *Reformation of Charity: the Secular and the Religious in Early Modern Poor Relief*.

BARBARA FOWLES is Chairperson and professor in the Media Arts Department at C.W. Post, where she teaches media ethics, media culture and media theory. Having earned a Ph.D. in Developmental Psycholinguistics, and served as Director of Research for the Children's Television Workshop Program *The Electric Company*, she developed an interest in the cognitive impact of television on children, especially in the area of literacy and interest in reading. Extending her interest in the relationships among language, thinking and mass media, she is now pursuing research on the language and structure of television news stories as they pertain to the communication of risk.

ERICA FROUMAN-SMITH is Associate Professor of Spanish in the Foreign Languages Department at C.W. Post, where she teaches undergraduate and graduate courses in Spanish, Spanish-American culture and literature, and Spanish-American women writers. She has published critical studies on the works of Argentine writers Silvina Bullrich and Liliana Heker as well as the works of Mexican writers Amparo Dávila and Inés Arredondo in journals such as *Chasqui, Discurso Literario, Letras Femeninas, Review* and *Revista de Estudios Hispánicos*. Frouman-Smith has also translated several of these authors' works. Her latest translation is a book-length study of the Spanish poet Federico García Lorca, by Angel Sahuquillo, titled *Federico García Lorca and the Culture of Male Homosexuality*.

CARA GARGANO is Chair of the Department of Theatre, Film and Dance and Professor of Dance and Theatre at C.W. Post. A former dancer, stage director, and choreographer, she studied at the New York School of Ballet under Richard Thomas and Barbara Fallis and later taught at the school. Her concert choreography has received warm reviews from the *New York Times* and has been presented in France and Switzerland as well as in the United States. She holds a PhD in French and has published in both English and French. A member of the Association for Theatre in Higher Education, the National Association of Schools of Dance, the Modern Language Association, and the Society for Dance History Scholars, she is the current President of the Congress on Research in Dance.

ANKE GROSSKOPF is Assistant Professor in the Department of Political Science at C.W. Post. She teaches courses on European Politics, the European Union, Comparative Politics, Introduction to Political Science, as well as interdisciplinary Honors courses such as "One Ideology to Rule Them All? Ideological Readings of *The Lord of the Rings*" and "The Good, the Bad, and the Ugly: A Political Psychology Research Seminar." Her research, which often crosses disciplinary and sub-disciplinary boundaries, focuses on the various intersections of public opinion, European integration, and constitutional courts. She has published articles in journals such as *Political Research Quarterly* and the *Law and Society Review*, among others. Currently, she is working on a book project entitled "Explaining the Democratic Trust Conundrum—Lessons from the Re-United Germany."

ESTELLE KAMLER, an associate professor in the Department of Educational Leadership and Administration at C.W. Post, teaches courses centered on the foundations of leadership. Kamler also coordinates the Aspiring Superintendents' Study Group, a mentoring collaborative in partnership with local administrative organizations. Previously, she served as a school superintendent, and her research focus continues to be on access to the superintendency. In recent publications,

Kamler examines the use of technology, comentoring, and mentoring mosaics—alternative mentoring practices—to support entrée of women and people of color to the superintendency.

BELINDA KREMER directs The Writing Center and coordinates First-Year Writing at C.W. Post, where she also teaches writing and literature. Her research interests include the conditions that tend to produce plagiarism, and how we might reduce the prevalence of those conditions; as well, she is interested in the rapidly shifting and tech-heavy conditions under which contemporary actors compose texts. Her poetry appears in literary journals (*FENCE, Calyx*, etc.), chapbooks (*Lake Diary, FIELD*, etc.), limited edition collections (*Blue: Poems for New York*, etc.), and as the graphic poem *All Begin Guy Walks into a Bar*. Her most recent manuscript is *get ahold of you*, and she is currently at work on the tentatively titled *Chat*.

RICHARD MCNABB is an associate professor in the Department of English and former Director of Composition at C.W. Post, where he teaches a variety of rhetoric and composition courses. His research interests focus primarily on the history of rhetoric and writing instruction in the Middle Ages. His publications in this area include "Remapping Medieval Rhetoric: Reading Boethius from a Grassian Perspective," "Innovations and Complications: Juan Gil de Zamora's *Dictaminis Epithalamium*," and "To Father Juan, with Love, Bishop Alexander: Juan Gil de Zamora's Medieval Art of Letters."

LORI MCNEIL is an Assistant Professor in the Sociology and Anthropology Department at C.W. Post. She teaches courses in feminism and gender, family, research methodology and statistics. Her research interests focus on issues typically defined as "women's issues." Examples of her publications include "Funding Drug Elimination in Public Housing: Effective or Wasteful?," "Understanding Childcare Through Experiential Knowledge," and "Assessing Childcare Need Under Welfare Reform." Her current research explores how women combine their work expectations with maternal duties and expectations and how oral histories contribute to marginalized knowledge bases.

EDMUND MILLER, Chair of the Department of English at the C. W. Post Campus of Long Island University, is the author of *Drudgerie Divine: The Rhetoric of God and Man in George Herbert, George Herbert's Kinships: An Ahnentafel with Annotations*, and other books and articles about seventeenth-century

British literature. In addition, he has published articles about rhetoric, linguistics, and the literature of other periods and is also a widely published fiction writer and poet. His most recent book is *The Go-Go Boy Sonnets: Men of the New York Club Scene.*

STEVEN NATHANSON is an assistant professor of literacy in the Department of Special Education and Literacy in the School of Education at C.W. Post. He teaches undergraduate and graduate courses in literacy and education and supervises graduate literacy clinicians at the reading/learning centers at C.W. Post and the LIU Brentwood campus. Recent publications include "Thinking about the Brain to Balance Classroom Literacy Programs," in the New York State Reading Association magazine *The Language and Literacy Spectrum* and "Harnessing the Power of Story: Using Narrative Reading and Writing Across Content Areas," published in *Reading Horizons.* Currently Dr. Nathanson has been conducting a research study about the literacy/reading habits of graduate students.

BARBARA SHORTER is an assistant professor and the Director of the Didactic Program in Dietetics in the Nutrition Department at C.W. Post. She is a Registered Dietitian and Certified Dietitian/Nutritionist. Barbara teaches courses in nutrition, nutrients through life cycles, food science, community nutrition, professional issues, and related topics. Her research interest is Interstitial Cystitis/Painful Bladder Syndrome. Her articles include "Effects of Comestibles on the Symptoms of Interstitial Cystitis" in *The Journal of Urology* (7/07) and "The Role of Dietary Services in the Treatment of Interstitial Cystitis/Painful Bladder Syndrome." She is currently researching the effects of foods and beverages on the symptoms on Chronic Prostatitis/Chronic Pelvic Pain Syndrome.

MARK PIRES is Associate Professor of Geography in the Earth and Environmental Science Department at C.W. Post. A broadly trained geographer with a regional specialization in Africa, he teaches courses in human and physical geography and environmental conservation. Pires's research interests focus on the political ecology of natural resource management. His recent publications include several articles on watershed protection for the New York City water supply system.

ANGELA PISANO is a graduate of C.W. Post. As an undergraduate, she studied graphic design; she went on to earn her Master's degree in Interactive Multimedia in

2007. While working at Post's Writing Center in the summer of 2005, she collaborated on the design of, and created the art and graphics for, *All Begin Guy Walks into a Bar*. In the future, Angela would like to work in an organization where she can utilize her skills and knowledge in interactive multimedia.

NICHOLAS J. RAMER, an assistant professor in the Department of Chemistry at C. W. Post, teaches courses in Basic Organic Chemistry, Basic Biochemistry and the honors program sequence, Chemistry in Daily Life. He has published several articles on inorganic ferroelectric materials and improvements in pseudopotential formulation for use in density-functional theory calculations. His most recent publications describe the determination of the structure and vibrational properties of different phases of poly(vinylidene fluoride), an organic ferroelectric material, using density-functional methods. These articles are co-authored with undergraduate students. He has also recently co-authored an article on the extraction of potassium from tuberous root vegetables common in the diets of Latin and Caribbean cultures.

JEROME TOGNOLI is a professor in the Psychology Department at C. W. Post. He teaches the undergraduate courses Advanced Experimental Psychology, Social Psychology, and Environmental Psychology, and a doctoral course in Social and Community Psychology. Tognoli's research interests revolve around the meaning and loss of home. His published articles include "Leaving home: Homesickness, place attachment, and transition among residential college students," "Adjustment and adaptation among World War II evacuees to loss of and disruption of home," "The privilege of place: Domestic and work locations of characters in children's books," "The role of home in adult development," and "The flight from domestic space: Men's roles in the household."

AMY WYSOKER is a professor in the Department of Nursing at C.W. Post. She is a certified clinical specialist in psychiatric mental health nursing and a psychiatric nurse practitioner. She is also in private practice as a psychiatric/mental health consultant and as a medical-legal nurse consultant in Forest Hills, NY. Dr. Wysoker teaches professional issue courses in the undergraduate and graduate nursing programs. She also teaches a graduate course on family, social, ethical and policy issues. She has published extensively on ethical and legal issues in psychiatric nursing. Her research interests and publications pertain to obesity, bariatric surgery, and weight loss and weight gain.

WHEN LANGUAGES COLLIDE

TODD ZIMMERMAN is an assistant professor in the Biology Department at C. W. Post. He received a B.A. from Wittenberg University, M.S. degrees from The University of Southwestern Louisiana and The University of Southern California, and a Ph.D. from UCLA. His research interests focus on ecology and evolution of crustaceans, and biodiversity of Caribbean marine invertebrates. The classes he teaches include Evolution, Marine Biology, Invertebrate Zoology, and General Biology.